Praise for *Theologies on the Move*

"*Theologies on the Move* is a crucial addition to theological conversations on religion, migration, and pilgrimage in the World of Neoliberal Capital. It has come at the right time when migration is top on the list of the signs of our times. The combination of migration and pilgrimage gives new insight to understanding ancient and modern movement of people from a theological perspective and highlights the World Council of Churches methodology of pilgrimage of Justice and Peace. Its methodological claim of doing theological reflection based on everyday experiences gives authenticity as a contribution to liberation theology. It is a must read for academics, students, religious leaders and policy makers who want to make a difference in understanding and acting for people on the move."—Isabel Apawo Phiri, Deputy General Secretary: Public Witness and Diakonia, World Council of Churches

"This collection of critical essays by scholars from across the Majority World challenges readers to rethink how they understand the human quest for survival, identity, belonging, and religious meaning within the massive contemporary waves of humanity on the move, driven by the overwhelming forces of neoliberal globalization, transnational capitalism, as well as unbridled economic greed and exploitation of humans. The authors are to be commended for their thought provoking essays offering much needed analysis, critique, and constructive theological responses on the complexities of border crossings, identity constructions, uprootedness and exile, religious longing and belonging within the intersectionality of migration and pilgrimage as two sides of the contemporary movements of people across the globe."
—Jonathan Y. Tan, Case Western Reserve University

Theologies on the Move

Decolonizing Theology

Series Editor: Jione Havea

This series aims to demonstrate the character and shape of the future of theology, which is a diversity of theologies "decolonized" of Western captivity and influence. Each volume of the series, as such, will highlight and explore indigenous expressions of Christian theology from a thickly contextual perspective. At the heart of the project is the goal of providing readers an array of theologies from around the globe, many unknown or often overlooked by Western audiences, as a way of demonstrating the availability of non-Western Christian development and de-centering the study and methods of Christian theology from Western domination and standards.

Titles in the Series

Resisting Occupation: A Global Struggle for Liberation, edited by Miguel de La Torre and Mitri Raheb

Theologies on the Move: Religion, Migration, and Pilgrimage in the World of Neoliberal Capital, edited by Joerg Rieger

Forthcoming

Horizons of Contextuality: Theological and Hermeneutical Explorations from the Great South Land (Australia), edited by Jione Havea

Theologies on the Move

Religion, Migration, and Pilgrimage in the World of Neoliberal Capital

Edited by
Joerg Rieger

LEXINGTON BOOKS/FORTRESS ACADEMIC
Lanham • Boulder • New York • London

Published by Lexington Books/Fortress Academic
Lexington Books is an imprint of The Rowman & Littlefield Publishing Group, Inc.
4501 Forbes Boulevard, Suite 200, Lanham, Maryland 20706
www.rowman.com

6 Tinworth Street, London SE11 5AL, United Kingdom

British Library Cataloguing in Publication Information Available

Library of Congress Control Number: 2020942148
ISBN 978-1-9787-0708-5 (cloth)
ISBN 978-1-9787-0710-8 (pbk)
ISBN 978-1-9787-0709-2 (electronic)

Contents

Acknowledgments

The chapters in this book were first presented and discussed at a conference sponsored by the Council for World Mission (CWM) in Mexico City in 2018, under the auspices of the Discernment and Radical Engagement (DARE) program. I am grateful for the leadership of Professor Jione Havea, Charles Sturt University, and Rev. Sudipta Singh, mission secretary, Research and Capacity Development, CWM. Thank you also to Dr. Neil Elliott, senior acquisitions editor, for his helpful input and suggestions, to Zachary Settle, Ph.D. candidate in theological studies at Vanderbilt University for his contributions to the editing process, and to Dr. Haley Feuerbacher for preparing the index.

Chapter One

Reclaiming Theology and Religious Traditions in the Tensions of Neoliberal Globalization

The Challenges of Pilgrimage and Migration

Joerg Rieger

Around the globe, more people are on the move today than ever before. Two very different expressions of this are migration and pilgrimage, both of which are at peak levels, linked to enormous transformations of life that impact everything, including religion. Even though migration and pilgrimage are seemingly unconnected examples of being on the move, they are both deeply impacted by particular experiences of powerlessness and empowerment under the conditions of globalizing neoliberal capitalism, which links the two phenomena in surprising and intriguing ways.

In this book, the connections between these experiences of powerlessness and empowerment, as well as the implications for and contributions of theology and religion, are being examined by an international group of scholars working in the Americas, Asia, Europe, and Oceania. Theological and religious examples are drawn mostly from Christianity, in conversation with its Jewish lineage, two global religious traditions that, in their own ways, have developed on the move.

RELIGIOUS TRADITIONS ON THE MOVE

For all the traveling activity that has shaped religious traditions like Judaism and Christianity, it is strange that religion is often treated as a static thing. Communities of faith often locate themselves in buildings, as is exemplified by many Christians who confuse the church with a building. In this case, "going to church" means going to a building rather than being part of a particular community. As a result, it never occurs to them that religion may have something to do with paying attention to what is happening outside of those buildings, in neighborhoods, cities, and the world. Both connections to others and vital opportunities to experience the divine are lost in this approach.

In this context, phenomena as seemingly disparate as pilgrimage and migration can help us reclaim religious traditions at deeper levels. To begin with, the people of Israel spent a good amount of time on the road, and their stories speak of slavery in the lands of a foreign empire called Egypt, of an exodus from this empire, and of forty years of wandering in the wilderness. On this journey, they learned important theological lessons, many of which were not easy or pleasant. These lessons included a deepening of their understanding of God as well as profound challenges to outdated images of God. What they learned along the way was that God was not the God of empires like Egypt but the God of the people, an insight that became the bedrock of the preferential option for the poor and the margins. [1]

Even though the Israelites developed their own imperial fantasies (consider the traditions of the conquest of the promised land in the book of Joshua, which is hardly a realistic option for a band of slaves), they found themselves under the gun of empires again, starting with Babylonia. During the Babylonian exile, they developed another set of fresh and earth-shattering theological insights. Many of the biblical traditions of creation, for instance, were produced in this exile, as the people began to understand that their God was not subject to the empire that enslaved them, but was instead the creator of a world that allowed for alternatives and the flourishing of the marginalized— including the widows, the orphans, and the strangers.

In the New Testament, Jesus's ministry takes place almost entirely on the road. As a person who has "no place to lay his head" (Luke 9:58), he travels in the company of others who shared in his mission. Travel provides the setting of Jesus's birth on the road on which his family found itself by Roman decree, with no room in the inn. Jesus's subsequent travels include migration as a refugee to Egypt as a child, ministerial journeys to various remote areas of Galilee, entry into budding economic centers around the Sea of Galilee, journeys along the border and into the borderlands, and a journey to metropolitan Jerusalem. The Gospel of Luke adds a journey to Jerusalem as a child, and the Gospel of John speaks of several journeys to this metropolis. Following Jesus often literally meant being on the road with him, and the number of those who traveled was not limited to the twelve disciples, whom we recognize by name. Among those who were on the road with Jesus were others, men and women, and even a group of wealthy women who chose to be in solidarity with his work, including the wife of one of Herod's officials (Luke 8:2–3).

The apostle Paul was locationally challenged in his own way, covering much larger distances than Jesus and presenting challenges to the Roman Empire wherever he went. On his travels, Paul established churches in various parts of the Roman Empire, often in situations of great pressure and tension, which he describes in this way: "Three times I was shipwrecked; for a night and a day I was adrift at sea; on frequent journeys, in dangers from rivers, dangers from bandits, danger from my own people, danger from Gentiles, danger in the city, danger in the wilderness, danger at sea, danger from false brothers and sisters; in toil and hardship, through many a sleepless night, hungry and thirsty, often without food, cold and naked" (2 Corinthians 11:25–27). For good reasons the book of Acts, which describes many of these travels, calls Christians the people of "the Way" (Acts 9:2; 19:9, 23; 22:4; 24:14, 22).

Being on the move has thus been a central topic of the Jewish and Christian traditions from their origins. Travel often has to do with tensions and challenges, which are experienced in solidarity with the common people rather than the rulers. Travelers who are not in control—migrants and some pilgrims, in contradistinction to tourists and many business travelers—display habits of thinking on one's feet, including the broadening of horizons, flexibility, challenging the status quo, and a much-needed awareness of their own limits and finitude, all of which are tied to experiences of God that elude those who think they have arrived.

Such travelers experience in their very being what is at the heart of the logic of the Jewish and Christian traditions and what took philosophers thousands of years to understand: a new appreciation for particular experiences of the tensions of life, in relation to which bigger ideas not only get shaped but also reshaped. This appreciation is where theology, philosophy, and cultural understanding started when religion took place on the road, in contradistinction to the big concepts and ideas proposed by the powers that be and their empires.

COMPLEXIFYING MIGRATORY TRAVEL

Just as tourism began its ascent in the United States and Europe after World War II, a reverse movement took shape that increasingly brought people from around the world into the centers of wealth and power in the United States and Europe, presenting new challenges and opportunities. Migratory travel is an old phenomenon, as people have probably migrated since the beginning of time. What is new, however, are the steadily increasing numbers of migrants discussed in the chapters of this book. The massive and growing migrations we witness today are tied to various kinds of tensions, some of which are of a political nature. For good reasons, people who have been persecuted for political reasons and whose lives are in danger often seek asylum in countries where they assume that they will be safer.

The immigration policies of many European countries and of the United States generally allow for asylum in cases of particular political persecutions. Those whose proofs of political persecution are accepted by the immigration authorities are allowed to stay; others are sent back to their countries of origin, a situation that has created many hardships. According to the United Nations Geneva Convention of 1951, refugee status is granted only on grounds of persecution for reasons of race, religion, nationality, or membership of a social group or political opinion; persecution for reasons of gender was added only in the 1990s. Not included in these categories, however, are reasons related to matters of economic hardship, which can be equally severe.

Today, migratory travel for political reasons is widely accepted. What is much less accepted, however, is migratory travel for economic reasons. Whereas political refugees are sometimes admired for their integrity and courage, economic refugees are often portrayed as duplicitous and opportunistic. While it is recognized that political refugees are faced with life-and-death situations, economic refugees, by contrast, are often seen as shallow freeloaders in search of more comfortable lives. In this climate, economic refugees are not even recognized as refugees; rather, for lack of official recognition by the authorities they are classified as "illegal immigrants" or "undocumented immigrants," to use a slightly more politically correct term. Yet the line that separates the various reasons for migratory travel is blurry.

It is commonly understood that millions of migrants in today's world are following the flow of money. What is less clear, especially in the current climate in the United States, where hostility against migrants is high and rising under the presidency of Donald Trump, is that for the most part migratory travels are anything but voluntary. In addition to economic necessity, migrants are sometimes lured to other places with false promises because of capitalism's appetite for cheap labor, as M. P. Joseph notes in the second chapter of this volume. This lure is all the more effective because many migrants live in situations where making a living feels impossible. Conversations with migrant workers along the US-Mexico border, for instance, have helped some of my students understand these often-unacknowledged facts. A large number of the migrants with whom we talked in the early years of the twenty-first century came from the state of Chiapas, Mexico, and similar places where they were pushed off their own lands by multinational corporations. Many of these migrants did not feel like they had the option to stay at home. Another reason for migration at the time was the North American Free Trade Agreement (NAFTA), which allowed US farmers to sell their corn at such low prices that many Mexican farmers lost their livelihood. Not only political refugees are confronted with life-and-death situations—the same is increasingly true for economic refugees.

These forced travels of migration remind us of a paradox that marks our age: while money is allowed to travel ever more freely across borders, people are increasingly restricted in their movements. At a time when free trade continues to be celebrated (despite some hiccups with the Trump administration in the United States), more fences and walls are being built along the US-Mexico border. Those migrants who still attempt to cross from Mexico into the United States, following the flow of money often out of necessity, are risking their lives to ever greater degrees. The death toll keeps growing despite a declining number of people who make it across the border.[2]

Migration is a complex global phenomenon. The majority of migrants do not head for wealthy countries in the North but travel within the so-called "intraperiphery" world—another important dynamic that is often overlooked—and the second-largest number of migrants travel within the wealthy countries. Only the third place is occupied by migrations between center and periphery. Countries like India, China, and Brazil have a lot of internal travel, mostly from rural to urban areas. A more recent phenomenon of labor-related migration in the wealthiest countries has been called the "outsourcing" of production, which reduces immigration of men from poorer countries, while work in the domestic sector (like care for children and elderly, domestic labor) increases, so that immigrant women are more in demand, as is discussed in various chapters of this book. These women are more closely related to the host families than male workers, with all the resulting benefits and problems.[3] If religious communities and scholars want to learn from migration, we need to consider its complexity in greater depth.

While there is a clear power differential between migrants and their hosts, we should not assume that migrants are without power, as migrant communities are also changing the worlds of their hosts, introducing postcolonial experiences of ambivalence and hybridity.[4] From new hybrid cultural forms and emerging communication networks that are produced by migrant communities, a certain revolutionary potential arises. Tourism scholar Dean Mac-Cannell talks about a "post-tourist" or "composite community."[5] It may not be an accident that much of what we now call "critical theory" emerged at these times of increasing migration, including decolonialism, postcolonialism, and subaltern studies.

The experiences of migratory travelers display the challenges of both ambivalence and hybridity. Advances in transport and electronic communications allow them to maintain not only multiple identities but multiple localities as well. "Migrants and refugees develop new, globally oriented identities and pluri- or trans-local understandings of 'home,'" note anthropologists Nadje Al-Ali and Khalid Koser. The same could be said about religion, as Wanda Deifelt's and Gemma Cruz's contributions in this book show. As a result, home and religion become spaces and communities "created within the changing links between 'here' and 'there.'"[6] This was different in the earlier days of migration, when it was much more difficult to maintain contact with home due to the difficulties of communication and travel. Even as recently as two or three decades ago, talking on the phone was still outrageously expensive. For migratory travelers and refugees today, however, mythical images of home as a static place that undergird dominant forms of patriotism and nationalism make little sense. This does not mean that notions of home are disappearing; rather, home consists of a variety of places, many of which are often in tension with each other.

The early Christians seem to have held similar sentiments. In the letter to the Hebrews, the author puts it this way: "Here we have no lasting city, but we are looking for the city that is to come" (Hebrews 13:14). Much like contemporary migrants, the early Christians had no choice but to live in the midst of the tensions of their world. They resisted Roman patriotism and nationalism because of their allegiance to the way of Christ, which was not primarily a pious idea of the future or the afterlife but a reality, embodied in their communities here and now. As Al-Ali and Koser observe regarding migrants, "One of the defining characteristics of transnational migrants is that they have multiple allegiances to places."[7] Yet not all places are alike, and migrants, like the early Christians, tend to have their priorities straight.

Today, an additional layer of complexity is added by the fact that migrant remittances are increasingly important for the economic well-being of their families and their countries of origin. This serves as another reminder of the fact that migrants are never disconnected from their places of origin. More importantly yet, remittances signify that migrants continue to shape what is going on in their places of origin.

In sum, migratory travel helps us expose the deep relationships of power that are at work in our times, and it can provide models for how to negotiate them. This forces us to rethink our own identities, including religious ones. The difference between migration and tourism clarifies what is at stake. Tourists expect to return home safely, assuming that their homes are waiting just as they left them. Migrants, on the other hand, can have no such expectations. This sort of travel, to which any of us who ever bought a one-way ticket might be able to relate in some small way (I happen to be an immigrant myself), resembles many of the travels in the Jewish and Christian traditions. Deep lessons for faith and life grow out of this experience, throwing new light on the meanings and potential of pilgrimage.

The power differentials manifest in migratory travel can also be expressed in the difference between what has been called "transnationalism from above and from below."[8] While transnationalism from above describes dominant forms of globalization where the elite expand their power across the globe, transnationalism from below describes the sort of relationships where common people—the multitude[9]—develop their own agency in the midst of hostile environments. Many migrant communities are already embodying this agency but nonmigratory travelers—pilgrims in particular—may also have an opportunity to align themselves with these alternative powers.

PILGRIMAGE

Sociologist of religion Luigi Tomasi defines pilgrimage as a religious search for the divine, "a journey undertaken for religious purposes that culminates in a visit to a place considered to be the site or manifestation of the supernatural—a place where it is easier to obtain divine help."[10] Others, seeking to erase the sharp distinctions between pilgrimage and tourism, have argued that travel in search of authenticity and self-renewal also constitutes a search for the sacred and should thus also be understood as a form of pilgrimage.[11] A comparison of pilgrimage and migration may help clarify what is at stake, challenging some of our assumptions and pushing us to develop broader horizons.

In Western Christendom, pilgrimages originated as forms of itinerant devotion in the seventh century C.E. The number of these itinerant devotions kept growing and peaked in the twelfth and thirteenth centuries. Pilgrimages in those periods were seen as a "major investment in eternal life."[12] The use of economic language to describe pilgrimage as an investment reminds us that in the past religion, politics, and economics were not considered separate phenomena. Everything was at stake in these travels: not only religion but also politics and economics. Pilgrimage affected all of these realms, not only in the context of the lives of the travelers themselves, but also in the broader religious, political, and economic context of the communities to which the travelers belonged.

As far as individual travelers were concerned, pilgrimages were dangerous and risky undertakings, not unlike some of the migratory travels of today. Many things had to be given up, and others were lost along the road. There was even a good chance that travelers would not return home. But even if everything went according to plan for individual travelers, there were political and social consequences that could not be avoided. Such forms of pilgrimage can thus be considered in terms of a "civil death" because it put the pilgrims outside of the structures of their communities and societies. According to medieval law, pilgrims were declared physically dead if they had not been heard of for a year and a day.

While physical death was a constant companion of life for pilgrims in the Middle Ages, the pilgrims' bigger concern was for what they considered to be spiritual death. To contemporary ears, this may sound like a simple trade of one world for another (the heavenly world for the physical world). But these acts of risking one's life can also amount to putting up resistance within the physical world, as the physical world was not brushed aside but put in its place. A pilgrim would have intuitively understood that life is more than what the status quo can offer and promise. In other words, giving up the physical world of the status quo would have empowered pilgrims to envision not only the heavenly world but also an alternative physical world where the rules of the status quo are challenged in order that (borrowing from contemporary language) "another world is possible."

Here we might find a parallel between the travels of medieval pilgrims and contemporary migrants, whose search is for alternative physical worlds where life transcends the pressures and confinements of the status quo they experience. In both cases, transcendence is a matter not just of heaven but also of an alternative earth.

In modernity pilgrimage underwent important changes. The emphasis was now on the freedom of the individual, and funded by the economic developments of budding capitalism, pilgrimages could now also be undertaken as a demonstration of freedom and personal independence. As a result, in the seventeenth and eighteenth centuries, pilgrimages morphed into the travel of elites who set out to view examples of fine art and other cultural artifacts. In the nineteenth and twentieth centuries, the invention of tourism further changed pilgrimage, as sightseeing, tourism, and pilgrimage were increasingly combined and made available to the emerging middle class. Whatever contradictions remain between travel for the purposes of enjoyment and travel for reasons of faith have been further eroded as the tourism industry has gotten ahold of pilgrimage.

What has changed over the years are not just the forms of pilgrimage but also popular definitions of the sacred and how people relate to it. Where once the pilgrims' search for the sacred implied a challenge and had to do with concepts like penitence and an intentional commitment to the hardships and dangers of the journey, now the search for the sacred is more likely connected with concepts of personal growth and self-realization. Where once the search for the sacred implied a search for how best to conform to it, now the search for the sacred comes with the assumption that the sacred conforms to the interests of the pilgrim, affirming (or perhaps gradually improving) the status quo rather than challenging it. Here, the difference between pilgrimage and migrant travels is most pronounced, as migrants are still forced to conform, with no expectation that reality would conform to them.

In addition, the hardships and dangers of the journey have been reduced to such an extent by modern forms of tourist travel that the journey itself has been all but abandoned as a meaningful part of most pilgrimages. What matters most today is what happens between arrival and departure. Tomasi describes the World Youth Rally in Rome on August 20, 2000, which attracted 2.5 million young people, with these words: "The stone used as a pillow, typical of the pilgrim of the past and symbolic of penitence, had given way to the cellular phone, the paramount symbol of comfort in the modern age."[13] Many modern-day pilgrims would be unaware that things have ever been different.

The loss of the more challenging aspects of the encounter with the sacred that characterizes modern pilgrimages is paralleled by a certain domestication of the sacred in contemporary religiosity. Modern pilgrims assume the approval of the sacred and are interested in how they can better integrate the sacred with their own concerns, while ancient pilgrims would have assumed the challenge of the sacred, seeking to adjust their concerns to the concerns of the sacred. This is similar to the difference between wondering whether God is on our side (the typical quest of modernity and of those who benefit from its political and economic structures) or we are on God's side (the quest of those who understand that things are not as they should be, which today is also the quest of various liberation theologies).[14] Once again, the experiences of migrants throw light on this difference, as migrants, too, are searching for something beyond their control, however pragmatic and needs driven this search may be.

How might we recover some of the challenging aspects of traditional pilgrimages in such a climate? And what difference might this make? A first step, mirrored to some extent by the challenges of migration, would be to gain a better awareness of what happens when the worlds of the pilgrim are put in touch with other worlds, however limited these experiences are for contemporary pilgrims. Anthropologist Victor Turner's concept of liminality might be helpful here in that it refers to a situation of finding oneself in between different worlds. Liminality, which means being on the threshold or on the border, challenges established hierarchies and can thus create space for new kinds of relationship.[15] Eventually, these more challenging examples of relating might create space for new relations with the divine as well.

Decolonial scholar Walter Mignolo's notion of border thinking takes this experience of liminality to the next level, exploring what happens when people find themselves in border situations where various worlds collide. The topic of power differentials, a key experience of those who are forced to migrate, is of particular importance here. Migrants, as those who find themselves marginalized by borders, are best positioned to see both sides in new light, enabling them to raise questions of the status quo and begin pushing beyond it.[16]

Pilgrims open to examining their own positions of power and who enter into solidarity with those on the margins based on those new insights can learn to share in these alternative perspectives. The same is true for migrants who—even though they are usually more aware of positions of power—also need to develop deeper understandings of what is going on. And both pilgrims and migrants cannot remain neutral but need to take sides: as Latin American liberation theologians have pointed out, even the poor need to make an option for the poor.[17] In virtually all of the chapters of this volume it is becoming clear that romanticizing migrants and displaced people is as problematic as merely ignoring them altogether.

The fact that traditional places of pilgrimage are often located in remote places further supports the potential benefits of pilgrimages. Those pilgrims who have the courage and nerve to venture further off the beaten path might encounter some aspects of hybridity—the fused nature of identity that welds together dominant and repressed aspects of life in one's own person. Hybridity is a crucial part of the experience of colonized peoples and those who have come under pressure from the dominant system, such as migrants. For some pilgrims, hybridity can be experienced in a small way when they are no longer in control, off the beaten path, and subject to the multiple pressures of their surroundings, from having to find their own food to adopting the survival skills that have long been mastered by others. These experiences not only help to examine, challenge, and destabilize the dominant system, but also enable fresh encounters with other people and the divine Other, all of whom are kept at arm's length by the status quo.

The image of pilgrimage has also been invoked when Christians understood that assimilating to the status quo was not an option. The text of a German hymn, written during the Third Reich in Germany by Christians who refused to go along with the fascist status quo that sought to shape not only politics but also the Christianity of the time, reflects their resistance. Titled *"Wir sind nur Gast auf Erden"* ("We Are But Guests on Earth"), the hymn talks about the restless march through time on paths that are deserted and lonely. When all others forsake the faithful, the first stanza continues, Christ continues to walk with them. The first stanza ends with the prayer to God to put out a light so that the faithful will be able to find the way home.[18]

What may sound like an expression of sentimental feelings of loneliness and abandonment reflects the experience of those who have mustered the courage of pilgrims to step outside of the religious, political, and economic status quo, and to take a stance against it. This hymn was written by Christians who endured the consequences for their defiance against a dominant system that claims Christianity and God. Perhaps this was the reason why my father and some of the older people in the German Methodist church where I grew up remembered it so well. Contemporary American Christians of mainline traditions still mostly lack such experiences of defiance and its consequences, even in the age of Trump.

In the context of the United States, where religion today is often employed in support of the status quo, resistance is, at times, fueled by the experiences of the oppressed and the exploited, whether they are oppressed and exploited for reasons of race, ethnicity, class, gender, or even sexuality.

When the status quo blocks the roads for those who are different, forces us to travel the alleyways and secondary roads of the world, and sometimes discourages travel altogether, religion can expect to be reshaped as well.

One of the key challenges of pilgrimages and migration is being forced to leave the familiar places of home, of family and friends, and to forgo the affirmation of familiar religious communities. Yet these can be healthy challenges for people of faith who have grown comfortable with the status quo, as they need to learn that none of their familiar places must ever assume the place of God. The Christian God is not the God of the familiar (or of the family, Mark 3:31–35) but the God who calls us to embark on journeys that engage the struggles of life ("follow me," Luke 5:27). This journey ultimately points us to our true home, which is found at last where we least expect it: in the presence of God, who is often encountered in special ways in the unfamiliar. This insight is exemplified for Christians in a special way in the life, death, and resurrection of Jesus Christ, who walked the dusty roads of Galilee in the past, alongside emigrants and refugees (Matthew 2:13–15) and who continues to walk the alleyways and secondary roads with migrants today, as various authors in this book demonstrate.[19]

This challenge is further deepened in Christ's presence at the margins of the world, as expressed in the words of Jesus in the Gospel of Matthew that keep haunting self-centered Christianity: "Truly I tell you, just as you did it to one of the least of these who are members of my family, you did it to me" (Matthew 25:40). This concern reverberates through many of the books of the Bible, both in the Hebrew Bible and the New Testament.

To be sure, leaving familiar places is not merely an act of deconstruction. For the vagrants and hermits of the Middle Ages, "their pilgrimage to God was an exercise in self-construction," notes sociologist Zygmunt Bauman.[20] People moving out of their established homes also moved out of the religious, political, and economic control of the status quo and often found alternative visions and constructed new ways of life. The established church resented these movements because it understood itself as the only connection to God, seeking to organize vagrants into monastic orders. Yet the challenges posed to the status quo by these kinds of pilgrims proved too strong, so the powers that be were never completely able to control them.

PILGRIMS, MIGRANTS, AND NEOLIBERAL CAPITALISM

Under the conditions of neoliberal capitalism, lives are not grounded in traditional relations as much as they once were. As a result, some have argued that pilgrimage has become a way of life, as grounding in families, traditional communities, and geographical locations can no longer be presupposed as a given. Even the economic security that many members of the modern middle class once took for granted is becoming more and more elusive, and Zygmunt Bauman observes that one of the foremost strategies of pilgrimage, "saving for the future," makes less and less sense as pension plans and other provisions for the future are failing to deliver.[21] The experiences of migrants can further deepen the urgency of these experiences and might provide some guidance.

Over a century ago, Karl Marx described a feeling of being lost and suspended in time and space, reminding us of the underlying cause of Bauman's concern—a capitalism that constantly needs to reinvent itself in order to stay competitive: "Constant revolutionising of production, uninterrupted disturbance of all social conditions, everlasting uncertainty and agitation distinguish the bourgeois epoch from all earlier ones. All fixed, fast-frozen relations, with their train of ancient and venerable prejudices and opinions, are swept away, all new-formed ones become antiquated before they can ossify." Marx's famous conclusion is that "all that is solid melts into air, all that is holy is profaned, and man is at last compelled to face with sober senses his real conditions of life, and his relations with his kind."[22] More and more of us can relate to the disturbing feeling that all that is solid melts into air, and migrants are at the forefront of these experiences.

In this context, as poststructuralism and other postmodern theories have taught us, meaning is never fixed but is shaped in relation. According to Bauman, "The pilgrim and the desert-like world he walks acquire their meanings *together*, and *through each other.*"[23] When seen in light of Marx's challenge, however, Bauman's description is too general. Even in a neoliberal capitalist context, relationships are never as open ended as they might seem—an insight that many migrants would be able to confirm. Capitalism is not a matter of open-ended relationships but is structured in such a way that one class builds its wealth and power on the back of another class—the few extract the profit produced by the labor of the many. This is hard to deny at a time when it is generally acknowledged that the rich get richer and the poor get poorer. This is the context in which more and more people are beginning to wake up, as it is when the pretensions of seemingly stable traditions melt away that people can see their "real conditions of life" and "[their] relations with [their] kind."

In this context migrants might be the ones who resist this "melting into air" of capitalism and who keep seeking alternatives, "saving for an alternative future," and pilgrims might be able to join them in these efforts. In this way, they are defying the future projected by the capitalist economy and create an alternative vision connected to an alternative way of life.

This process begins when migrants remind us of the basic objective of capitalism, which is the production of profits at all cost, on the back of both humanity and the earth. Migrant workers experience the deepest tensions of the system, being both lured and pushed into migration as cheap labor and played off against other workers, linked to deteriorating circumstances in their locations. The rest of us need to learn from these experiences because, even though most of us also experience some of these tensions, we simply cannot be aware of the extent of destructive forces at work with the same existential intensity. Only when persons of faith, who also understand themselves as pilgrims in the deeper sense, get in touch with these struggles and engage in them can we begin to think about real change. To be sure, no academic (theologian or sociologist) studying or writing about migration and pilgrimage will make any progress without some forms of participation.

Under the pressures of global neoliberal capitalism a form of solidarity emerges (what I have elsewhere called deep solidarity)[24] that is based not primarily on extraordinary and heroic moral commitments but on the simple insight that we find ourselves in the same boat. Deep solidarity is based on the insight that what challenges the lives of migrant workers also challenges the lives of the proverbial 99 percent, all those who also have to work for a living under the conditions of capitalism. This goes a long way to address a problem that Alice Heo mentions in her chapter, namely that workers are suspicious of intellectuals, because they often abandon the struggle. This response is no longer possible once we understand that all of us are affected, even though some more and some less. When there is a sense that we are connected—if only because the capitalist system puts us in the same boat and challenges our existence and the future of life on planet earth in ways that previous generations could never have imagined—things can change.

Reflections on capitalism and class, therefore, need to become part of the project, including the study of theology and religion. Class, in this discussion, is not a matter of stratification (a common sociological understanding) but a matter of unequal relationships of power that include class struggle waged by the dominant class against everyone else, including the earth.[25] Those in the trenches—migrants—experience these class tensions in their own bodies but still need to develop a clearer understanding of what is going on, as too many are still drawn by the clichés of the "American Dream." People of faith—pilgrims—also need to pay attention because they are affected by class as well, yet in such a way that they pay closer attention to what is going on in the margins and engage in solidarity without erasing differences. Our relationships to the divine and to each other, including images of God and of ourselves, can be rethought on this basis in unprecedented ways that will make even the insights of the celebrated giants of theology seem flat.

The parallels between the experiences of pilgrims and migrants—despite all differences—resonate with Sam Cooke's blues song "A Change Is Gonna Come."[26] In this song, the protagonist talks about his birth in a small tent by a river and the fact that he had to run his whole life. Yet while living is hard, dying is even worse because of the worry about "what's up there beyond the sky." Yet despite these hardships, each stanza concludes with the confidence that change is coming. To be sure, neither pilgrims nor migrants are ultimately in control. Becoming a pilgrim used to mean relinquishing one's connections to the dominant powers, and the same is true for migrants. Cooke's character, however, finds himself in worse trouble than pilgrims could ever imagine—resonating deeply with the reality of migrants. The cards are stacked against him to such an extent that even the eternal home, to which pilgrims look forward in hope, has been replaced by a question mark. For Cooke's character, who may have been a slave in the past but who could also be a migrant in today's economy, not even heaven or the divine is a safe option.

This should not be surprising because the powers that be not only claim this world; they seek to claim any world on which they are able to lay their hands, including the world that is to come. Nevertheless, Cooke's character remains hopeful, an inspiration to pilgrims and migrants alike: change is on its way, and it is going to come. Both migrants and pilgrims know what the status quo of neoliberal capitalism (that infuses politics, economics, culture, faith, and even the academy) does not want them to know: none of the powers that be will last forever, and no empire is here to stay, despite prominent claims to the contrary. The kingdom of God, or God's empire, as M. P. Joseph calls it, must be something altogether different.

Rolf Potts, not a scholar of theology or religion but a travel writer dealing with the contemporary trends of vagabonding, puts his finger on one of the most powerful lessons that can be learned on the road: "If you travel long enough, you'll find that your spiritual revelations are invariably grounded in the everyday."[27] This may sound trite coming from someone who may have to worry little about day-to-day existence. Yet here is the lesson that can be learned from migrants and embodied by pilgrims. That God is at work in the everyday rather than "beyond the sky" is also the experience of many of the biblical travelers, from the Hebrew slaves in the desert to the people of God on the way in the book of Acts.

More specifically, these lessons are learned not on the mountaintops but in situations of pressure and trouble, from where they can inform all those who care enough to pay attention. As Paul says regarding the body of Christ, if one member suffers, all suffer together with it—and only then is it possible that if one member rejoices all rejoice together with it (1 Corinthians 12:26). The path on which we are called to walk as people of faith, in the histories of Judaism and Christianity, has been blazed by migrants, and it continues to be blazed by them today. What if these migrants were accompanied by true pilgrims, thereby ushering in glimpses of the reign of God in ways that might surprise us, without need for protective gates nor temples (Revelation 21:1–26) and without all the tired ways of status quo religion?

PLAN OF THE BOOK

In chapter 2, M. P. Joseph details the complexities of migration, taking into account not only the existential struggles of migrants but also the competing interests of migrants and those who employ them under the conditions of neoliberal capitalism. Migration is not just a matter of migrants being pushed out of their places of home; it is also a matter of pulling them to places where capital benefits from cheap labor and from the ability to play workers off against each other. Considering God's concern for working people, as manifested by the prophets of the Hebrew Bible and by Jesus, can serve as a challenge to the exploitation of migrant labor and creates new conditions for life.

In chapter 3, George Zachariah addresses the challenge of the commons as communal spaces that are increasingly colonized as neoliberal capitalism advances into all areas of life. His primary example is coastal communities in the south of India—a context where traditional concepts of pilgrimage often support spiritualities that perpetuate unjust social orders. Hope emerges where working people and religious communities reclaim the commons, engaging alternative pilgrimages and alternative interpretations of their traditions closely connected to social movements that refuse to be controlled by the dominant powers and, in the process, open up new encounters with each other and with God.

Deenabandhu Manchala, in chapter 4, discusses the experiences of those who are forced to migrate or have become victims of human trafficking, contrasting experiences of migration and pilgrimage, which are two important experiences of our time that have the potential to put people and their theologies in motion. The result is not only a deeper and reconstructed sense of what pilgrimage might mean but also a sense of how more appropriate theological understandings of pilgrimage as a "pilgrimage of life" might help deal more constructively with the problems of migration.

Chapter 5, by Alice Heo, addresses the struggles of working women in Asia under the conditions of capitalism and narrates their resistance as supported by communities of faith. Migration is part of the experience of these women as well, including long-standing sex tourism to Korea. In these contexts, the story of Women Church is one encouraging example of the practice of solidarity, as it provides support especially for women, who even today continue to be the "minjung of the minjung" and the oppressed of the oppressed. In the process, the agency of all women is affirmed and encouraged.

The notion of pilgrimage is further complicated in the relation of Jews and Christians in contemporary Israel. In chapter 6, Marc H. Ellis describes the problems with traditional notions of pilgrimage in situations where Christians engage in pilgrimage to sites of the Jewish Holocaust. Instead of life and the presence of God, these pilgrims experience and are challenged by visions of death and the absence of God. In the meantime, new forms of pilgrimage have arisen, led by Palestinians in Israel, and Ellis expresses some hope that the "broken middle of Jerusalem" could be maintained as a site of pilgrimage where injustice and death are mourned and justice and life are celebrated.

Wanda Deifelt, chapter 7, investigates what happens when patron saints such as Our Lady of Guadalupe are brought along on migratory journeys. What changes take place, and what kind of affirmation is experienced by the migrants and their faith? However, because the symbolism of these saints is malleable, they can support either the ecclesial and political status quo—as often happens—or those who are relegated to the margins and who experience unimaginable challenges. And even though migrants have managed to find support in religious symbolism in many cases, the struggle continues.

In chapter 8, Eliseo Pérez-Álvarez shifts the perspective to matters of migration, noting that people have been migrating since the earliest beginnings of humanity. Following along important developments in the complex histories of migration, Pérez-Álvarez points out the tensions and inconsistencies of the powers that be and how the concept of migration is now turned against those who are forced out of their places of home, and how migration is racialized and turned even against women and children. People of faith, in this context, need to learn to name things for what they are (Luther), thus "speaking truth to power."

Gemma Tulud Cruz, in chapter 9, discusses the concept of pilgrimage in the context of popular religion. Roman Catholic Latino/a migrants in the United States maintain constructive and creative roles for religion in their lives, thus bringing together experiences of migration and pilgrimage in new ways. To begin with, even the search for a better life, with all of its challenges, could be considered a pilgrimage. God is encountered in everyday life, and religion anchors the identities of individuals and communities not only on the journey itself but also in the places where migrants end up working, functioning in terms of resistance and the empowerment of the powerless.

Luis N. Rivera-Pagán, in the final chapter, develops a theology of migration in the increasingly xenophobic climate of the United States. The situation, which increasingly affects even children and teenagers and tears apart families, is dire and requires a response. Acknowledging the limits of the biblical traditions, which at times get caught up in xenophobia themselves, Rivera-Pagán interprets certain biblical motifs such as the Exodus and prophetic traditions as moving from xenophobia to xenophilia (the love of the stranger). That movement exemplifies a new form of solidarity.

To be sure, none of these struggles is likely to conclude any time soon or to disappear by itself, so ongoing investigation and involvement is required. Yet no matter how powerful and far reaching the consequences of global neoliberal capitalism, no empire in history has yet escaped finitude and collapse, and so there is reason for hopefulness in the midst of what now sometimes seems hopeless.[28]

NOTES

1. In the early days of Latin American liberation theology, Gustavo Gutiérrez repeatedly pointed out that the option for the poor was not based on the goodness of the poor but on the goodness of God.

2. Agence France-Presse, "US-Mexico Border Migrant Deaths Rose in 2017 Even as Crossings Fell, UN Says," *The Guardian*, February 6, 2018, sec. US news, https://www.theguardian.com/us-news/2018/feb/06/us-mexico-border-migrant-deaths-rose-2017.

3. Christiane Harzig, Dirk Hoerder, and Donna R. Gabaccia, *What Is Migration History?*, 1st ed. (Cambridge, UK, and Malden, MA: Polity, 2009), 134, 136.

4. For the notions of hybridity and ambivalence and their use in postcolonial theory see Homi K. Bhaba, *The Location of Culture* (London and New York: Routledge, 1994).

5. Dean MacCannell, *Empty Meeting Grounds: The Tourist Papers* (London and New York: Routledge, 1992), 2.

6. Nadje Al-Ali and Khalid Koser, "Transnationalism, International Migration, and Home," in *New Approaches to Migration?: Transnational Communities and the Transformation of Home*, ed. Nadje Al-Ali and Khalid Koser (London and New York: Routledge, 2001), 6.

7. Al-Ali and Koser, "Transnationalism, International Migration, and Home," 8.

8. Al-Ali and Koser, "Transnationalism, International Migration, and Home," 9.

9. For the notion of the multitude see Joerg Rieger and Kwok Pui-lan, *Occupy Religion: Theology of the Multitude*, reprint ed. (New York: Rowman & Littlefield Publishers, 2013).

10. Luigi Tomasi, "Homo Viator: From Pilgrimages to Religious Tourism via the Journey," in *From Medieval Pilgrimage to Religious Tourism: The Social and Cultural Economics of Piety*, ed. William H. Swatos, William H. Swatos Jr., and Luigi Tomasi (Westport, CT: Praeger, 2002), 3.

11. Ellen Badone and Sharon R. Roseman, "Approaches to the Anthropology of Pilgrimage and Tourism," in *Intersecting Journeys: The Anthropology of Pilgrimage and Tourism*, ed. Ellen Badone and Sharon R. Roseman (Urbana: University of Illinois Press, 2004), 2.

12. Tomasi, "Homo Viator," 4–21.

13. Tomasi, "Homo Viator," 21.

14. Joerg Rieger, *God and the Excluded: Visions and Blindspots in Contemporary Theology* (Minneapolis, MN: Fortress Press, 2000), chapter 4.

15. Badone and Roseman, "Approaches to the Anthropology of Pilgrimage and Tourism," 3.(reference to Victor Turner).

16. Walter Mignolo, *Local Histories/Global Design: Coloniality, Subaltern Knowledges and Border Thinking* (Princeton, NJ: Princeton University Press, 2000).

17. Gustavo Gutiérrez, "Church of the Poor," in *Born of the Poor: The Latin American Church since Medellin*, ed. Edward L. Cleary, 1st ed. (Notre Dame, IN: University of Notre Dame Press, 1990), 16.

18. Georg Thurmaier and Adolf Lohmann, 1935/1938, *Gesangbuch der Evangelisch-methodistischen Kirche* (Stuttgart, Germany: Medienwerk der Evangelisch-methodistischen Kirche, 2002), 1210.

19. Dietrich Bonhoeffer, according to his biographer Eberhard Bethge.

20. Zygmunt Bauman, "From Pilgrim to Tourist—or a Short History of Identity," in *Questions of Cultural Identity*, ed. Stuart Hall and Paul du Gay, 1st ed. (London and Thousand Oaks, CA: Sage, 1996), 21.

21. Bauman, "From Pilgrim to Tourists," 23.

22. Karl Marx and Friedrich Engels, *The Communist Manifesto* (New York: Pocket, 1964), 63.

23. Bauman, "From Pilgrim to Tourist," 22.
24. Rieger and Pui-lan, *Occupy Religion*; Joerg Rieger and Rosemarie Henkel-Rieger, *Unified We Are a Force: How Faith and Labor Can Overcome America's Inequalities* (St. Louis, MO: Chalice Press, 2016).
25. Joerg Rieger, ed., *Religion, Theology, and Class: Fresh Engagements after Long Silence* (New York: Palgrave Macmillan, 2013).
26. Sam Cooke, "A Change Is Gonna Come," on *Ain't that Good News* (Camden, NJ: RCA Victor, 1964).
27. Rolf Potts, *Vagabonding: An Uncommon Guide to the Art of Long-Term Travel* (New York: Villard, 2003), 190.
28. In conversation with Miguel A. De La Torre, *Embracing Hopelessness* (Minneapolis, MN: Fortress Press, 2017).

BIBLIOGRAPHY

Al-Ali, Nadje, and Khalid Koser. "Transnationalism, International Migration, and Home." In *New Approaches to Migration?: Transnational Communities and the Transformation of Home*, edited by Nadje Al-Ali and Khalid Koser. London and New York: Routledge, 2001.
Badone, Ellen, and Sharon R. Roseman. "Approaches to the Anthropology of Pilgrimage and Tourism." In *Intersecting Journeys: The Anthropology of Pilgrimage and Tourism*, edited by Ellen Badone and Sharon R. Roseman. Urbana: University of Illinois Press, 2004.
Bauman, Zygmunt. "From Pilgrim to Tourist—or a Short History of Identity." In *Questions of Cultural Identity*, edited by Stuart Hall and Paul du Gay, 1st ed. London and Thousand Oaks, CA: Sage, 1996.
Bhaba, Homi K. *The Location of Culture*. London and New York: Routledge, 1994.
France-Presse, Agence. "US-Mexico Border Migrant Deaths Rose in 2017 Even as Crossings Fell, UN Says." *The Guardian*, February 6, 2018, sec. US news. https://www.theguardian.com/us-news/2018/feb/06/us-mexico-border-migrant-deaths-rose-2017.
Gutiérrez, Gustavo. "Church of the Poor." In *Born of the Poor: The Latin American Church Since Medellin*, edited by Edward L. Cleary, 1st ed. Notre Dame: University of Notre Dame Press, 1990.
Harzig, Christiane, Dirk Hoerder, and Donna R. Gabaccia. *What Is Migration History?* 1st ed. Cambridge, UK , and Malden, MA: Polity, 2009.
MacCannell, Dean. *Empty Meeting Grounds: The Tourist Papers*. London and New York: Routledge, 1992.
Marx, Karl, and Friedrich Engels. *The Communist Manifesto*. New York: Pocket, 1964.
Mignolo, Walter. *Local Histories/Global Design: Coloniality, Subaltern Knowledges and Border Thinking*. Princeton, NJ: Princeton University Press, 2000.
Potts, Rolf. *Vagabonding: An Uncommon Guide to the Art of Long-Term Travel*. New York: Villard, 2003.
Rieger, Joerg. *God and the Excluded: Visions and Blindspots in Contemporary Theology*. Minneapolis, MN: Fortress Press, 2000.
———, ed. *Religion, Theology, and Class: Fresh Engagements after Long Silence*. New York: Palgrave Macmillan, 2013.
Rieger, Joerg, and Rosemarie Henkel-Rieger. *Unified We Are a Force: How Faith and Labor Can Overcome America's Inequalities*. St. Louis, MO: Chalice Press, 2016.
Rieger, Joerg, and Kwok Pui-lan. *Occupy Religion: Theology of the Multitude*. Reprint ed. New York: Rowman & Littlefield Publishers, 2013.
Tomasi, Luigi. "Homo Viator: From Pilgrimages to Religious Tourism via the Journey." In *From Medieval Pilgrimage to Religious Tourism: The Social and Cultural Economics of Piety*, edited by William H. Swatos, William H. Swatos Jr., and Luigi Tomasi. Westport, CT: Praeger, 2002.
Torre, Miguel A. De La. *Embracing Hopelessness*. Minneapolis, MN: Fortress Press, 2017.

Part I

On the Move under the Conditions of Global Capital

Chapter Two

"Buy Our Bodies and Our Land That We May Live"

The Story of the Faceless Migrant Laborers

M. P. Joseph

Perhaps the story of Andrea Baguiold, a Filipino live-in domestic worker in Taiwan, depicts the plight of migrant laborers around the world. In an interview with a group of theology students, Bagauilod said:

> I came to Taiwan with the expectation to work as an auxiliary nurse, for which I signed a contract. When I landed at the Kaohsiung airport, [my passport was taken and] was sent to a house in Tainan. The local sponsor informed me that my primary responsibility is to work as an auxiliary nurse but initially need to take care of ailing grandfather. However, needs of the household was not just a caregiver, but a live-in domestic worker, expected to shoulder all the burdens of the daily chores. There isn't any specific job description for a live-in domestic worker. Consequently, no end to the list of responsibilities either. The family was good to me in many ways. Strangely they demanded that I should stay inside the house always, no freedom to go to the 7-11 shop, which is around the corner, to procure goods for personal needs, to the post office to send mail to the loved ones in the Philippines or to the Catholic Church with a sizable number of Filipino members, despite the knowledge that I am a devout Catholic. I have seen the sun and moon only through the windows for almost two years.[1]

Baguilod later realized that this treatment of live-in domestic maids was not uncommon among families who employed such people. They were denied a social life to avert the risk of migrants coming together and sharing their joys and frustrations. Despite the experience of incarceration, Baguilod observed that she was one of the privileged among domestic workers. The stories of others are more gruesome and bizarre.[2]

Baguiold had three children between the ages of two and ten when she left her country. She had led a rather comfortable life in Iloilo, central Philippines. She is a trained auxiliary nurse, and after marriage, she joined her husband in a grocery shop business, which offered them sufficient income to meet their household needs. But their dreams came tumbling down when the city of Iloilo "invited" a multinational retailer to open a supermarket in the town. "Initially our regular customers stayed with us, but it was only for a short time," she said. The supermarket had a fully air-conditioned space, neatly packed groceries, and occasional "surprise" sale items. "It was impossible for us to compete with them." Votaries of the free market say it offers fair competition, but Baguiold's experience testifies otherwise. They lost to the competition miserably. The couple had even sold their ancestral land in the village to raise capital to start the grocery shop. "Failing to locate any alternative, I made use of my auxiliary nurse certificate to locate this job," she said.

The story of Baguiold is not an isolated one. By 2015, the average number of Overseas Filipino Workers [OFWs] leaving the Manila airport reached a phenomenal 6,092 per day.[3] This means that OFWs outnumber locally employed Filipinos. In 2013, the number of OFWs breached the 2 million mark while the number of locally employed Filipinos was 1.02 million, depicting the narrowing of job opportunities in the nation. This phenomenon has not arrested the flow of migrants from the rural areas to the urban centers. With the rural economy experiencing a strain, a large number of people are moving out of rural areas in search of a living.[4] According to the International Migration Report (United Nations), the number of international migrants worldwide reached 258 million in 2017, up from 220 million in 2010 and 173 million in 2000.[5]

Baguiold's reality and similar cases lead to four primary assumptions:

1. Migration in itself is not the major issue that workers and nations presently face. Rather, migration is a symptom of the much more profound crisis visiting poor communities around the world. People are forced to migrate due to the destruction of the living possibilities in their own domicile.
2. Migrants are not often making subjective decisions informed by a cost-benefit analysis on whether and when to migrate. Those decisions are made beyond the migrant's agency. This has been true throughout the history of mass migration, which includes the forceful removal of able-bodied people as slaves and indentured laborers during European colonialism.

3. The primary function of migration is to satisfy the interest of capital. The relative benefit of migration to international capital is enormous when compared to the gains of the individual migrants. This function is contrary to what is depicted as the primary vocation of labor in the creation narrative in the Bible. According to biblical reminders, the cardinal concern of labor is the reproduction of life, and thus, labor becomes a spiritual function. But the quality of human life rests on the ability to have subjective control over labor such that through labor life finds fulfilment. Origin of evil amounts to the attempt to control the subjective relation of other to the objective world (Genesis 3:1–6), thereby depriving others of the ability and rights to make independent decisions about how to organize their life and their relationship to the material world. In the Genesis narrative the snake controlled the decisions of the primordial human community through deception. The evil distorts the goal of human relationship to materiality. Besides when labor is for capital, humanity is deprived. A person does not exist as a laborer, but the ability to labor becomes a means to celebrate life with subjectivity.

4. The response of churches and social movements around the globe to the growing phenomenon of migration is centered around the concepts of hospitality, compassion, human rights, and human dignity. Though these approaches are cardinal, they are, perhaps, not sufficient to address the profound crisis that the people and nations now confront.

The history of migration is as old as the history of humankind. Fish, birds, and animals migrate when their own domiciles are not adequate to meet the needs of survival. The biblical stories of Cain, Abraham, Jacob, and others often perpetuate the idea that migration is a social option to sustain life.

COLONIAL DISCOURSE ON MIGRATION

Migration is not always perceived in negative terms. Within the genre of social sciences, for instance, several efforts have been made to establish the notion that the development of civilization owes its credit to migration. The colonial schools of sociology created the understanding that culture and civilization were developed in certain centers of the world and subsequently diffused throughout the rest of the world through migration and colonization. Though this was a colonial construct, the histories of many nations were reconstructed to rationalize the assumption. One apt example is the Aryan invasion myth created to delineate Indian history.[6] According to this theory, the Aryan tribe, from the northern steppes, invaded India about 1500 B.C.E., bringing the sophisticated Hindu civilization with them. The Aryan invasion theory not only offered a racial justification for the caste system (allegedly the upper caste hails from the invading white northerners and the lower caste were composed of the dark-skinned Dravidians, who in prehistoric times originated from the black tribes of African and Austroasiatic communities), but it also legitimized European colonialism.[7] This myth is constituent of modernization theories, especially those that belong to the sociological schools.[8] Mission agencies are not different. They have rationalized their participation in the colonial project by alluding to this fictitious construction and perceive mission as a God-given mandate to salvage the rest of the world from barbarity.

Incidentally, migrations reached phenomenal levels during the time of colonialism. The period from 1850 to 1913 was one of mass migration, when some 51 million people left Europe to settle in other parts of the world. In the first three decades after 1846, the numbers averaged around 300,000 a year, doubled in the following two decades, and then exceeded a million a year by the turn of the century.[9]

The invading migrants from Europe[10] gained subjecthood of their own lives to various degrees while the fate of the people who were forcefully shipped as objects was rather different.[11] These early migrations radically amended the economic, political, and cultural geography of the world.

The world's economic development since colonialism was directed by the enormous economic power Europe gained through the control of resources. The demonetization of people in the colonies[12] led to their becoming pawns to any form of migration. Like pieces on a chessboard, people were uprooted from their own domiciles and moved around the world. There was no attempt to create labor opportunities for people in their respective nations or to prevent these large-scale migrations.

Search for Economic Subjectivity

Post-independent nations around the world attempted new economic beginnings with more protective markets. Governments in the newly independent nations realized that in the absence of protection of their production relationship, their economies would remain blocked systems with structural impediments against growth.[13] Restrictions on imports, exports, and capital movements appeared as a policy among Third World nations to ensure the safety of their budding industries and the economic security of the people. One of the professed goals was the creation of employment opportunities within the Third World, in hopes of equipping laborers by imparting new skills in science and technology. Most of these nations strengthened their welfare systems as well as the public education systems by investing more in the life of the people. Tanzania, under the leadership of Julius Nyerere, is one such example. As Colin Legum and G. R. V. Mmari report:

Tanzania under Nyerere made great strides in vital areas of social development: infant mortality was reduced from 138 per 1000 live births in 1965 to 110 in 1985; life expectancy at birth rose from 37 in 1960 to 52 in 1984; primary school enrollment was raised from 25% of age group (only 16% of females) in 1960 to 72% (85% of females) in 1985 (despite the rapidly increasing population); the adult literacy rate rose from 17% in 1960 to 63% by 1975 (much higher than in other African countries) and continued to rise. [14]

These initiatives by the newly independent nations resonate with the observation of Amartya Sen that poverty is the consequence of the deprivation of the capability to live a good life. Building capabilities was hence taken as the primary objective for the planned economy.

Protectionist policies in the Third World resulted in the slow growth of global capitalism. The determination for capability building and the protection given to the economics of the Third World resulted in the stagnation of economic growth in rich nations. Two factors probably have contributed to the stagnation. One is the apparent deficiency of investment avenues for the growth of capital due to the protectionism of the Third World. The second is that the wages of the working class in the West remained the same or even lower due to the lack of access to the labor market outside their own economic domain. Consequently, their purchasing power remained the same and the ability to participate in the commodity market stagnated. To prevent stagnation and to invigorate growth, capital faced the urgent need to find new ways of expansion and control of labor.

Apart from control over primary resources and unfettered access to markets, capitalist growth is structurally dependent on the creation of conditions that ensure the oversupply of labor. Large masses of people should enter and leave the labor market according to the needs of the capital. Surplus labor is not an upshot of the respective growth of population. Labor becomes surplus when the economy is regulated by a profit regime that creates artificial excess supply as the rule for accumulation for the sake of accumulation.

Promotion of Migrant Labor to Ensure Autonomy of Capital

To accelerate growth, autonomy of capital over all other possible economic forces is considered to be imperative in neoliberal economic models. The two forces that demonstrate a threat to the autonomy of capital are national governments and unionized workers. Enforcement of International Monetary Fund (IMF) policies systematically curtailed the ability of state power to govern economic matters. Furthermore, the IMF and other global economic structures created by global capitalist forces have demonized the term "state power" and its role in welfare, education, health care, and other civic responsibilities. As a result, individuals without marketable capital have to offer their bodies to be purchased as a commodity in order to keep themselves alive.

To ensure the total control of capital over all other production relationships in order to accelerate accumulation, global capitalism employed two strategies: (1) converting capital to a nomadic state by creating conditions to ensure mobility of capital to all corners of the world, and (2) promoting (non-unionizable) aliens to flock into national labor markets. When the pool of reserve labor is large, the labor price remains extremely cheap, and, as a result, the rate of profit will reach the highest possible ranges. In the process known as globalization, terms like "free market" and other terms preceded by the adjective "free" were deceptions used by global capitalists to make this pool of reserve surplus labor large enough to ensure unfettered growth of capital. Western economies, with the aid of multinational corporations, systematically derailed the economic structures of the Third World and promoted the process of labor export. They moved capital and labor to one place in order to accelerate production, but they did so under the strict control of capital. These measures also helped weaken the power of unionized workers and granted total autonomy for capital over the entire economic process. Stories of the total defeat of labor struggles, echoed from Detroit to Seoul and from Bombay to Sao Paulo, reiterate this fact. Uprooted workers, with the absence of any citizenship rights, remain economic variables. They have no political subjectivity and no right to participate in the political process, neither in the sending countries nor in the so-called receiving countries, and they thus live in noncivil entities with no claims or rights to any civil or political rights. In the present scenario, where capital and labor have assumed this nomadic character, labor is reduced to an economic variable with no rights of protection, while capital gains political subjectivity and thus the highest level of protection. For example, when Taiwanese capital sets up companies in Cambodia and employs labor from Myanmar, Taiwanese capital receives protection from the Cambodian government while Myanmar workers receive zero protection from any legal structures.

From the history of slavery onwards, capitalists learned that as the vulnerability of labor increases, the power and autonomy of capital also increase. Although locally available labor was more than sufficient to maintain competitive production relationships, the logic of the importation of labor from other countries to destabilize the local labor reiterates the urge of capital to establish autonomy. The uprooted labor abetted colonial masters to maintain total control over production and resources. At the present time, the lack of any legal framework to protect the migrants helps the capitalist production relationship keep this labor force completely dependent. The rule in the game of survival dictates that they shall compete with each other to express their total and unflinching loyalty to their capitalist masters.

It is indeed deplorable that migrant labor is now used as the mercenary of capital to defeat the spirit of unionization among the working class. Trade unions are seen by capital as agencies with potential to form counter-hegemony to capital. Though it is not intentional, the survival needs of the migrants ended up positioning them into the role of mercenaries of capital. If there is a lack of solidarity between migrant workers and local workers, it is the result of this reactionary position into which the migrants are pushed.

Demographic Changes

Apart from the strategy of gaining autonomy for capital, a second reason for the promotion of migrant labor, as is often cited, is the changing demographic patterns in middle-income nations such as Taiwan, Korea, Japan, and others. Societies such as Taiwan, while experiencing a sharp decline in birthrate, have witnessed a significant rise in life expectancy, granting the nation the title of a super-aged society. The percentage of the population classified as elderly in the country in 2017 was 14.05, and by 2025 it is expected to cross 20 percent.[15] Meanwhile, the working age population of people between 15 and 64 years has decreased by 180,000 each year (out of a total population of 22 million) since 2015.

This leads to two challenges: (1) to find more human labor for the growing service industry and (2) to locate additional labor in the industrial sector to replace the declining labor population of natives to maintain the current rate of production.

The escalating need of personnel in the service sector has, in turn, changed the gender ratio among migrants. In 2014, when 186,243 Indonesian men migrated to other countries to join the labor force, 243,629 women migrated for work.[16] In the Philippines, by 2010, the female-male ratio of new hires was 135,168 females to 19,367 males, showing the rapid change in the demand for labor in the service sector.[17] Men are largely employed in the industrial and construction sectors; women occupy the service sector. When the government of Indonesia announced its policy to stop sending women as live-in domestic workers to East Asian nations, a special delegation from Taiwan visited Indonesia to request the policy makers to reconsider their decision.

MIGRANTS, AN INEVITABLE FORCE TO MAINTAIN GLOBAL ECONOMY

In spite of this reality, conservative rhetoric voices the myth that the presence of migrants is economically and socially destructive to host nations. This rhetoric is important both to gain political sympathy among the group of unemployed who lost their jobs because of the nomadic character of the capital[18] and to increase the feeling of vulnerability in the minds of the migrants, making them more docile and submissive.

The popular argument from anti-migrant political movements assumes that migrants consume the social security privileges meant for the natives, creating a strain on the ability of nation-states to provide adequate care for all. Moreover, migrants are viewed as people that siphon off the resources of the host countries to the sending countries. Figures provided by the International Labor Organization (ILO) debunk this assumption. They show that the majority of the industrialized economies would be significantly crippled without the help of a strong migrant workforce. A report titled "Foreigners Contribute to the Korean Economy" observed that migrant laborers "have become the spine of corporate Korea."[19] *Taipei Times* ran a similar report: "In the past it was Taiwanese laborers that went abroad to find employment. Now we import foreign labor. These workers have been indispensable to the nation's economic development and we could not do without them, in terms of both their contribution to the economy as well as our society."[20]

The economic contribution of migrants to the respective host societies is immensely high; a large number of the major economies would find it difficult to pull on without the economic contribution from this segment of workers. The ability to compute the financial contribution of the migrants to host economies seems to be lacking, though. Hence, the surplus generated through their labor to the productive forces in host countries remains unaccounted. Yet it seems that they are appallingly underpaid for the labor that they invest in the production lines of host countries. There are now several ongoing efforts to calculate migrant contributions to the economy. These studies suggest that migrant workers transfer "on average 13 per cent of their income back to their country of origin, which means they spend 87 percent in the host country."[21] These figures lead to the conclusion that "the contribution of migrant workers to host countries worldwide has a value of more than US \$1 trillion."[22]

The Logic that Creates Slavery

The logical reasoning that capital uses to "manufacture" migrant workers is an improvised strategy found in the biblical narrative that Joseph, Pharaoh's minister, employed in Egypt to institute slavery (Genesis 43–47). The legendary wise man did not employ his wisdom to help people under his jurisdiction to overcome famine; he used the natural calamities as a means for enslaving them.

Joseph employed four economic initiatives:

1. *Creation of artificial scarcity.* During the time of the seven good years of bountiful harvest, Joseph filled the state granaries with grain and

consequently depleted the storage facilities of the people. Scarcity is not the deficiency of resources; it is the insufficient means for people to procure those resources. Both abundance and scarcity are relative terms. With the act of hoarding grain, Joseph created scarcity.

2. *Demonetization of the currency.* During the succeeding years of scarcity (famine), Joseph did not provide free food to the people in distress, but he *sold* the grain that they had accumulated until he "gathered up *all* the money" (Genesis 47:13–14), ultimately bringing all of it "into Pharaoh's house." Joseph removed all the currency (the silver and shekel) from circulation and thereby deprived the poor of their purchasing capacity. This act of removing currency pushed the Egyptian economy into an economic depression, which only exacerbated the famine. If currency had stayed in circulation, folks might have had the option of buying food from other places, including Canaan. (Note that when Jacob sent his children to buy food, he filled their bags with good nuts, fruits, and other food stuff, indicating that non-availability was not the problem.) The people would perhaps even have had the ability to find ways to work their way through the famine. But with no food and no money (purchasing power), the economy collapsed, and people eventually were trapped in a spiral of famine and poverty, becoming absolutely *dependent* on the rulers who hoarded capital and resources.

3. *Depriving people of their economic subjectivity.* After establishing total control over money (cash economy), Joseph turned his attention to divesting people of their infrastructure for production. He forced people to barter their livestock for food. This plan lasted for almost a year, and Joseph collected horses, goats, cattle, donkeys, and all the required supplements to engage in agricultural production.

4. *Finally, appropriation of land, resources, and "bodies."* The final stage of slavery was a natural corollary. Once deprived of any control over the money economy and participation in production due to lack of implements, the Egyptians, fearing death by starvation, sold their land and "their bodies" to the ruling establishment. They turned to Joseph and pleaded, "Buy us . . . we will be slaves to Pharaoh" (Genesis 47:19).

The economic logic that Joseph employed is repeated several times, with various different forms of narrative grammar.[23] The phenomenon of migrant labor, ever since the advent of speculative finance capital, is predominantly a corollary of the implementation of this economic logic of slavery. Neoliberalism first introduced the "growth model" as the only panacea to address an artificial scarcity alleged by the global economic powers, and it followed by aiding the global economic forces to monopolize production and distribution. The immediate ramification was the conversion of common people into wage laborers, waiting to sell their labor power to find a means for living. Petty producers, traders, and farmers have lost their space in the monopoly market and are forced to abandon their subjective identity. The process of de-peasantisation has contributed to the largest number of job seekers. Two factors have accelerated the death of the peasantry:

1. *Monopolization of agricultural production.* Marginalization of peasants from agricultural relations, through the monopolization of agriculture by big agro-business corporations who have replaced the small producers around the world, commenced the debacle of the peasantry.[24] With the absolute control of big agro-business companies over seeds, fertilizers, and farm products, farmers are forced to abandon agricultural activities and turn themselves into wage laborers. Some of them take the most extreme step to escape this reality—the total number of farmer suicides in India between 1995 and 2014 was more than 300,000.[25]

2. *Primitive accumulation of land and natural resources.* Appropriation of land and resources by big business has pushed millions of farmers off their own land and turned them into daily wage laborers. Close to 50 percent of arable land in Madagascar, for instance, is in the hands of Daewoo Logistics of Korea.[26] As many as 3.2 million hectares have been taken for 99 years at a meager rate of US $12 a hectare per year. As of 2013, mega-corporations had bought 49 million hectares of land in the Third World, mainly in Africa. People who lost their land were forced to join the army of job seekers, whose number has swollen from 1.5 billion to 3.3 billion in the last 20 years.

Petty traders have also met the same fate. According to a United Nations Conference on Trade and Development report, 80 percent of global trade is controlled by 147 global corporations, but 95 percent of the investment by the 147 companies is in the hands of just four investment firms. This is the bizarre reality of monopolization. Small retailers have lost their livelihood in the competition with mega-corporations and have subsequently entered the job market.

A third group to have greatly suffered is the petty commodity producers. Handloom weavers in India, once the pride of Indian nationalism, demonstrate the plight of the petty producers. Official surveys published by the Office of the Development Commissioner (Handlooms) recounted that the number of weaver families has been reduced from 12.4 million in the 1970s to 6.4 million in 1995, and further down to 4.4 million in 2010.[27] By 2010, more than 70 percent of the textile market was controlled by big textile manufacturers.

The growth of reserve labor has made the labor crisis precarious. When the ability to find jobs in one's own country is limited, people are forced to move around the world with billboards announcing the sale of their bodies.

Demonetization has substantially increased the flow of migrant labor. After the East Asian monetary crisis of 1997, the number of migrants leaving the poorer East Asian nations has nearly tripled.[28] The devaluation of currency wiped out the savings of the people, and they were left only with the option of seeking employment elsewhere. Illegal migration also increased in the post-1997 crisis period.

These realities question the dominant assumption that "migrants make a cost-benefit analysis and migrate only when the benefits of migration outweigh the cost."[29] The poor are not free to make rational choices. Life in the market society is rather "choreographed."[30] Free choice is an unrealistic concept in a choreographed existence. The poor who lose their subjectivity to capital are instructed what to do. This has been true in the past and repeats itself in history. Migration is not an outcome of the subjective decision of laborers. On the contrary, the migrants are forced to sell themselves as cheap labor by deliberately destabilizing their means of living by the global capitalist class. Policies of primitive accumulation in the early stages of industrial capitalism adopted the same dynamic. They made rural life untenable, and, as a consequence, farmers left their farming activities and migrated to industrial centers as wage laborers.

As the traditional logic accentuates, when the population making up the reserve surplus labor enlarges, those who control capital gains also obtain absolute control over the forces of production. As such, the labor force is deprived of any bargaining power. According to International Labor Organization (ILO) figures, 630 million workers in the industrial sectors receive less than US $1.25 a day.

Victims of a Perceived Economic Insecurity

Historically, as discussed above, labor migration did not stem from the personal will of the individual worker, but rather from of the needs of capital. Early migration from Asia during colonial times reiterates this observation. The Dutch colonial regime sent thousands of Javanese to Suriname as cheap labor, as coolies on plantations. Thousands of Indians were forcefully taken to various African countries and the Pacific—Fiji in particular. They were displaced from relatively comfortable economic zones and converted into cheap human capital.

Contrary to this reality, labor anthropology suggests that "migration is the simple response to poverty,"[31] meaning that the majority of those who migrate are poor and that they benefit from the process of migration. Empirical realities speak otherwise. Interviews with domestic workers in Taiwan have pointed out that a majority of the migrant workers are university degree holders, some with teacher training certificates, engineering degrees, and law degrees from their respective countries. But they are victims of a collective feeling of economic insecurity. The feeling of economic insecurity has been consciously constructed among the commons by the forces that control production and market. This feeling has been converted as "a common sense" that regulates their life and their decisions. This perception creates fear of a potential vulnerability in the minds of laborers who, as a result, submit themselves to the interest of capital. This strategy of capital to manipulate public consciousness in order to preserve the prevailing exploitative economic reality is contrary to what Joerg and Rosemarie Rieger identified as the approach of Jesus. The objective of Jesus was to "exchange a broken material reality for a new one."[32]

The ideology of "economism," constructed by neoliberal market forces, has a tremendous impact on the creation of a sense of economic insecurity. Economism, among other proposals, suggests that prosperity equals a better life. Since the search for a better life is a constituent of human nature, economism implies that the unending search for accumulation is ethical, informed by the urge for goodness. That feeling makes people refuse to be satisfied by any given conditions of life.

A Political Product

Globalization has also promoted the growth of a rather small elite lumpen class, totally dependent on the international monopoly capital, in the Third World, who are intoxicated with an incessant savor for luxury goods. Their hedonistic desire for new technologies and luxury gadgets places pressure on national governments to find foreign capital to facilitate the import of these luxury items. Defeated by multinational corporations in the field of consumer goods production, along with a fall in the price of raw materials exported from the Third World, the only exchangeable commodity that can be produced and exported to earn foreign currencies needed to import luxury items for the elites is human bodies.[33] As a result, governments have started to set up special ministerial centers to promote the sale of human bodies to international capital. For example, the government of India—the largest remittance-receiving country from migrant workers, with an estimated $79 billion in 2018—set up the India Centre for Migration in July 2008. The center serves as a research think-tank to facilitate migrant labor flows and to advise the government on all matters relating to "international migration." The center undertakes empirical-, analytical-, and policy-related research, and initiates pilot projects to advise job seekers to find jobs outside India. Even the state governments in India initiated their own centers to assist the migrants. Non-Resident Keralites (NORKA) of the government of Kerala is one such institution. Several universities in the sending countries are running special programs to manufacture this export commodity labeled "migrant labor."

Commodification of Virtue

Most of these new migrants fall under the category of live-in domestic workers or caregivers, who have no specific job description, working hours, or leave rules. The expectation is not to "work for a family," but "work in a family." The workplace is the only place of belonging. Thus, the requirement is to convert the work space into a real family by suspending all other family affinities. All tasks that are necessary for the upkeep of a family (cooking, cleaning, caring for children, caring for parents, emotionally accompanying family members, etc.) fall under the job requirements. There is no moment when a domestic worker can think that her task is finished; it always remains undone.

The dynamics that operate in the live-in domestic worker system are akin to that of slavery, except for the fact that there was no monetary contract between a slave and the slave master in a slaveholding system like there is for live-in domestic workers. Like a slave, the domestic worker submits her being, not just her labor power, to the one who has purchased her from the labor market. The figure of the slave was captured by brutal force; the live-in domestic worker is appropriated by creating uninhabitable economic conditions in poor nations. A domestic worker sells her very being, her spiritual abilities to love and care, and her faculties of reproduction of life. Emotional accompaniment is brought under the realm of market exchange. This reality raises a few ethical questions:

1. Live-in domestic labor reifies and commodifies virtues such as love, care, responsibility, goodness, and everything else that constitutes this genre.
2. The discussion of justice is rather erroneous in this condition. In the traditional labor market, it is assumed that the price of labor is measured in terms of output. When virtues such as love and goodness are brought under the wage economy, how does one find an appropriate price? How can one measure the output with respect to love and emotions?
3. The new phenomenon is often described as "care drain," where mothers are forced to "abandon" their young children or daughters or leave their elderly parents without any alternative to offer care. They sell their spiritual abilities to be a mother or a daughter to those who have the financial ability to buy their caring abilities. As a result, centers of capital hold an abundance of care,[34] while the children of poor neigh-

borhoods are deprived of any affectionate caring concern from anyone.[35]

4. Live-in domestic workers, similar to slaves, transcend the distinction
   between private and public. The public is often considered to be the
   space of wage labor, while the private is imagined to be free from such
   concerns. Live-in labor is reproductive labor because the output is
   social, cultural, or even spiritual instead of material. Live-in labor
   reproduces life and nurtures human beings with subjectivity, dignity,
   and personhood. The capacity to transcend the exchange rules of the
   market is the spiritual strength of the realm of the reproduction of life.
   This is in danger now. Live-in domestic workers reduced the gift of
   reproduction of life as a commodity for exchange in the market. As
   Carol Gilligan has observed, the spiritual ability of care is the foundation for a moral society, and the death of that spiritual faculty signifies
   the death of the ethical.[36]

Deified God

Migrant laborers become nonpersons under the regime of speculative capital.
Being reduced to economic variables, they are shipped around the globe
under the exchange rules of the market and are condemned to remain without
any citizenship rights or freedom.

The living labor is objectified. Since the face of living labor is the highest
point of God's revelation in history, as God's own image, capitalism objec-
tifies God. The objectification of God is the root of idolatry in the present
system.

Biblical accounts do not delineate how the descendants of Joseph became
victims of slavery, but it was arguably designed by Joseph.[37] Perhaps it is
rational to consider that Pharaoh, abetted by Joseph's knack in creating the
logic of slavery, amassed enough power to subvert the relatively decentralized political system of the tribal configurations, and constructed a hegemonic imperial order with centralized governance. Joseph reduced most of the
Egyptians to slaves and took over all farmland and implements for production. The groups that were spared were the priests and the descendants of
Jacob. As a constituent logic of imperialism, an emperor would need to be
vigilant and thwart the possibility of any forces growing as a counter-power.
Besides, an empire cannot allow different models of economics to coexist
within the regime. As a result, the Israelites became the victims of the same
centralized empire that Joseph helped to build.

Prophetic imperatives of the later period were aimed at preventing the
construction of centralized power structures, thus averting the emergence of
empires. To ensure democratic decentralized systems, the prophets said: "At
the end of every seven years you shall grant a remission of debts. This is the

manner of remission: all creditors shall release what they have loaned to their neighbors; they shall not exact it of their neighbors and their siblings, because the LORD'S remission has been proclaimed. In this year of jubilee, you shall return, every one of you, to your property" (Deuteronomy 15:1–2; Leviticus 25: 13). Restoring equity among all our neighbors is the precondition to establishing a just society.

Deuteronomic instruction aimed to prevent the germination of imperialism, but it is morally deficient because of the provision granted to subjugate and objectify foreigners (Deuteronomy 15:3). An alternate vision with a comprehensive and profound rejection of an exploitative economic order was offered by the prophet Isaiah. Channeling the voice of God, the prophet exhorted: "Behold, I create new heavens and the new earth. . . . They shall build houses and inhabit them; they shall plant vineyards and eat their fruits. They shall not build and another inhabit; they shall not plant and another eat; . . . They shall long enjoy the work of their hands. They shall not labor in vain, or bear children in calamity" (Isaiah 65:17–23). As Marc Ellis has reminded us, embodying the possibility of meaning in history is the prophetic task, "and by embodying the prophetic, prophets embody the possibilities of God."[38] Isaiah embodied this vision of history at a time when Jerusalem was converted to a synonym for rampant form of exploitation of peasant communities under the monarchic systems supported by tributary systems of taxes that led the poor to debt slavery.

Although the quantification of the extent of exploitation of the poor peasants by King Solomon, through various forms of taxes, appears to be imprecise or symbolic, the writer(s) of 1 Kings observed: "The weight of gold which Solomon received every year was 666 talents of gold, besides what came from tradesmen, from the traffic of the merchants, and from all the kings of Arabia and the governors of the regions" (1 Kings 10:14; also 2 Chronicles 9:13). This enormous wealth (perhaps equivalent to around 25 tons of gold per year) is a reified form of the sweat and blood of the farmers and the working people, since wealth could be created only through the interaction of labor and nature and the so-called rulers and wealthy class hardly invest any labor in the production process. "Wealthy" denotes the conditions that enabled a few to appropriate the "fruits of the labor" of the others. The prophet Isaiah, speaking for God, negates the system that controls and commoditizes labor: "They shall plant vineyards and eat their fruits." Production is for the celebration of life. The prophet Isaiah embodies the possibility of God and thus profoundly delegitimizes the exploitative practice.[39] The existing Jerusalem, where religion and monarchic power cohabitate to ensure the objectification of the people as economic variables, will be of past memory (Isaiah 65:18). In its place a new reality will emerge where people rejoice in the blessings of life.

AN ECONOMY OF LIFE: THE PARABLE OF THE
WORKERS IN THE VINEYARD

Jesus employed a direct political term, *Basileia tou Theou* (Empire of God), to offer new value to his prophetic vision. "Empire of God" depicts an alternate vison of a just and loving society where each individual lives for the other. An Empire of God also delegitimizes the existing imperial regimes built as irreplaceable totalities. Jesus used parables rather than philosophical expositions to explain the values of the Empire of God. A majority of the parables were aimed at subverting an existing worldview, which took rationalizing the prevailing economic order as its primary task. Matthew's gospel speaks of one such subversive parable, often known as the parable of the workers in the vineyard (Matthew 20:1–15).

Prior to the parable itself, Matthew tells of a series of encounters with Pharisees and others connecting gender, children, and purity issues. The immediate reference to the parable was a conversation with the rich young ruler on the question of wealth. It should be recalled that through the story of the temptations of Christ (Matthew 4:8), Matthew had already established the notion that the devil is the one who claims ownership of wealth. The discussion with the rich young ruler also centered around the dominant perceptions regarding wealth. After reminding him of the limitation of religious traditions, Jesus asked him to sell his property in order to inherit the Empire of God. The rich young ruler and Jesus's disciples were perplexed by this advice. As perceived by this young ruler and others, the rejection of private property stood in direct conflict with their cherished religious dogmas, which depict God as one who bestows land and enormous wealth on God's chosen and righteous people (Psalms 37:18; 112:2, 3). Selling their property amounted to rejecting God's blessings. The parable of the workers in the vineyard expands this question of wealth and calls attention to the inbuilt injustice in the forces of production, which, as Rieger argues, are more foundational for establishing justice than the issue of just distribution.[40]

Jesus introduces two categories of people in this parable. The landowning class (the house holder in Matthew's narrative), and the daily-wage laborers. During the first century, the absentee landowners who lived in urban centers and owned land in rural areas (the majority of them were latifundial in character), enforced production of export-oriented crops, such as grapes and olives, at the expense of the basic food production of the people. The daily laborers were a specific social class referred to in different contexts throughout the gospels. Many miracle stories and parables speak directly about this social class (Luke 13:10–17; 14:25; Mark 5:1–13). According to Matthew, the Empire of God belongs to this social class, the crippled, the blind, and the expendable. In short, the gospel belongs to all the nonpersons.

A marked feature of the society during the time of Jesus was its dependence on slave labor, both for domestic work and for production of goods, including agriculture. Apart from slaves, the bulk of the population consisted of poor wage laborers, fisherfolk, free artisans, small peasantry, and tenants working on the land of absentee landlords (Matthew 21:33). Prisoners of war were forced into slave labor, and their numbers were greater than the debt farmers.[41] War radically fashioned the relations of production in two ways: (1) it displaced the small peasants who were called to serve in the army, leaving the land to be accumulated by the rich landlords, and (2) war produced an influx of slave laborers into the land, sinking the price for slaves in the market.

Isaac Mendelsohn explains that the large agricultural farms of the absentee landlords were managed through the appropriation of the labor of either tenant farmers or slave labor.[42] In certain cases, absentee landowners leased parcels of their land to freeborn tenant-farmers. These tenant-farmers received seed, animals, and implements for the cultivation of the land, mostly in the form of loans from the landlords, who in turn also received a definite ratio of the produce at the end of the harvest. However, the landlord in Jesus's parable may not fit in this category as he was hiring daily-wage laborers. Thus, the farm in the parable falls in the second category of farms, dependent on slave labor for production. Slave labor pushes down the production cost substantially as slave labor is a fixed capital. The majority of slaves were sold with the land on which they settled.[43] The surplus of slaves could be traced to the numerous military conquests of Emperor Octavian (Augustus), during which were acquired a large number of slaves to please the wealthy landowners. The slaves, in general, were similar to stable property. They produced a greater amount of surplus in comparison to the cost of hiring a wage laborer. In addition to being a form of fixed capital, slaves maintained a steady production record. The result was the total alienation of wage laborers from the forces of production. Completely out of the pale of economic activity, they were forced to live on the charity of others or as robbers. Since the condition of the wage laborers was worse than that of the slaves, there were occasions when slaves refused the offer of freedom to avoid becoming daily wage laborers.

The parable begins with an invitation extended to this social class to become part of the relations of production (v.2). Under the logic of the capitalist economics and their management theories, this landlord might be considered "stupid" and illiterate. He should have employed slaves rather than daily-wage labors. Capitalism promotes the migration of laborers because their condition is like that of the slaves, people without rights and bargaining power. Labor without bargaining power, as in the case of slave economy, keeps production cost low and increases the profit margin. By inviting wage laborers to the vineyard, Jesus shatters the prevailing economic logic that focuses on profit at the expense of the right to life of everyone, including those who are considered expendables. The householder ensured the participation of the alienated, deprived people in the process of production. The act of the householder declares that the right to work is not charity as much as a universal right. Participation in the forces of work should not be determined by the logic of profit. People are forced out as migrants because their right to participate in meaningful production in their own domain was denied by the profit-oriented production relations.

The Jewish audience of the parable could be invoked in their faith affirmation that land belongs to God and that the participation with the creative productivity is the religious right of all. Each individual should seek bread through the sweat on their face (Genesis 3:19). A just working relation is a right of all.

The parable also conveys a second message. The householder went out in the morning, in the third hour, sixth hour, ninth hour, and eleventh hour to the marketplace where the daily-wage laborers sit around hoping for a contract to work. This picture depicts the life of the migrants. They wait in every street corner looking for work, knock on all doors, and yet have been driven out from the labor market. The landlord's invitation for people to work at the eleventh hour reiterates the concept of "right to work" as a strong message of the parable.

Verse 9 speaks of an unusual practice in the distribution of wages. The living laborer is a vendor in the labor market selling her/his labor capacity as a commodity. The buyer of this commodity exerts power to bargain in order to reduce the price of this specific commodity and then engage in a contract. Exercising the right and power to bargain is a basic lesson in the management schemes of feudal and capitalist societies alike. The right to bargain ensures profit. Contemporary capital and labor assume a nomadic character due to the realization that bargaining power of capital increases when the laborer is not granted civic rights that come with citizenship. In economic theory, the accumulation of surplus is vital to sustain the growth-oriented system. It is often said that a growth-oriented system "can no more be 'persuaded' to limit growth than a human being can be 'persuaded' to stop breathing."[44]

The householder in this parable breaks this economic law. The householder engaged laborers even when the sun was setting. But he paid a full day's wage, though these workers worked only one-twelfth of the regular work. A "wise" householder would pay only one-twelfth of a denarius to this last group. Jesus introduced a different landlord, "stupid" in the eyes of neoliberal pundits, but affirming the universal right of all to life and work. This landlord refused to follow the wisdom of exploitative economic theories that suggest "everyone is rewarded according to what they contribute."[45] In the

Empire of God, gratuitous love regulates life, and not wealth (mammon), and thus all are invited to the feast of life.

CONCLUSION

Production for profit and capital accumulation will keep labor as a disposable commodity. And as a result, labor becomes a dehumanizing act. However, the prophet Isaiah reminds us that the act of production should be an act of freedom overflowing one's own being into time and space. The covenant of creativity made between God and the first human being, as depicted in the Genesis narrative, reiterates this cardinal concern: that production under the conditions of freedom is to objectify one's faculties, truth, value, and beauty in things and nature in order to satisfy the social needs of others. Thus, production becomes an extension of oneself in space and time—a process that enables our subjectivity to unfold. Labor is to assist oneself and others to discover our true identity. Creative faculties enable one to participate in the re-creative process of the divine. But when work is brought under conditions set by mammon and being a process of dehumanization, it negates the divine presence in history.

NOTES

1. The name is changed to conceal the identity of the worker. Interview was conducted in April 2016.

2. On February 16, 2018, the body of Joanna Daniela Demafelis, an OFW working in Kuwait, arrived at the Manila airport. The tragic story of her death shocked the public. For over a year, her corpse was stuffed inside a freezer, and initial investigations revealed signs of torture. Several more cases of OFW deaths in Kuwait are also under investigation, and, according to President Duterte, as many as 120 Filipinos died in Kuwait last year. See "Kasammako Statement on the SSS-NPS Security Agreement," Migrante International, accessed May 14, 2019, https://migranteinternational.org/.

3. Daily embarkation of OFWs from Manila airport was only around 2,500 in 2009. Department of Economic and Social Affairs, *International Migration Report 2017* (New York: United Nations, 2017).

4. The number of migrant workers who moved from rural areas to the cities in China alone was approximately 274 million in 2014, accounting for around 20 percent of the total population. National Bureau of Statistics of China, "China: Number of Migrant Workers 2018," accessed May 14, 2019, https://www.statista.com/statistics/234578/share-of-migrant-workers-in-china-by-age/.

5. Department of Economic and Social Affairs, *International Migration Report 2017*.

6. Romila Thapar, *The Aryan: Recasting Constructs* (Delhi: Three Essays Collective, 2008).

7. Samuel Laing, the finance minister of the colonial government in India in 1862, spoke on the virtues of Aryan brotherhood to pacify Indian feelings in the wake of the sepoy mutiny of 1857. He exhorted that "two races so long separated meet once more. . . . [T]he younger brother has become the stronger, and takes his place as the head and protector of the family. . . . We are here on a sacred mission, to stretch out the right hand of aid to our weaker brother, who once far out-stripped us, but has now fallen behind in the race." Samuel Laing, *Lecture on the*

Indo-European Languages and Races (Calcutta: G. C. Hay, 1862); Martin Maw, *Visions of India: Fulfilment Theology, the Aryan Race Theory, and the Work of British Protestant Missionaries in Victoria India* (Frankfurt: P. Lang, 1990), 37.

8. Alvin Y. So, *Social Change and Development: Modernization, Dependency, and World-System Theories* (Newbury Park, CA: Sage, 1990).

9. Charlotte Erickson, *Leaving England: Essays on British Emigration in the Nineteenth Century* (Ithaca, NY: Cornell University Press, 1994), 19. From 1884 to 1900, the outward passengers from Britain and Ireland alone were over 200,000 per annum. See J. A Hobson, *Imperialism: A Study* (London: Allen and Unwin, 1905), part 1, chapter 3.

10. Hobson observed that migration from Europe was promoted to avoid an economic collapse of the European economies. "The mass migrants were typically young and single, and about two thirds of them were male. More than three quarters of the immigrants entering the United States between 1868 and 1913 were aged 16–40. Among men emigrating from England and Wales, only one in nine traveled with other family members compared with more than half in the 1830s." Erickson, *Leaving England*, 143.

11. This group includes the people who were turned into slaves and indentured laborers. In the early phase of indentured labor, people were largely shipped from China and India and later from Korea and Japan to the Americas and the Caribbean. But as the powers of colonialism strengthened, laborers were moved around the world as people on a chessboard: Chinese to Indonesia, Koreans to Japan, and Indians to Malaysia, Sri Lanka, and many parts of Asia, Africa, the Pacific, the Caribbean, and around Europe. The sale price of the labor covered the shipping cost, and the comparison of this price with the value of the servant's expected productivity over and above maintenance determined the length of bonded labor—usually between four and seven years—after which the servant was freed.

12. Computing the economic drainage from India to Britain during colonial period, Romesh C. Dutt writes: "One-half of the net revenues of India, which are now forty-four millions sterling, flows annually out of India. Verily the moisture of India blesses and fertilizes other lands." Romesh Dutt, *Economic History of India: Under Early British Rule* (Great Britain: Kegan Paul, 1902), xv. Eduardo Galeano offers a detailed account of the demonetization of the people in Latin America by early colonial masters. He writes: "Between 1503 and 1660, 185,000 kilograms of gold and 16,000,000 of silver arrived at the Spanish port of Sanlucar de Barrameda. Silver shipped to Spain in little more than a century and a half exceeded three times the total European reserves, and it must be membered that these figures are not complete." Eduardo Galeano, *Open Veins of Latin America: Five Centuries of the Pillage of a Continent*, 25th anniversary ed. (New York: Monthly Review Press, 1997), 23.

13. Erick S. Reinert observed that Western industrial nations also achieved growth through strong protectionism. Quoting William Ashworth, Reinert writes: "If here was a unique English/British pathway of industrialization, it was less a distinct entrepreneurial and technocratic culture than one predominantly defined within an institutional framework spearheaded by the excise (tax) and a wall of tariffs." Erik S. Reinert, *How Rich Countries Got Rich and Why Poor Countries Stay Poor* (New York: Public Affairs, 2009), 21–22.

14. Colin Legum and Geoffrey Mmari, *Mwalimu: The Influence of Nyerere* (London: Britain-Tanzania Society in association with J. Currey, 1995), 127.

15. Cheng Hung-ta and Jake Chung, "Taiwan Could Become Hyper-Aged within Eight Years," *Taipei Times*, April 17, 2018.

16. United Nations ESCAP, *Asia-Pacific Migration Report 2015 Migrants' Contributions to Development* (New York: United Nations, n.d.), Table 1.1, 21.

17. "20 Years after Flor Contemplacion's Death, More Women OFWs Abused, Exploited and Enslaved under Aquino's Term," *Migrante International* (blog), March 8, 2015, https://migranteinternational.org/2015/03/08/20-years-after-flor-contemplacions-death-more-women-ofws-abused-exploited-and-enslaved-under-aquinos-term/.

18. Growth of unemployment in Detroit corresponds largely to the flight of capital and industries to other locations where cheap labor is abundant.

19. "Dispelling the Migrant Myth," *World of Work*, September 2006, 20–21.

20. "Editorial: Riots Rooted in Injustice," *Taipei Times*, August 23, 2005, http://www.taipeitimes.com/News/editorials/archives/2005/08/23/2003268855/1.

21. "Dispelling the Migrant Myth," 21.

22. "Dispelling the Migrant Myth," 21.

23. Naomi Klein described this logic of monopoly capitalism as "Disaster Capitalism." Naomi Klein, *The Shock Doctrine: The Rise of Disaster Capitalism* (New York: Metropolitan Books, 2007).

24. US agricultural exports to the Third World nations more than doubled between 2006 and 2014. The value of US exports of soybeans to China (one of the traditional crops in China) accounts for double the value of US exports of aircraft. The value of cotton yarn is more than the value of automobiles. US exports of agricultural product to Taiwan totaled 3.1 billion in 2013, while US export of aircraft to Taiwan was 1.8 million.

25. P. Sainath, "The Slaughter of Suicide Data," *Frontline: India's National Magazine*, August 21, 2015, https://frontline.thehindu.com/social-issues/the-slaughter-of-suicide-data/article7495402.ece.

26. The nationalist movement under Gandhi promoted handloom weavers as the political medium for the independence movement. The *swadeshi* movement, promoted by Gandhi, was made possible because the weavers in India took responsibility of producing indigenous textiles to prevent the Britain manufactures from gaining absolute control over the market.

27. Some of the weavers' communities were totally wiped out by the big textile corporations. For example, Mangalagiri in Guntur, one of the traditionally known weaving village, had approximately 20,000 weavers in the early 1990s; that number is estimated to have come down by nearly 75 percent and only about 6,000 active handloom weavers were left by 2010. See B. Syama Sundari, "Handlooms Are Dying—and It's Because of Our Failure to Protect Them," The Wire, accessed May 14, 2019, https://thewire.in/culture/handlooms-are-dying-and-its-because-of-our-failure-to-protect-them. Similar to the crisis among farmers, suicide due to the marginalization from the forces of production is common among handloom weavers. In a study conducted by Rashtra Cheneta Jana Samakhya, a leading trade union of handloom weavers, over 1,500 weavers committed suicide in the last three years across the country. Vivek Kumar, "The Dying Handloom Industry Is a Serious Issue for Indian Economy," The Companion, August 3, 2017, https://thecompanion.in/dying-handloom-industry-serious-issue-indian-economy/.

28. Chris Manning, "The East Asian Economic Crisis and Labour Migration: A Set-Back for International Economic Integration?," Departmental Working Paper (The Australian National University, Arndt-Corden Department of Economics, 2001), https://econpapers.repec.org/paper/paspapers/2001–03.htm.

29. Tisha M. Rajendra, "Justice Not Benevolence: Catholic Social Thought, Migration Theory, and the Rights of Migrants," *Political Theology* 15, no. 4 (July 2014): 293.

30. The term "choreographed" is borrowed from Elisabeth Schüssler Fiorenza, *Wisdom Ways: Introducing Feminist Biblical Interpretation* (Maryknoll, NY: Orbis Books, 2006).

31. Quoted in Tisha M. Rajendra, *Migrants and Citizens: Justice and Responsibility in the Ethics of Immigration* (Grand Rapids, MI: Eerdmans, 2017), 6.

32. Joerg Rieger and Rosemarie Henkel-Rieger, *Unified We Are a Force: How Faith and Labor Can Overcome America's Inequalities* (St. Louis, MO: Chalice Press, 2016), 7.

33. In 1983, the export of human as commodity was privatized by the Ministry of Manpower (sic) by the government of Indonesia by giving license to private agencies to recruit migrant workers promoting the remarkable growth of migrants. The income generated through sending migrant labor prompted the political leadership to establish the Centre for Overseas Employment within the Ministry of Manpower in 1984 (renamed as the Directorate of Overseas Manpower Services in 1994) with a mandate to increase the number of labor exported every year, both by negotiating with the receiving countries and giving special training to the prospective human capital waiting for export. This story repeats itself in almost all the "sending countries."

34. The majority of the wealthy families in the receiving countries do have more than one live-in domestic workers. It is also considered that having one or two domestic workers at home is a status symbol to reinforce their elite social status. M. I. Finley observed that slaves were considered as a status symbol for the elites in Graeco-Roman societies and, therefore, the

more one had, the better. Live-in domestic workers have replaced slaves as status symbols. See M. I. Finley, *Ancient Slavery and Modern Ideology* (Princeton, NJ: Markus Weiner, 1998).

35. Rhacel Salazar Parreñas, "Mothering from a Distance: Emotions, Gender, and Intergenerational Relations in Filipino Transnational Families," *Feminist Studies* 27, no. 2 (Summer 2001): 361–90.

36. Carol Gilligan, *In a Different Voice: Psychological Theory and Women's Development* (Cambridge, MA: Harvard University Press, 1982).

37. The narrative describing the growth of population is a phenomenon under slavery. The unknown factor is how they became slaves in the first place.

38. Marc H. Ellis, "On Performing the Indigenous Jewish Prophetic at the End of Jewish History: Further Notes on a Jewish Theology of Liberation," *CrossCurrents* 66, no. 2 (June 2016): 193.

39. It may not be just a coincidence but deliberate that the writer of Revelation uses the same number 666, which denotes the booty of Solomon as the mark of the beast (Revelation 13:17–18).

40. Joerg Rieger, "Christianity, Capitalism, and Desire: Can Religion Still Make a Difference?," *Union Seminary Quarterly Review* 64, no. 1 (2013): 6.

41. M. A. Dandamaev, *Slavery in Babylonia: From Nabopolassar to Alexander the Great (626–331 B.C.)*, ed. Marvin A Powell, trans. Victoria A. Powell (DeKalb: Northern Illinois University Press, 2009), 67–80.

42. Isaac Mendelsohn, *Slavery in the Ancient Near East: A Comparative Study of Slavery in Babylonia, Assyria, Syria, and Palestine from the Middle of the Third Millennium to the End of the First Millennium* (Westport, CT: Greenwood Press, 1978), 109.

43. "The preamble of such a sale document reads: 'X measures of land together with the people.' For when an absentee owner sold his farm with its implements, livestock, and houses, it was quite natural that he should include in the sale also its unfree laborers." Mendelsohn, *Slavery in the Ancient Near East*, 111.

44. Murray Bookchin, *Remaking Society* (Boston: South End Press, 1990), 93–94.

45. Joerg Rieger, *Jesus vs. Caesar: For People Tired of Serving the Wrong God* (Nashville, TN: Abingdon Press, 2018), 84.

BIBLIOGRAPHY

"20 Years after Flor Contemplacion's Death, More Women OFWs Abused, Exploited and Enslaved under Aquino's Term." *Migrante International* (blog), March 8, 2015. https://migranteinternational.org/2015/03/08/20–years-after-flor-contemplacions-death-more-women-ofws-abused-exploited-and-enslaved-under-aquinos-term/.

Bookchin, Murray. *Remaking Society*. Boston: South End Press, 1990.

Dandamaev, M. A. *Slavery in Babylonia: From Nabopolassar to Alexander the Great (626–331 B.C.)*. Edited by Marvin A Powell. Translated by Victoria A. Powell. DeKalb: Northern Illinois University Press, 2009.

Department of Economic and Social Affairs. *International Migration Report 2017*. New York: United Nations, 2017.

"Dispelling the Migrant Myth." *World of Work*, September 2006.

Dutt, Romesh. *Economic History of India: Under Early British Rule*. Great Britain: Kegan Paul, 1902.

"Editorial: Riots Rooted in Injustice." *Taipei Times*, August 23, 2005. http://www.taipeitimes.com/News/editorials/archives/2005/08/23/2003268855/1.

Ellis, Marc H. "On Performing the Indigenous Jewish Prophetic at the End of Jewish History: Further Notes on a Jewish Theology of Liberation." *CrossCurrents* 66, no. 2 (June 2016): 193–203.

Erickson, Charlotte. *Leaving England: Essays on British Emigration in the Nineteenth Century*. Ithaca, NY: Cornell University Press, 1994.

Finley, M. I. *Ancient Slavery and Modern Ideology*. Princeton, NJ: Markus Weiner, 1998.

Fiorenza, Elisabeth Schüssler. *Wisdom Ways: Introducing Feminist Biblical Interpretation.* Maryknoll, NY: Orbis Books, 2006.

Galeano, Eduardo. *Open Veins of Latin America: Five Centuries of the Pillage of a Continent.* 25th anniversary ed. New York: Monthly Review Press, 1997.

Gilligan, Carol. *In a Different Voice: Psychological Theory and Women's Development.* Cambridge, MA: Harvard University Press, 1982.

Hobson, J. A. *Imperialism: A Study.* London: Allen and Unwin, 1905.

Hung-ta, Cheng, and Jake Chung. "Taiwan Could Become Hyper-Aged within Eight Years." *Taipei Times*, April 17, 2018.

"Kasammako Statement on the SSS-NPS Security Agreement." Migrante International. Accessed May 14, 2019. https://migranteinternational.org/.

Klein, Naomi. *The Shock Doctrine: The Rise of Disaster Capitalism.* New York: Metropolitan Books, 2007.

Kumar, Vivek. "The Dying Handloom Industry Is a Serious Issue for Indian Economy." The Companion, August 3, 2017. https://thecompanion.in/dying-handloom-industry-serious-issue-indian-economy/.

Laing, Samuel. *Lecture on the Indo-European Languages and Races.* Calcutta: G. C. Hay, 1862.

Legum, Colin, and Geoffrey Mmari. *Mwalimu: The Influence of Nyerere.* London: Britain-Tanzania Society in association with J. Currey, 1995.

Manning, Chris. "The East Asian Economic Crisis and Labour Migration: A Set-Back for International Economic Integration?" Departmental Working Paper. The Australian National University, Arndt-Corden Department of Economics, 2001. https://econpapers.repec.org/paper/paspapers/2001-03.htm.

Maw, Martin. *Visions of India: Fulfilment Theology, the Aryan Race Theory, and the Work of British Protestant Missionaries in Victoria India.* Frankfurt: P. Lang, 1990.

Mendelsohn, Isaac. *Slavery in the Ancient Near East: A Comparative Study of Slavery in Babylonia, Assyria, Syria, and Palestine from the Middle of the Third Millennium to the End of the First Millennium.* Westport, CT: Greenwood Press, 1978.

National Bureau of Statistics of China. "China: Number of Migrant Workers 2018 | Statistic." Statista. Accessed May 14, 2019. https://www.statista.com/statistics/234578/share-of-migrant-workers-in-china-by-age/.

Parreñas, Rhacel Salazar. "Mothering from a Distance: Emotions, Gender, and Intergenerational Relations in Filipino Transnational Families." *Feminist Studies* 27, no. 2 (Summer 2001): 361–90.

Rajendra, Tisha M. "Justice Not Benevolence: Catholic Social Thought, Migration Theory, and the Rights of Migrants." *Political Theology* 15, no. 4 (July 2014): 290–306.

———. *Migrants and Citizens: Justice and Responsibility in the Ethics of Immigration.* Grand Rapids, MI: Eerdmans, 2017.

Reinert, Erik S. *How Rich Countries Got Rich and Why Poor Countries Stay Poor.* New York: Public Affairs, 2009.

Rieger, Joerg. "Christianity, Capitalism, and Desire: Can Religion Still Make a Difference?" *Union Seminary Quarterly Review* 64, no. 1 (2013): 1–13.

———. *Jesus vs. Caesar: For People Tired of Serving the Wrong God.* Nashville, TN: Abingdon Press, 2018.

Rieger, Joerg, and Rosemarie Henkel-Rieger. *Unified We Are a Force: How Faith and Labor Can Overcome America's Inequalities.* St. Louis, MO: Chalice Press, 2016.

Sainath, P. "The Slaughter of Suicide Data." *Frontline: India's National Magazine*, August 21, 2015. https://frontline.thehindu.com/social-issues/the-slaughter-of-suicide-data/article7495402.ece.

So, Alvin Y. *Social Change and Development: Modernization, Dependency, and World-System Theories.* Newbury Park, CA: Sage, 1990.

Sundari, B. Syama. "Handlooms Are Dying—and It's Because of Our Failure to Protect Them." The Wire. Accessed May 14, 2019. https://thewire.in/culture/handlooms-are-dying-and-its-because-of-our-failure-to-protect-them.

Thapar, Romila. *The Aryan: Recasting Constructs.* Dehli: Three Essays Collective, 2008.

United Nations ESCAP. *Asia-Pacific Migration Report 2015 Migrants' Contributions to Development*. New York: United Nations, n.d.

Chapter Three

Commoning

Toward an Alternative Pilgrimage of the Economy of Life

George Zachariah

Colonization of the commons is a contemporary manifestation of imperialism, which destroys the economy of life. In India, coastal commons are desecrated and plundered for the blue economy in the name of progress and development. Though India is known for pilgrimages, a critical engagement of the concept informs us that pilgrimages, in general, tend to reinforce a spirituality that perpetuates the unjust social order and the colonization of the commons. Such pilgrimages are rituals that draft us into the logic of the prevailing order. Neoliberal development has become a fetish in our times; colonization and corporatization of the commons are celebrated with religious fervor, marking the nation's pilgrimage toward progress. It is in this context that this chapter attempts to engage with the alternative pilgrimages of the subaltern social movements of the coastal communities displaced from their commons by the neoliberal pilgrimage of the dominant. Our ecumenical resolve to initiate a pilgrimage of justice and peace requires the nerve to contest the dominant pilgrimages of our times and to join the subaltern pilgrimages to make justice and peace tangible realities. This chapter, therefore, is an attempt to develop an alternative model of commoning in terms of pilgrimage by drawing on the contestations and struggles of coastal communities to protect their commons.

COMMONS: AN ALTERNATIVE POLITICS AND
ETHICS OF ECONOMY OF LIFE

Commons are nature's gift to the community of creation; they are shared, protected, and nurtured by the community for the community's mutual flourishing. Traditional commons signify an organic connection between land, water, forest, and subsistence communities who are marginalized by the prevailing social order. The commons are intimately and organically intertwined with the struggles, aspirations, and joys of these vulnerable communities as they sustain each other through their life together. For the coastal communities and fishers, rivers and oceans are their mother, while for the indigenous communities the sacred grove is seen as the space where ancestors dwell. The legal systems of the nation-state do not define or regulate this relationship with the commons. Market economies have no sway over their bond with the commons. The commons are therefore alternative spaces and relationships that contest the rules and ethos of the system world in and through their practicing and propagating the politics, ethics, and spirituality of an economy of life.[1]

The commons are more than particular geographical spaces. In a political sense, the commons are a paradigm—a paradigm of organic socio-economic and ecological relationships, social ethics, shared socio-economic practices, and a covenant of shared responsibility and obligation. Commons are the commonwealth. It is this distinctive politics of the commons that makes them an alternative economy of life in the neoliberal, market-driven world. "The ethos of the commons knit people together with their neighbors and with the land, plus the local fens, forest and bodies of water, with no one or nothing treated as exempt, nor as an externality. Inhabitants and habitats are one inseparable whole."[2] The politics and ethics of the economy of life that is practiced in the commons has the audacity to contest the logic of the neoliberal market economy and to offer moral and spiritual energy to believe in the possibility of something beyond the prevailing order.

DE-COMMONING: COLONIZATION AND
COMMODITIZATION OF THE COMMONS

The British enclosure movement, progressively unfolding from the twelfth century through the nineteenth century, is the precursor of de-commoning whereby pastures, forests, and water bodies used by subsistence communities were stolen and declared private property by the kings, the aristocracy, and the landholding nobility. In the Marxian analysis, enclosure represents "primitive accumulation," a historical process through which the producer is forcefully alienated from the means of production. As David Harvey rightly observes, enclosure was "accumulation by dispossession," which resulted not only in the alienation of subsistence communities but also in their pauperization.[3] The enclosure movement was perhaps the oldest attempt to convert the commons into commodity and capital. More than a mere landgrab, the enclosure movement was determined to destroy the potential of the commons paradigm and a politics and ethics of mutual flourishing of the flora and fauna through self-governance. De-commoning, therefore, is a hegemonic, violent act of erasing the memory of alternative socio-economic ecological relations and ethical practices at the grass roots. The very fact that such enclosures were legitimized by the British Parliament through various acts exposes the role of the state in legalizing de-commoning—a practice that continues in our times.

Enlightenment rationality, combined with an anthropocentric Judeo-Christian theology, further contributed to the paradigm of de-commoning. Since the commons defies the logic of market control and state control, it embodies an alternative paradigm to the prevailing models of socio-economic relations. The organic understanding of everything as interrelated and interconnected affirms the possibility for mutual flourishing through self-governance and a covenantal relationship of mutual custodianship. Elevating the rational human being and considering it the crown of creation endowed with the vocation to subdue the earth and to have dominion over the rest of the creation took away the intrinsic worth of nonhuman beings. As a result, the indigenous ethic of mutual respect and coexistence was replaced by an ethic of domination and alienation.

David Bollier's observations of the impact of the British enclosure movement on the commoners are very important: The enclosure movement transformed commoners from beings concerned with collective interests into "creatures of the market-place." They were made into individual consumers and wage slaves obedient to the satanic mills of the Industrial Revolution. De-commoning further led to the separation of production and governance, as the market took charge of production and the state took charge of governance.[4] In short, de-commoning through enclosures led to the "dissolution of communities, deep economic inequality, an erosion of self-governance and a loss of social solidarity and identity."[5] This is how John Clare, the eighteenth-century British poet, articulates the tragedy of the enclosures:

> "Inclosure came and trampled on the grave
> Of labour's rights and left the poor a slave
> And birds and trees and flowers without a name
> All sighed when lawless law's enclosure came."[6]

Karl Polanyi's observations and analysis of the British enclosure movement are also instructive here.[7] He argues that the enclosure movement initiated a

shift from a habitat-centered society and economy to a market-centered society. When commons were forcefully converted into private property, they
became commodities, and production and profit became the objective of
human engagement with nature. The ethos of organic and subsistence economy of life was thus replaced by the new axiom "accumulation by dispossession." Put differently, the enclosure movement helped to shift from a society
wherein economic relations and practices were "embedded" in the socio-
ecological relations to a society colonized by the hegemonic logic of accumulation and private property.

Colonialism further contributed to the destruction of the subsistence ethics of the commoners by alienating them from the commons. Colonial legal
systems declared the commons as *tera nullius* and occupied them as the
eminent domain of the colonial state. Alien legal and administrative systems
were imposed and enforced, desecrating the commons by destroying the
earth-healing sacred ethos and practices of the subsistence communities. For
colonialism, nature was either a resource pile waiting to be plundered and
engineered or wilderness needing to be fenced off from the traditional subsistence communities. Through the semiotic metamorphosis of "jungle" into
"forest," made possible by the colonial forest acts, the jungle previously
considered to be the organic abode of the commoners became forest—a
stockpile of resources under state control. In India, the state enacted various
forest acts, which resulted in the exclusion of commoners from their traditional habitats in the name of conservation, social forestry, biological reserves, and natural parks. "Eighty percent of the nation's mineral wealth and
seventy two percent of the forests, water, and other natural resources are
found in tribal lands. Thus mines, industrial estates, hydroelectric projects,
urban centers and planned population transfer signaled the internal colonization of tribal homelands."[8]

The postcolonial state in India has continued de-commoning for the last
seven decades. Today, the remaining commons in India are sites of contesta-
tion and resistance where commoners, with their indigenous weapons of
slings and arrows, are confronting the state and the corporations in order to
reclaim their commons. We see the resilience of the commoners in the words
of Mukta Jhodia, a tribal woman from the state of Odisha:

> You did not create these mountains, water flowing in the streams or the culti-
> vated lands which have been giving us life and livelihood from generation to
> generation . . . and it will also nurture our future generations. These are given
> to us by the god of nature. Who are you to snatch away the gifts of nature from
> us? We shall not allow you to destroy our resources. You have killed three of
> my sons. Many more of us are prepared to die.[9]

TRAGEDY OF THE COMMONS: IDEOLOGICAL
LEGITIMIZATION OF DE-COMMONING

Garrett Hardin's 1968 essay, "The Tragedy of the Commons," offered ideological legitimization to the process of de-commoning through state appropriation, corporate colonization, and commodification of the commons. For Hardin, the British commons disappeared because they were unsustainable in a context where people's attitude towards nature was informed and inspired by utilitarianism. According to him, establishing open and free access to all in common grazing lands would create problems. Every rational herdsman would send more sheep to maximize his profit. This would lead to overgrazing and would exceed the capacity of the pastureland. "Each man is locked into a system that compels him to increase his herd without limit—in a world that is limited. Ruin is the destination toward which all men rush, each pursuing his own best interest in a society that believes in the freedom of the commons. Freedom in a commons brings ruin to all."[10] One commentator summarizes Hardin's opinion by noting that "what belongs to all belongs to none, and only private or state ownership can rescue a commons from the sad fate that will otherwise befall it."[11]

Hardin's essay has played a major role in propagating the gospel of neoliberal economic ideology because it argued prosperity and contentment can only be achieved through individual freedom, private property, and trade. Hardin's theory was contested by economists like E. P. Thompson and Elinor Ostrom. Hardin's hypothetical pastureland and herdsmen are problematic because they do not accurately represent the commons. As Bollier rightly observes, "A commons has boundaries, rules, social norms and sanctions against free riders. A commons requires that there be a community willing to act as a conscientious steward of a resource. . . . The commons, properly understood, is about the practice and ethic of sufficiency."[12] So why is Hardin's theory so popular even today? Perhaps, its popularity is due to the remedy Hardin prescribed for the tragedy of the commons—privatization. Privatization, in our times, means corporate appropriation of the commons for profit and plunder.

COLONIZATION OF THE COMMONS:
INDIA'S TRYST WITH DESTINY

India's "tryst with destiny" on the midnight of August 14, 1947, was not just the inauguration of an independent nation, but also the beginning of a regime of de-commoning.[13] The development gaze, which came out of the nationalist mold, perceived the commons—consisting of land, water, and forests—as untapped resources to be plundered for the "common good" and "national interest." De-commoning emerged as a sacred patriotic mission, much like the ways big dams and big industries were equated with nation building. "If you are to suffer, you should suffer in the interest of the country."[14] This appeal by Jawaharlal Nehru, the first prime minister of India, to the subsistence communities displaced from their commons for a mega-dam project, testifies to the ways in which the rhetoric of patriotism and common good was used to legitimize the violence of forceful enclosure of the commons and displacement of the commoners.

Among the major nation-building projects that independent India initiated were the multipurpose river valley projects. As Arundhati Roy observes, "Not only did they build big dams and new irrigation systems, they took control of small, traditional systems [commons] that had been managed by village communities for thousands of years, and allowed them to atrophy."[15] De-commoning is nothing but the desacralization of the traditional communities' sacred commons. But the state addressed this legitimation crisis by fetishizing the big dams and other projects constructed through enclosure and displacement. The following statement by Prime Minister Nehru explains how God-talk was used to cover up and legitimize the violence of de-commoning: "As I walked around the [dam] site I thought that these days the biggest temple and mosque and gurdwara is the place where man works for the good of mankind. . . . Where can be a greater and holier place than this, which can be regarded as higher?"[16]

COLONIZATION OF THE COASTAL COMMONS: FROM THE ECONOMY OF LIFE TO THE BLUE ECONOMY

The coastal commons are very important for a nation and the community, not because of the abundance of marine resources, but because coastal commons are the habitats and source of life for the traditional fishing communities. Further, coastal commons play a significant role in influencing climate conditions and preventing natural disasters. Coastal commons are filled with mangroves, which offer abode for countless species of fish and protect the coastal communities from natural calamities like cyclones and tsunamis. Traditional fishing communities cherish and celebrate their organic relationship with the coastal commons on both material and symbolic levels. The very fact that seas and oceans cannot be divided into segments, enclosed by boundaries, or owned as private property inspires the coastal communities to resist the state appropriation and corporate takeover of those coastal commons. In spite of the resilience and resistance of these communities, the state has declared the coastal commons to be commodities to be auctioned off to the highest bidder in the market.

Prior to the 2004 tsunami, which destroyed the coastal regions in India and Sri Lanka, these coastal commons were invaded by a different type of tsunami, which prepared the way for the actual tsunami. Neoliberal globalization had invaded them through commercial tourism and aquaculture. Tourist resorts and hotels conquered the coastline and destroyed the tropical mangrove forests, one of the world's most important ecosystems. Mangrove swamps function as natural protection against large waves. The habitats of the traditional fisher people were converted into tourist resorts and shrimp farms. Thousands of hectares of mangrove forests and bushes were cleared to make the resorts beautiful for the tourists. Traditional communities were displaced from their land and livelihood to welcome in the transnational corporations who would eventually abuse their land, water, and environment. In short, the tsunami was the consequence of the commoditization and corporatization of the coastal commons.

Coastal commons are the new economic frontier of our times. Blue economy is the new catchphrase, and a wide range of actors are now converging together to occupy and plunder the coastal commons. Coastal commons are vital for the food sovereignty of fishing communities. It was in the name of "protecting" the beaches and the coastal regions that the Indian government began declaring the coastal regions as regulation zones in 1981. But the coastal zone management policies eventually led to ocean grabbing, and the casualty in this seemingly conservationist and sustainable governmental intervention is the traditional fishing community. In the coastal zone management initiatives, all coastline users (resource intensive and resource based) are clubbed together as coastal stakeholders, and coastal degradation is attributed to all of them. The traditional fish workers (resource-based communities), who have been protecting their commons from time immemorial, are thus pronounced as destroyers of the oceans. Further, use, access, and control of the coastal commons are transferred from the traditional fishing communities to the corporations, who, according to the state are involved in the sustainable economic activity called blue economy. Put differently, neoliberal ideology privileges the interests of the corporations and investors over against the interests of the traditional fishing communities.

It is in this context that a critical engagement with the recent coastal regulation zone (CRZ) notification of the Indian government becomes crucial. The US $145 billion Sagaramala Project is one of the ventures the government is trying to implement through this initiative. The Sagaramala Project is expected to modernize several existing ports and build six new mega-ports. The project will also develop at least 14 coastal economic zones (CEZ) and 29 coastal economic units (CEU). Further, the project will facilitate the development of mines, industrial corridors, railways, and roads. Airport connectivity with the ports is expected to yield an export revenue growth of US $110 billion and generate over 150,000 new jobs.[17]

As traditional fishing communities and environmental activists have rightly noted, the main objective of the Sagaramala Project is to develop a coast-based industrial model that will uproot traditional fishing communities from their habitats and livelihoods in order to hand over the coastal commons to private investors and corporations. This corporate plunder and theft will lead to the genocide of the subsistence communities in the coastal regions and to ecocide. According to T. Peter, general secretary of the National Fishworkers Forum (NFF), "The new CRZ was issued only to help the industrialists, especially those in the tourism sector. When this CRZ will be adopted, the port and tourism sector will steal the coastline from the fishing communities." He observed that the purpose of this new initiative is "to sell the coastline to businessmen, without bothering about the traditional fishing communities, their livelihoods, their rights and the coastal ecology and marine biodiversity."[18]

The Vizhinjam International Deepwater Multipurpose Port in the state of Kerala is an example of the colonization of the coastal commons. The ongoing construction work of this US $65 million project of the Adani Group is a threat both to the coastal commons and the traditional fishing communities. As part of the construction work, a 3.8-kilometer-long breakwater has been developed, and it is estimated that, when the project is completed, it will adversely affect at least 15 kilometers of the coast and 30,000 people from that coastal region. Over 700 houses of the fishing community have already been damaged by coastal erosion caused by the work during the monsoon season. The National Fishworkers' Federation and other environmental movements are protesting against this project, and they demand the state "recognize the inalienable traditional and customary rights of the fishing communities over coastal lands and waters, and . . . enact a national act for the conservation of coastal and marine biodiversity that inter alia protects traditional fish workers' preferential access and historic use to coastal and marine resources."[19] The comptroller auditor general (CAG) of India concluded that "the Vizhinjam project is against the interests of the Kerala State and that only the Adani Group will benefit from the agreement." The report further points to "widespread discrepancies in the Concession Agreement as well as grave irregularities in breakwater construction and land acquisition resulting in a substantial loss to the government."[20]

Blue economy is a threat to the economy of life as it propagates an ideology that commoditizes the coastal commons and alienates the traditional fishers from their habitat and livelihood. For the Indian state, blue economy is the panacea of all the accumulated problems that the country faces today. As the Indian Ocean Rim Association (IORA) points out, blue economy will "contribute to food security, poverty alleviation, the mitigation and resilience to the impacts of climate change, enhanced trade and investment, enhanced maritime connectivity, enhanced diversity, job creation and socio-economic growth."[21] That is, the blue economy is said to offer sustainable development and ecological restoration with economic growth. The Research Collective Delhi's succinct observation about this capitalist vision of ecological and socio-economic growth is important:

> By combining economic growth, environmental protection, and livelihoods security under its framework, it creates an optimistic narrative of harmony and hope. Ports exist alongside villages. Coastal Industrial Zones prosper along-side biodiversity hotspots. Industrial fishing vessels ply in the deep oceans. Tourists flock to the beaches, and the coasts become a site of perpetual recreation.[22]

Blue economy—the neoliberal paradigm of the colonization of the coastal commons—is a grave threat to the economy of life packaged as a gift of socioeconomic and ecological flourishing. Through the monetization of the coastal commons, the life-sustaining and flourishing economy of the commons is destroyed and grafted into the market regimes. In this process, the organic coastal commons are converted into commodities. Accumulation by dispossession further deligitimizes the traditional coastal communities, their cultural practices, and their ethical visions. The vocation of the state also undergoes radical transformation in this process. The state can no longer be seen as a source of welfare ensuring the flourishing of its citizens and the traditional commons. Rather, the state has become a broker on behalf of the transnational corporations, and its vocation is to facilitate the corporate take-over of the commons. The biggest threat from the blue economy is

> its attempt to sanitize dispossession. By co-opting the demands of the fishing communities for coastal protection and food sovereignty, it pitches these as business opportunities for International Financial Institutions, Trans and Multi-national Corporations. However, for the livelihoods at stake the Blue Economy is merely ushering a new regime of dispossession, this time disguised under the combined global narratives of ocean health, sustainable development, poverty alleviation and food security.[23]

COMMONING: THE PRAXIS OF ENLIVENING THE ECONOMY OF LIFE

The commons challenge us to see the world through eyes that are not blinded by the logic of neoliberal market economy, and they thereby enable us to reimagine the cosmos as an economy of life. They enable us to discern our vocation as commoning—to realize an economy that flourishes and celebrates life. Commoning is reclaiming our organic connectedness with nature and each other by coming out of the imperial worldview of conquest and plunder. It is the ethical courage to denounce the morality of the market forces and to affirm the potential of human solidarity to transform the face of the earth by midwifing the economy of life.

Commoning offers a credible alternative to the neoliberal development paradigm. "Commons-based models are not just policy mechanisms that are inserted into a situation to solve a problem; they generally embody a very different vision than that of Western industrialization and consumerism. . . . Commons is not just about managing resources; it's an ethic and inner sensibility."[24] The notion of *Buen Vivir*, from the cosmovision of the indigenous peoples of Abya Yala in Latin America, provides us a fascinating model for communing:

> *Buen Vivir* is foremost a decolonial stance. . . . It calls for a new ethics that balances quality of life, democratization of the state and concern with biocentric ideals . . . a lived practice against commodification, a way of doing things differently . . . a new paradigm of social and ecological commons—one that is community-centric, ecologically balanced and culturally sensitive. It's a vision and a platform for thinking and practicing alternative futures based on a "bio-civilization."[25]

Put differently, commoning is an alternative to the neoliberalism. It facilitates the flourishing of an economy of life by reducing inequality and social exclusion and celebrating life in abundance. Commoning is practiced in several indigenous and subsistence communities through concepts and practices such as *Buen Vivir*. It is a vision and ethic that are antithetical to the logic of neoliberal capitalism. Commoning, therefore, facilitates the enlivening of an economy of life.

The creation narratives that we read in the book of Genesis remind us that the commons are sanctuaries of the community of creation committed to continuing God's creative work by birthing, nurturing, protecting, and celebrating life in abundance. As the Yahwist tradition in its creation narrative upholds, it is in the commons that we practice our vocation to till and to keep the earth. The commons are the sacred spaces wherein we celebrate communion with the Creator in the community of our siblings—the plants, the birds, the water bodies, and the air. The book of Genesis further affirms the mutuality between the commons and the commoners. In Genesis 4, we see the connection between fratricide and ecocide. The lives of the commons and the commoners are integrally connected The commons are the scriptures that reveal the glory of God, and our life together as community of creation in the commons is the true doxology. The colonization of the commons is a desecration of this sacred space and sacred communion, and it is therefore a sin against God. God created the commons so that humans and nonhuman beings can live in community with each other. Economy of life is, from a theological perspective, primarily a critique of the dominant economy of greed and accumulation. It "engenders participation for all in decision-making processes that impact lives, provides for people's basic needs through just liveli-hoods, values and supports social reproduction and care work done primarily by women, and protects and preserves the air, water, land, and energy sources that are necessary to sustain life."[26] Commoning is hence the voca-tion of enlivening the economy of life.

COMMONING: TOWARD AN ALTERNATIVE PILGRIMAGE FOR AN ECONOMY OF LIFE

The "Pilgrimage of Justice and Peace" is an alternative ecumenical journey initiated by the Tenth Assembly of the World Council of Churches in Busan, South Korea. This journey affirms the churches' commitment to celebrate unity as we *travel* together resisting injustice and violence. As pilgrimage communities, the churches are called to become alternative communities realizing God's justice and peace through their transformative presence in the world. A pilgrimage of justice and peace begins with a deeper experience of *metanoia* (conversion), where genuine self-reflexivity and system-threaten-ing political interventions work together to enable the churches to come out of the empire and to witness publicly to the gospel of justice and peace. It is a leap of faith from our comfort zones to a dangerous journey in solidarity with the wretched earth and the wretched of the earth. It is a pilgrimage in which we experience deeper meanings of comradeship and spirituality. In this pil-grimage, we celebrate our diverse gifts, visit the wounds of the earth and the earth community, and bring about healing through our acts of compassionate justice. Our pilgrimage of justice and peace offers us new epiphany experi-ences as we meet the journeying God—the pilgrim God in our praxis of justice and peace.[27]

Pilgrimage is a contested category in our times. We are familiar with pilgrimages that promise us blessings in the form of prosperity and privi-leges. In a metaphorical sense, the neoliberal development paradigm is also a sort of pilgrimage. Development has become a fetish, and the colonization of the commons is a movement toward "progress." We also witness alternative pilgrimages emerging out of the process of de-commoning pushed by the dominant pilgrimage. These are the movements of the commoners—climate refugees, landless agriculture workers, coastal communities, forest dwellers, indigenous communities, and a host of internally displaced people who are uprooted from their commons by the neoliberal pilgrimage of the dominant. Stated differently, while the fetishization of market economy leads to the pilgrimage of de-commoning, commoning is the alternative pilgrimage hap-pening at the margins to enliven the economy of life.

As a subversive literature that emerged from a colonized community, the book of Revelation articulates the stories of subaltern resistance and alternative visions. In Revelation, we come across two contrasting pilgrimages: the imperial pilgrimage that is the colonization of the commons, and the pilgrimage of the colonized who work to bring healing and restoration to the commons. Revelation continues to invite the communities to come out of the empire and to transform Babylon into New Jerusalem. This is a call to participate in the alternative pilgrimage of commoning.

In the eschatological vision of Revelation, the redeemed earth has no sea. "And the first earth had passed away and the sea was no more" (Revelation 21:1). Here, Revelation portrays the sea as a political and economic category, and the disappearance of the sea in the New Jerusalem is hence a critique of the political economy of the Roman Empire. The sea was the means for colonizing the commons and the commoners in the Roman-occupied territories. The list of cargos mentioned in chapter 18 reveals how the commons and the commoners were colonized and commodified by Rome. The list included "cargo of gold, silver, jewels and pearls, fine linen, purple, silk and scarlet, all kinds of scented wood, all articles of ivory, all articles of costly wood, bronze, iron, and marble, cinnamon, spice, incense, myrrh, frankincense, wine, olive oil, choice flour and wheat, cattle and sheep, horses and chariots, slaves—and human lives" (Revelation 18:12–13). The list reveals how the fruits of the commons and the fruits of the labor of the commons were colonized and plundered by the Roman imperial power. The list of cargos also included "slaves and human beings." Artisans and farmers engaged in the creative vocation of tilling and keeping the commons were enslaved and commodified for slave trade. So the disappearance of the sea in the redeemed earth is not the disappearance of water per se; rather it is the alternative vision of commoning, which is antithetical to the imperial political economy of greed, commodification, and accumulation.[28] Living in a context of de-commoning, the vision of the absence of the sea in the redeemed earth inspires us to take up the pilgrimage of commoning to celebrate an economy of life.

While proclaiming the absence of sea in the redeemed earth, the pilgrim community of Revelation proposes an alternative vision of water: water is a free gift for all. "To the one who is thirsty I will give to drink from the spring of the water of life as a gift" (21:6). "Let everyone who is thirsty come. Let everyone who wishes take the water of life as a gift" (22:17). The pilgrimage of Revelation is a salvific mission to restore the water commons by de-commodifying it and offering it as a free gift to the entire community of creation. Here the water commons are brought out of the logic of neoliberal capitalism. Revelation's pilgrimage of commoning is a prophetic judgment on the capitalist economy of de-commoning. The pilgrimage of commoning propagates the vision of a gift economy where nature's bounty is available to all, not just to people with money. Through this pilgrimage we participate in the redemption of our water and coastal commons—oceans, lakes, rivers, estuaries, and wells. The promise of free access to clean and pure water is the divine rejection of the prevailing political economy of privatization and commodification of water and coastal commons.

The book of Revelation ends with the vision of the river of the water of life—a pilgrimage of tiny water drops—flowing from the throne of God and of the lamb through the middle of the street of the city. This is a therapeutic pilgrimage. The healing of the earth comes through the leaves of the tree that is nourished by the river of the water of life. This apocalyptic vision affirms the salvific nature of commoning. Revelation proclaims an alternative doctrine of salvation by affirming the agency of the leaves and the water in the healing of the nations. Said differently, the leaves and the waters participate in the divine mission of redemption in history, and hence our pilgrimage of commoning is a form of participation in God's redemptive work in our midst. Commoning is the pilgrimage against all manifestations of imperial conquest in the name of enlivening the economy of life.

The alternative pilgrimage of communing is where we meet God in our times. We see commoners and their social movements spearheading this movement of life. Movements like the National Fishworkers Forum (NFF) are co-redeemers as they participate in the salvific work in history to renew the face of the earth. For such a time as this, the church is called to witness to the in-breaking of this new eon—an alternative eon of communing, where the movement of life is flourished and celebrated.

NOTES

1. I am thinking of the distinction between system world and life world proposed by Habermas.

2. Heather Menizes, *Reclaiming the Commons for the Common Good* (Gabriola Island, BC: New Society Publishers, 2014), 27.

3. David Harvey, *A Brief History of Neoliberalism* (Oxford: Oxford University Press, 2007), 159.

4. "Dark satanic mills of the Industrial Revolution" is a metaphor used by William Blake in one of his poems to describe the destruction of the commons and the commons people by Industrial Revolution. "Satanic" here refers to the desacralization of the sacred earth by the Industrial Revolution

5. David Bollier, *Think like a Commonder: A Short Introduction to the Life of the Commons* (Gabriola Island, BC: New Society Publishers, 2014), 43.

6. George Monbiot, "John Clare, the Poet of the Environmental Crisis—200 Years Ago | George Monbiot," *The Guardian*, July 9, 2012, sec. Opinion, https://www.theguardian.com/commentisfree/2012/jul/09/john-clare-poetry.

7. Karl Polyani, *The Great Transformation* (New York: Farrar and Reinhart, 1944), 73.

8. Pradip Prabhu, "In the Eye of the Storm: Tribal Peoples of India," in *Indigenous Traditions and Ecology: The Interbeing of Cosmology and Community*, ed. John A. Grim (Cambridge, MA: Center for the Study of World Religions, 2001), 62.

9. Quoted in Prafulla Samantara, "Rural Commons: A Source of Livelihood and Sustainability," in *Vocabulary of Commons*, ed. Anita Cheria and Edwin (Anand, India: Foundation for Ecological Security, 2011), 107.

10. Garrett Hardin, "The Tragedy of the Commons," *Science* 162, no. 3859 (December 13, 1968): 1243–48.

11. Jonathan Rowe and Peter Barnes, *Our Common Wealth: The Hidden Economy That Makes Everything Else Work*, 1st ed. (San Francisco: Berrett-Koehler Publishers, 2013), 18.

12. Bollier, *Think Like a Commonder*, 24, 32.

13. Jawaharlal Nehru, "Tryst with Destiny—Jawaharlal Nehru Speech to Nation on Independence Day," IndiaCelebrating.com, December 21, 2016, https://www.indiacelebrating.com/speech/independence-day-speech-by-nehru/.

14. Jawaharlal Nehru, *Modern Temples of India: Selected Speeches of Jawaharlal Nehru at Irrigation and Power Projects*, ed. C. V. J. Sharma (Delhi: Central Board of Irrigation and Power, 1989), 41.

15. Arundhati Roy, *The Greater Common Good* (Bombay: India Book Distributors, 1991), 7.

16. Jawaharlal Nehru, *Jawaharlal Nehru's Speeches*, vol. 3 (New Delhi: Publication Division, Ministry of Information and Broadcasting, 1958), 3.

17. Rejimon K, "Draft Coastal Regulations Facilitate NDA's Sagarmala Project but Fishermen, Environmentalists Feel Threatened—Firstpost," First Post, May 5, 2018, https://www.firstpost.com/india/draft-coastal-regulations-facilitate-ndas-sagarmala-project-but-fishermen-environmentalists-feel-threatened-4457331.html.

18. Rejimon K, "Draft Coastal Regulations."

19. Rejimon K, "Draft Coastal Regulations."

20. "The Vizhinjam Port: Dream or Disaster" (Delhi: The Research Collective, 2017), 8, https://updatecollective.wordpress.com/2018/01/04/the-vizhinjam-port-dream-or-disaster/.

21. Member States of the Indian Ocean Rim Association, "Jakarta Declaration on Blue Economy" (Jakarta, Indonesia, May 2017), https://www.iora.int/media/8218/jakarta-declaration-on-blue-economy-final.pdf.

22. *Occupation of the Coast: Blue Economy in India* (New Delhi: The Research Collective, 2017), 6.

23. *Occupation of the Coast*, 9.

24. Bollier, *Think Like a Commonder*, 158–59.

25. Juan Francisco Salazar, "Buen Vivir: South America's Rethinking of the Future We Want," The Conversation, accessed May 3, 2019, http://theconversation.com/buen-vivir-south-americas-rethinking-of-the-future-we-want-44507.

26. Rogate R. Mshana and Athena Peralta, eds., *Economy of Life: Linking Poverty, Wealth and Ecology* (Geneva: World Council of Churches, 2015), 9.

27. World Council of Churches, "An Invitation to the Pilgrimage of Justice and Peace," Document, July 8, 2014, https://www.oikoumene.org/en/resources/documents/central-committee/geneva-2014/an-invitation-to-the-pilgrimage-of-justice-and-peace.

28. Barbara R. Rossing, *The Choice between Two Cities: Whore, Bride, and Empire in the Apocalypse* (Harrisburg, PA: Trinity Press International, 1999).

BIBLIOGRAPHY

Bollier, David. *Think Like a Commonder: A Short Introduction to the Life of the Commons*. Gabriola Island, BC: New Society Publishers, 2014.

Hardin, Garrett. "The Tragedy of the Commons." *Science* 162, no. 3859 (December 13, 1968): 1243–48.

Harvey, David. *A Brief History of Neoliberalism*. Oxford: Oxford University Press, 2007.

Member States of the Indian Ocean Rim Association. "Jakarta Declaration on Blue Economy." Jakarta, Indonesia, May 2017. https://www.iora.int/media/8218/jakarta-declaration-on-blue-economy-final.pdf.

Menizes, Heather. *Reclaiming the Commons for the Common Good*. Gabriola Island, BC: New Society Publishers, 2014.

Monbiot, George. "John Clare, the Poet of the Environmental Crisis—200 Years Ago | George Monbiot." *The Guardian*, July 9, 2012, sec. Opinion. https://www.theguardian.com/commentisfree/2012/jul/09/john-clare-poetry.

Mshana, Rogate R., and Athena Peralta, eds. *Economy of Life: Linking Poverty, Wealth and Ecology*. Geneva: World Council of Churches, 2015.

Nehru, Jawaharlal. *Jawaharlal Nehru's Speeches*. Vol. 3. New Delhi: Publication Division, Ministry of Information and Broadcasting, 1958.

———. *Modern Temples of India: Selected Speeches of Jawaharlal Nehru at Irrigation and Power Projects*. Edited by C. V. J. Sharma. Delhi: Central Board of Irrigation and Power, 1989.

———. "Tryst with Destiny—Jawaharlal Nehru Speech to Nation on Independence Day." IndiaCelebrating.com, December 21, 2016. https://www.indiacelebrating.com/speech/independence-day-speech-by-nehru/.

Occupation of the Coast: Blue Economy in India. New Delhi: The Research Collective, 2017.

Polyani, Karl. *The Great Transformation*. New York: Farrar and Reinhart, 1944.

Prabhu, Pradip. "In the Eye of the Storm: Tribal Peoples of India." In *Indigenous Traditions and Ecology: The Interbeing of Cosmology and Community*, edited by John A. Grim. Cambridge, MA: Center for the Study of World Religions, 2001.

Rejimon K. "Draft Coastal Regulations Facilitate NDA's Sagarmala Project but Fishermen, Environmentalists Feel Threatened—Firstpost." First Post, May 5, 2018. https://www.firstpost.com/india/draft-coastal-regulations-facilitate-ndas-sagarmala-project-but-fishermen-environmentalists-feel-threatened-4457331.html.

Rossing, Barbara R. *The Choice between Two Cities: Whore, Bride, and Empire in the Apocalypse*. Harrisburg, PA: Trinity Press International, 1999.

Rowe, Jonathan, and Peter Barnes. *Our Common Wealth: The Hidden Economy That Makes Everything Else Work*. 1st ed. San Francisco: Berrett-Koehler Publishers, 2013.

Roy, Arundhati. *The Greater Common Good*. Bombay: India Book Distributors, 1991.

Salazar, Juan Francisco. "Buen Vivir: South America's Rethinking of the Future We Want." The Conversation. Accessed May 3, 2019. http://theconversation.com/buen-vivir-south-americas-rethinking-of-the-future-we-want-44507.

Samantara, Prafulla. "Rural Commons: A Source of Livelihood and Sustainability." In *Vocabulary of Commons*, edited by Anita Cheria and Edwin. Anand, India: Foundation for Ecological Security, 2011.

"The Vizhinjam Port: Dream or Disaster." Delhi: The Research Collective, 2017. https://updatecollective.wordpress.com/2018/01/04/the-vizhinjam-port-dream-or-disaster/.

World Council of Churches. "An Invitation to the Pilgrimage of Justice and Peace." Document, July 8, 2014. https://www.oikoumene.org/en/resources/documents/central-committee/geneva-2014/an-invitation-to-the-pilgrimage-of-justice-and-peace.

Chapter Four

Pilgrimage of Life

Lessons from the Experiences of Forced Migrants and Victims of Human Trafficking

Deenabandhu Manchala

Forty–year-old Mingus, who was trafficked some ten years ago to work on a palm oil plantation in Malaysia, returned to Kupang, Indonesia, on April 7, 2018, in a coffin. His wife and children stayed back in an unknown location. Pneumonia was stated as the cause of death, as is typical with most of the six coffins that arrive on an average day at different Indonesian airports. As his body arrived, some of us who had gathered in Kupang for a Global Ministries Conference on "Partnership for God's Justice in Solidarity with Victims of Human Trafficking" went to the airport to express our condolences and to grieve in solidarity with his extended family. We were told that this is a common feature at many airports in Asia, from where thousands leave every day in the hope of or with the promises of better life. At this five-day gathering of these grassroots, anti-human-trafficking activists from many parts of Indonesia, South and Southeast Asia, and the world, we heard similar stories of people, mostly of rural, poor women and children, who were trafficked for forced labor, prostitution, begging, and even the harvesting of organs. These stories had some common content: experiences of passports taken away, no telephone and bank accounts, no contracts, no medical care, no clue about where they are, no off-days, long working hours (12–16 hours), crammed workplaces, wage theft, unpaid wages, inhuman living conditions, rape and sexual harassment, food depravation, physical violence, detention, deportation, and death. Another common feature was the fact of their governments benefitting a great deal from foreign exchange remittances while doing nothing to protect or support their overseas workers.

According to a recent report from the International Labor Organization, 24.9 million victims are trapped in modern-day slavery. Of these, 16 million (64 percent) are exploited for labor, 4.8 million (19 percent) are sexually exploited, and 4.1 million (17 percent) are exploited for state-imposed forced labor.[1] Furthermore, 71 percent of these trafficked victims are women and girls. Among them, 15.4 million victims (75 percent) are aged 18 or older, while the number of children under the age of 18 is estimated at 5.5 million (25 percent).[2] This horrific business earns traffickers profits of roughly $150 billion a year.[3] Modern slavery is cheap and disposable. Whereas a slave in 1850 regularly sold for the equivalent of $40,000 in today's economy, slaves today cost, on average, $90.[4] It thrives on the misery and vulnerabilities of people made and kept poor and powerless by political and economic structures. Those statuses, systems, and conditions are legitimized by dominant religious beliefs and cultures.

At the larger level, according to the United Nations High Commissioner for Refugees 2017 report, there were 71.4 million people of concern to UNHCR worldwide, more than half of whom were women and children. All had fled armed conflict, violence, insecurity, criminality, persecution, and human rights abuses.[5]

Extreme poverty and dispossession, disease and malnutrition, lack of access to education and health care, unemployment and loss of traditional livelihoods, droughts and floods, conflicts, wars, violence, and persecution are widely acknowledged reasons for people embarking on these risky journeys, subjecting themselves to all the dangers associated with this form of movement. With wars and warmongers active as ever, laborsaving economic growth policies that cause unemployment continue increasing poverty despite boastful economic growth. This obscene reality of millions being pushed beyond the margins, it seems, will continue for many years to come.

Even if some of these trends and forces are deemed responsible for this shameful global reality, no one can deny the fact that we are a part of a world that seems to believe in economic growth by way of abuse and exploitation along both environmental and human lines. We become complicit through our apathy, silence, and indifference, our tacit approval of and allegiance to certain unjust political and economic systems and structures, and our practice of certain cultures of domination and discrimination.

The conference in Kupang, mentioned above, asserted that

> in a context of these manifold assaults on human dignity, churches and faith communities not only have the responsibility to protect the victims, but also have a distinct role as conscience keepers and moral voice of the society, because human trafficking exposes:
>
> • a shameful aspect of our collective psyche that allows and legitimizes the devaluation of some human beings for profit and pleasure;

- the impact of the institutionalization of greed that numbs our capacities to view and affirm the sanctity of life and the worth and dignity of all human beings;
- the structurally-embedded and culturally-legitimized patriarchy, caste system and similar social hierarchies, and the associated concepts of power that glorify domination, intimidation, subjugation, exploitation and violation of the disempowered;
- the superficial concepts of nation, community and human solidarity that we profess;
- the skewed concepts of development that overwhelm our moral sensibilities; and
- the continued connivance of religious institutions and faith traditions with the greedy and the powerful.[6]

Against the backdrop of these atrocities, let me begin by contrasting experiences of migration and pilgrimage, two important phenomena of our time that put people and their theologies in motion. Can migration help deepen a Christian understanding of pilgrimage, and can pilgrimage help us deal more constructively with the realities of migration?

Commonly understood, pilgrimage is a deeply religious, spiritual, or personal initiative. It implies a journey, a movement towards a destination, a search in anticipation, perhaps, of divine blessings, and a sublime spiritual experience of enlightenment, inner peace, physical well-being, or prosperity. People from all major religious traditions and all sections of society—men and women, rich and poor, urban and rural, and educated and not so educated—embark on these journeys, voluntarily embracing physical discomfort because these are considered holy sources of divine blessing by their respective religious traditions. All of them know that they have a home to go back to and that they will.

Contrast this voluntary embrace of discomfort with the experience of those driven out or fleeing from harm, those who are forced to embark on often extremely dangerous, aimless, and uncertain journeys to find other possibilities to live somewhere.

Of course, not all those who migrate can be put into a singular social category. Some have skills and assets and migrate to improve their economic status. But many are forced to migrate on account of an absence of possibilities to survive in the places they live, as elaborated in the earlier section of this paper.

When we are talking about the poor who are fleeing from poverty, danger, death, and abuse, we might rethink the discourse of pilgrimage. If pilgrimage implies renunciation, what do these people have to renounce? If pilgrimage implies humility, humiliation is their everyday reality. If it implies a single-minded pursuit of a goal, they opt for any possibility that gives them hope to survive. If experiences of enlightenment and sublime joy are the anticipated results, these trafficked people, forced migrants, and refugees more commonly experience the opposite, like rejection, detention, deportation, torture, or indefinite separation from their families. They are traumatized and pushed into despair. They thus often run towards anyone—touts and traders, and smugglers and traffickers—who offer hope and reprieve from their poverty and consequent suffering, even if it is temporary or dubious. They are neither exploring nor searching but are fleeing from hunger, homelessness, abuse, and oppression. They are on the way to unknown destinations out of the sheer desire to survive as long as they can in whichever condition that they deem can offer them the necessary conditions.

At the same time, to view those fleeing from poverty within the broad category of migration might imply trivialization of the complexity of the sources of their poverty and predicament in each geo-political context. "The poor" are a broad but convenient category for those who do not want to dig up the terrains of injustice. As Javier Echeverria says,

> Poverty must be seen as the depravation of basic capabilities rather than merely as lowness of incomes. . . . Poverty implies violation of basic or elemental freedoms, like being able to avoid such deprivations as starvation, under nourishment, escapable morbidity and premature mortality, as well as the freedoms that are associated with being literate and numerate, enjoying political participation and uncensored speech and so on.[7]

Nevertheless, the language of pilgrimage does not necessarily help here either, as it might imply equating the experience of those who are made and kept poor and vulnerable with that of the privileged others in order to suggest that the poor too can overcome poverty on their own. The larger structures and cultures that create, perpetrate, and legitimize poverty thus remain unchallenged.

As the poor and the marginalized struggle for life with justice, freedom, safety, and dignity, can we reimagine pilgrimage in ways that are both relevant to and respectful of those who are in various struggles for life? In the context of our conversation on people and poverty, we need to ask ourselves: What then is pilgrimage? Whose pilgrimage is it? What does it do to those who participate? What do they achieve? How should they participate in it? In other words, what is the meaning, purpose, and character of pilgrimage?

PILGRIMAGE OF LIFE

Since its tenth assembly in Busan, South Korea, in 2013, the World Council of Churches has been promoting the idea of the pilgrimage of justice and peace. It has generated considerable reflection in many parts of the world, inspiring churches to reclaim their essential missional and movement character.[8] In fact, the concept of pilgrimage has been present in the church's long history and in various Christian theological traditions and ecclesial expressions. People from different walks of life in different contexts of time and space have always formulated and pursued their own ideas of pilgrimages.

In light of the experiences of displaced people, the meaning of pilgrimage changes for those who have the possibilities to effect changes but prefer to remain silent, inert, and indifferent. Pilgrimage challenges those who benefit from the inbuilt injustice of the system but erroneously believe that they deserve those experiences due to their hard work and intellect. Pilgrimage also challenges those who believe that another world is possible and have the courage and determination to pursue that goal in solidarity with the poor. As such, this pilgrimage is primarily and deeply introspective—a voluntary exploration.

Understood this way, pilgrimage of life is also a journey of many together towards the creation of wholesome conditions for the celebration of life whereby all human beings have the possibility to live with dignity, respect, and freedom. It is a journey inspired by a new awareness of life and the intricate interconnectedness that makes life possible for all members of creation.

Pilgrimage is inspired by a spirituality of life that is not conditioned by any religious dogma or belief system but draws on the life-affirming values of all persuasions, whether religious or ideological. It is a spirituality that echoes with and amplifies the yearnings of those who are pushed to and beyond the margins of our world. According to Hindu scholar and activist Swami Agnivesh, "It is not a formula but a dynamic phenomenon that expresses itself through an ongoing engagement with the human predicament."[9]

While making a connection between Christian faith and spirituality, Gustavo Gutierrez argues:

> Spirituality is not some immaterial realm pertaining to our soul but not our body, to our beliefs but not our actions. *Rather, our spirituality is the comprehensive way in which we live out our faith* . . . [and] the reason why spirituality is so connected to accompaniment of those battling material poverty—suffering the death of sickness and of social insignificance—is that Christians consider the creation of the world as a gift of life.[10]

Such a pilgrimage, in partnership with the other, strives to realize the values of mutuality, interdependence, human dignity, justice, peace, and the integrity of creation. It is not docile; it is bold and assertive in confronting death-dispensing forces. It resists commodification of people and earth's resources, which destroys the intricate web of life.

It not only confronts and resists but also nurtures alternatives to the current logic of the survival of the fittest. It invites people to be active collaborators for the affirmation of life. It is a journey for the moral regeneration of the world gone astray, toward a new world. The journey might seem endless, but that is what the pilgrimage of justice is all about. There are no finish lines except the joy of striving for the celebration of life and of keeping oneself away from values and habits that trample over the dignity and rights of others, especially of the weak and vulnerable.

Further, it is not only a movement but primarily a space for encounter with all life-affirming forces and initiatives. It is open and inclusive of all who strive for justice and human dignity. It is a mode of learning to challenge and to be challenged, of sharing in one another's vulnerabilities as well as visions of another world. It is, therefore, a journey in partnership, especially with those who are treated unjustly and with those who yearn for a new world.

I suggest we make use of a reconstructed notion of pilgrimage for three reasons: One is that it can substitute for "mission," which seems to evoke negative responses in most of the multireligious world. It could help present a Christian response to the world in more personal and participatory ways than with triumphalistic assertions and through patronizing projects. Two, as it accents exploration and introspection, it can also help nurture an attitude of humility and openness to other experiences, perspectives, and visions, thereby enabling partnerships and movement toward a new world for all. Such an understanding of pilgrimage offers possibilities for churches to reclaim the essential movement character of Christianity by shedding their institutional self-understanding. And three, as an endeavor with an expansive understanding of God and God's purposes, it could also expand the scope of Christian theological activity to include similar expressions of spirituality in the wider world and to be an ally of change makers.

SOME THEOLOGICAL CHALLENGES ALONG THE WAY

On the basis of these reflections on pilgrimage, from the perspective of the displaced and trafficked people, I would like to lift up a few areas of our public life for a more focused theological reflection.

The first is human dignity. The trafficked people, forced migrants, refugees, displaced people, racially oppressed groups, religious and ethnic minorities, indigenous people, Dalits in my country, India, women, children, elderly people, people with disabilities, and many such others are treated as disposable instruments, commodities, or playthings as well as liabilities and a drain on economies. When these and millions of others are not treated and allowed to live like human beings, when some human beings think they are better than others and that some should suffer and die to make others feel superior and comfortable, it is necessary that Christian theological activity address this collective insanity of the human species, especially of our generation. Such a return does not imply a return to the anthropocentrism of traditional theologies. Rather, it asserts and upholds the sanctity and dignity of human life. The time has come to acknowledge and address, from a theological perspective, the existential complexities that make some human beings more prone to abuse and exploitation by some others. We must question why some human beings are deliberately denied access to opportunities even if we affirm that all are created equal and in the image of God.

The experiences of the marginalized and exploited people amply illustrate this tendency of "othering" in which the dignity of certain human beings is denied because they are supposedly inferior to the groups in power. A WCC Consultation on "Affirming Human Dignity" puts it this way:

> This trait has been the origin of many violent structures, cultures and values, such as racial bigotry, ethnic hatred, slavery, gender discrimination and many other forms of hatred and exclusion. This has also given way to the emergence of certain oppressive symbols and assertion of power, such as religious, ethnic, racial, linguistic identities, that are used by the vested interests to consolidate and multiply their hegemony over opportunities, privileges and power. Consequently, solidarity degenerates into selfish obligation to care for one's own group and into denial of responsibility towards others.[11]

The second is the need to address the distinct moral challenges posed by the interplay of the two most dominant cultures of our generation—individualism and consumerism. Such consideration can only properly occur, though, when considered in conjunction with two other increasingly dominant ideological trends of our time—fundamentalism and secularization. While fundamentalism seems to lend legitimacy to the injustice and aggression of the dominant social and economic powers, secularized attitudes seem to nurture apathy, indifference, and immunity to human suffering and injustice. While power and domination through exclusivist versions of social, political, and national identities seem to feature the agenda of fundamentalist, right-wing forces, the individualistic pursuits of wealth, power, perfection, dispassionate rationalization, and social indifference seem to result from some secularization processes. Both seem to hold or justify the suffering and sacrifice of some as inevitable for the achievement of more basic common goals. How does the theological community see itself responding to the complexity of these challenges? How do we enhance the sense of community, the values of mutual responsibility, and a holistic understanding of life at a time of increasingly fragmented views of the same? I do not believe that any one particular religious or ideological resource has the answers. Perhaps a broader spirituality of life needs to be nurtured, and the pilgrimage mode might help in finding helpful companions along the way.

The third is an alternative to the way power is commonly understood and exercised. Current models of power seem to be based on the premise of feeling powerful in contrast to powerlessness. Power is pursued as an instrument to intimidate, terrorize, control, and abuse the powerless in addition to amassing more wealth and more power. Certain skewed theories of self-validation (such as race, gender, caste, nationhood, etc.) add their support to these belief systems. Therefore, violence, violation, exploitation, and dispossession seem to continue unabated in an ethos where such notions of power are the prevailing norm. This exposes the collective disorder of our generation—persons, communities, and nations alike—as we live with destructive, distorted, damaged notions of power and human capacities. How do we expose the shallowness of these concepts of power, and what alternative models do we propose and nurture?

And fourth is the necessity to expose greed and arrogance as the sources of poverty and abuse. The most common response has always been to problematize poverty as a challenge to be overcome. Much energy is therefore invested in strategies for poverty alleviation. Churches, in their patronizing missions, have always reached out to the poor but have often left out the need to expose greed for power and wealth as a moral and missional challenge. A study on *Christianity, Poverty and Wealth in the 21st Century* by Aprodev, (Association of World Council of Churches Related Development Organizations in Europe), initiated with partners in many parts of the world in 2000, advocated the need for talking about the "greed line" in addition to the "poverty line."[12] The point here is that confronting and denouncing the immorality of greed that destroys the earth, human beings, and human relationships is a more important moral challenge than eradicating poverty. It is, in fact, a prerequisite for any attempt to eradicate poverty. Gutierrez puts this sharply: "To speak of the poor, thus, without opposing the poverty that kills them, is a major obstacle to announcing the gospel."[13] We must acknowledge that the insatiable greed of some for power and wealth makes and keeps millions poor, hungry, homeless, dispossessed, and dehumanized.

Some statistics are helpful here: Globally, just 8 billionaires have the same amount of wealth as the poorest 50 percent of the world population.[14] In my country, India, the richest 1 percent own 58 percent of total wealth.[15] An Oxfam Study on the eve of World Economic Forum 2018 mentions some facts, such as women forming 60 percent of lowest paid wage labor, 5.8 million child laborers, 100,000 deaths every year because of the burning of coal, and the irony of many governments offering tax cuts to the rich while cutting funds for education and health care for the poor. It further highlights that "between 1988 and 2011, the incomes of the poorest 10% increased just by \$65, while the incomes of the richest 1% grew by \$11,800—182 times as much." Mark Goldring of Oxfam makes a poignant remark:

While one in nine people on the planet will go to bed hungry tonight, a small handful of billionaires have so much wealth that they would need several lifetimes to spend it. The fact that a super-rich elite are able to prosper at the expense of the rest of us at home and overseas shown how warped our economy has become.[16]

Added to this is the scandalous practice of wealth generation through the manufacturing and sale of firearms and weapons that provoke or perpetrate violent conflicts and wars. These not only kill and destroy but also turn millions into refugees. According to a recent report by the Stockholm International Peace Research Institute, the "United States accounts for 31% of arms exports and Russia accounts for 27% followed by China, Germany and France." It goes on to say that these arms are used elsewhere in Africa, Asia, the Middle East, and the Americas.[17] The realities of extractive mining and anti-people industrial development policies of many governments around the world are also problematic. At the conference of anti-human-trafficking activists in Kupang, Indonesia, many participants asserted time and again that people leave or fall into the traps of traffickers because there was no employment. Their lands were taken away for palm oil plantations or industrial manufacturing, and this had destroyed their local economies and traditional livelihoods.

The point here is that while diaconal expressions of mercy and compassion are necessary, the massive displacement of people presents a number of moral challenges that cannot be ignored. In fact, the struggle for justice and truth alone can validate the pilgrimage that we advocate as an expression of Christian witness in our world today.

PILGRIMAGE OF NURTURING PARTNERSHIPS FOR GOD'S JUSTICE

As I said earlier, the pilgrimage of life neither has definite finish lines nor is an exclusive struggle. It is not about the end result but about the means— creating and nurturing a culture of life. It is a collective endeavor. It is inclusive in that it brings together and draws on the experiences and visions of various sections of people who experience discrimination, marginalization, and exclusion. It involves meeting and learning from partners and creating and nurturing partnerships for justice. There is no place for patronizing expressions of partnership. Churches, church organizations, and their diaconal initiatives need to assume a new role of creating spaces and opportunities for partners for justice to meet and work together rather than being merely dispensers of charity and compassion.

I started this presentation by mentioning a conversation among partners working on human trafficking in Kupang, Indonesia. Let me end by quoting what their communique said about partnership for justice:

> Partnership for justice implies a commitment to uphold the sanctity and dignity of all people. This partnership is multi-directional and is inclusive of all who are committed to these values. It is authentic and transformative only when it is based on relationships of respect, trust, mutuality, and a common commitment for justice. This necessarily implies and involves partnering with victims by entering into their life-worlds of struggle and hope. . . . In a world dominated and plundered by such partnerships among forces of greed and evil, it is necessary for churches and Christians to actively create and nurture partnerships for life among people's and survivors' movements, civil society organizations, and all people of faith and goodwill. The church affirms that every human being is made in the image of God, and that God desires us to love and have compassion towards one another. Therefore, the church cannot but respond to the reality of suffering and dehumanization caused by human selfishness. Justice is love in action; indeed, seeking justice is not an option, but a necessary expression of authentic Christian witness.[18]

NOTES

1. "Walk Free | The Minderoo Foundation," accessed April 29, 2019, https://www.minderoo.com.au/walk-free/.

2. The Asia-Pacific region accounts for the largest number of forced laborers—15.4 million (62 percent of the global total). Africa has 5.7 million (23 percent) followed by Europe and Central Asia with 2.2 million (9 percent). The Americas account for 1.2 million (5 percent) and the Arab States account for 1 percent of all victims.

3. According to the ILO report from 2014, the following is a breakdown of profits, by sector: $99 billion from commercial sexual exploitation; $34 billion in construction, manufacturing, mining, and utilities; and $9 billion in agriculture, including forestry and fishing. Finally, $8 billion is saved annually by private households that employ domestic workers under conditions of forced labor. See Human Rights First, "Human Trafficking by the Numbers," September 2017, https://www.humanrightsfirst.org/resource/human-trafficking-numbers; https://www.globalslaveryindex.org/resources/media/.

4. Free the Slaves, "Our Model for Freedom: Slavery Today," accessed April 29, 2019, https://www.freetheslaves.net/our-model-for-freedom/slavery-today/; Kevin Bales, *Disposable People: New Slavery in the Global Economy* (Berkeley, CA: University of California Press, 2012), 16.

5. United Nations High Commissioner for Refugees, "UNHCR Global Report: 2017," 2017, 15, https://www.unhcr.org/publications/fundraising/5b4c89bf17/unhcr-globalreport-2017.html.

6. Deenbandhu Manchala, "Partnership for God's Justice: An Interpretive Account of the Conversations among Global Ministries' Partners Engaged in Anti-Human Trafficking Work in Asia, Kupang, Indonesia, April 5–9, 2018," Global Ministries, November 16, 2018, https://www.globalministries.org/partnership_for_god_s_justice.

7. Javier Maria Iguiñiz Echeverria, "The Multidimensionality of Poverty," in *The Preferential Option for the Poor beyond Theology*, ed. Daniel G. Groody, Gustavo Gutiérrez, and José O Aylwin (Notre Dame, IN: University of Notre Dame Press, 2014), 55, http://site.ebrary.com/id/10815888.

8. For more on this, see the World Council of Churches: https://www.oikoumene.org/en.

9. Svami Agnivesh, *Applied Spirituality: For Justice Unlimited* (New Dheli: Dharma Pratishthan, 2005), 35.

10. Gustavo Gutiérrez, "Saying and Showing to the Poor: 'God Loves You,'" in *In the Company of the Poor: Conversations between Dr. Paul Farmer and Fr. Gustavo Gutierrez*, ed. Michael P. Griffin and Jennie Weiss Block (New York: Orbis Books, 2013), 33, http://catalog.hathitrust.org/api/volumes/oclc/828892555.html.

11. Deenbandhu Manchala, "Introduction," in *Nurturing Peace: Theological Reflections on Overcoming Violence* (Geneva: WCC Publications, 2005), 5–16.

12. https://berkleycenter.georgetown.edu/publications/christianity-poverty-and-wealth-in-the-21st-century

13. Gutiérrez, "Saying and Showing to the Poor: 'God Loves You,'" 22.

14. Larry Elliot, "World's Eight Richest People Have Same Wealth as Poorest 50%," *The Guardian*, January 15, 2017, sec. Business, https://www.theguardian.com/global-development/2017/jan/16/worlds-eight-richest-people-have-same-wealth-as-poorest-50.

15. "Richest 1% Own 58% of Total Wealth in India: Oxfam," *The Hindu*, January 16, 2017, sec. Economy, https://www.thehindu.com/business/Economy/Richest-1–own-58–of-total-wealth-in-India-Oxfam/article17044486.ece.

16. "Richest 1% Own 58% of Total Wealth in India."

17. Aljzaeera Editorial, "The 10 Countries That Export the Most Major Weapons," February 22, 2017, https://www.aljazeera.com/indepth/interactive/2017/02/10–countries-export-major-weapons-170220170539801.html.

18. Deenbandhu Manchala, "Partnership for God's Justice Conference: Anti Human Trafficking Conversations and Theological Reflection," Global Ministries, November 16, 2018, https://www.globalministries.org/partnership_for_gods_justice.

BIBLIOGRAPHY

Agnivesh, Svami. *Applied Spirituality: For Justice Unlimited*. New Dheli: Dharma Pratishthan, 2005.

Aljzaeera Editorial. "The 10 Countries That Export the Most Major Weapons," February 22, 2017. https://www.aljazeera.com/indepth/interactive/2017/02/10–countries-export-major-weapons-170220170539801.html.

Bales, Kevin. *Disposable People: New Slavery in the Global Economy*. Berkeley, CA: University of California Press, 2012.

Echeverria, Javier Maria Iguiñiz. "The Multidimensionality of Poverty." In *The Preferential Option for the Poor beyond Theology*, edited by Daniel G. Groody, Gustavo Gutiérrez, and José O Aylwin. Notre Dame, IN: University of Notre Dame Press, 2014. http://site.ebrary.com/id/10815888.

Elliot, Larry. "World's Eight Richest People Have Same Wealth as Poorest 50%." *The Guardian*, January 15, 2017, sec. Business. https://www.theguardian.com/global-development/2017/jan/16/worlds-eight-richest-people-have-same-wealth-as-poorest-50.

Free the Slaves. "Our Model for Freedom: Slavery Today." Accessed April 29, 2019. https://www.freetheslaves.net/our-model-for-freedom/slavery-today/.

Gutiérrez, Gustavo. "Saying and Showing to the Poor: 'God Loves You.'" In *In the Company of the Poor: Conversations between Dr. Paul Farmer and Fr. Gustavo Gutierrez*, edited by Michael P. Griffin and Jennie Weiss Block, 27–34. New York: Orbis Books, 2013. http://catalog.hathitrust.org/api/volumes/oclc/828892555.html.

Human Rights First. "Human Trafficking by the Numbers," September 2017. https://www.humanrightsfirst.org/resource/human-trafficking-numbers.

Manchala, Deenabandhu. "Introduction." In *Nurturing Peace: Theological Reflections on Overcoming Violence*. Geneva: WCC Publications, 2005.

———. "Partnership for God's Justice: An Interpretive Account of the Conversations among Global Ministries' Partners Engaged in Anti Human Trafficking Work in Asia, Kupang, Indonesia, April 5–9, 2018." Global Ministries, November 16, 2018. https://www.globalministries.org/partnership_for_god_s_justice.

"Richest 1% Own 58% of Total Wealth in India: Oxfam." *The Hindu*. January 16, 2017, sec.
    Economy.   https://www.thehindu.com/business/Economy/Richest-1–own-58–of-total-
    wealth-in-India-Oxfam/article17044486.ece.
United Nations High Commissioner for Refugees. "UNHCR Global Report: 2017," 2017.
    https://www.unhcr.org/publications/fundraising/5b4c89bf17/unhcr-global-report-2017.html.
"Walk Free | The Minderoo Foundation." Accessed April 29, 2019. https://
    www.minderoo.com.au/walk-free/.

Chapter Five

Faith, Action and Subjectivity

J. Alice Heo

Who takes the initiative in the process of liberation in the Christian community? Gustavo Gutiérrez suggests that it is the poor that initiate this process,
and he refers to that process as "the irruption of the poor."[1] The poor reveal
their situation as active agents, and then theologians begin critically reflecting on this historical event in order to read the sign of the times in a theological register.[2] This commitment has brought a new theological perspective to
Christianity.

Liberation theology speaks of salvation in terms of liberation and thereby
strives to balance concerns for life after death with concerns for life on the
earth. The latter has received much less attention in the history of Christianity. Liberation theology treats human beings not only as sinners who violate
God's law (personal sin) but also as victims who are violated by structural
sin.[3] The concept of the poor in liberation theology thus applies to anyone
suffering from the various oppressions.[4]

Responding to the cry of the exploited during South Korea's socio-political and economic crisis of the mid-1970s, liberation-minded theologians formulated minjung theology by following in the footsteps of the liberation
theology that emerged in the late 1960s. Minjung theologians adopted some
unique terms from their traditional and cultural expressions, which had already existed in their vernacular language, in order to formulate their own
contextual theology. Their main terms, *minjung* and *han*, align with liberation theology's treatment of the poor and the experience of oppression caused
by structural sin.[5] The title of the most significant publication in minjung
theology, *Minjung Theology: People as the Subjects of History,* signifies that
this movement sees people as the subjects of history.

However, Korea-born ecofeminist Chung Hyun Kyung has drawn a helpful distinction between minjung theology and women's theology, referring to

the status of Korean women as the "minjung within the minjung."[6] In Latin America, the Final Document of the Third General Conference of Latin American Bishops (CELAM III) at Puebla, Mexico, January 27 through February 13, 1979, also regarded women as "doubly oppressed and marginalized" among the poor.[7] In women's theology, the woman's lived experience becomes the most important source, thereby increasing the import of analyzing specific forms of oppression related to the categories of sex and gender.[8] Chung also introduces the idea of Asian women's theology as God-praxis rather than God-talk, as defined by Elizabeth Tapia, a Filipina feminist theologian.[9] This refers to a theological approach wherein action (praxis) and reflection (theology) work together: on the one hand, "it is a commitment and participation in people's struggle for full humanity," but on the other, "it is discernment of God's redemptive action in history."[10]

How are action and reflection being worked together in the lives of women in the Christian communities? This article will briefly explore Christian women's praxis (and its theological implications) since the 1960s, paying particular attention to the movement's prominent figures.

WOMEN WORKERS SINCE THE 1960S

The South Korean economic miracle of the 1960s and 1970s can be largely credited to the hard work of young female workers in the export industries—textiles, garments, electronics, and chemicals.[11] The majority of employees in the textile industry were young women between 16 and 25 years of age.[12] They moved mostly from the countryside and lived under poor conditions in the big cities.[13] They worked long hours in the shops.[14] They had no weekly holiday, and they were only given a few public holidays off per year.[15] Some of them took medicine to keep them awake and ended up addicted.[16] Having to continuously run machines kept workers from taking meal breaks or going to the bathroom.[17] Worst of all, though, were the beatings their male supervisors and foremen would administer in the name of traditional obedience.[18] Some employers created excessive competition among workers to improve the productive outputs, and many collapsed from exhaustion.[19] Liberation-oriented Christians would not accommodate this sort of exploitation, and they thus walked into this underside of society.

In Western Europe since the late 1940s, Christians, particularly progressive Catholics, had been serving the working class as worker priests. These worker priests worked as laborers in factories and on the docks for periods of time ranging from six months to five years.[20] Despite the Roman hierarchy's orders to restrict themselves to part-time employments, more priests joined this ministry without authorization.[21] These priests stemmed from France, Belgium, Italy, the Netherlands, and other Western European countries.[22]

Worker priests started to organize teams and recruit lay activists.[23] When these worker priests started conversing with blue-collar workers, they began to understand the concerns and problems workers faced in their jobs.[24] In and through those encounters, these worker priests developed an expanded understanding of faith. Bruno Gandolfi, a worker priest, summarized his experience in this way:

> We left to evangelize, and what happened was the opposite. We have become evangelized. We have found Christ there where we thought we would need him to be introduced: within the working class.[25]

Half a world away in South Korea, a small but dedicated number of Catholic, Methodist, and Presbyterian clergy followed this example in the 1960s. They led two major Christian movements. The first is JOC (Jeunesse Ouvrière Chrétienne or Young Christian [Catholic] Workers), which is a Roman Catholic organization started in 1958.[26] The other is UIM (Urban Industrial Mission), which is a Protestant organization that formed in 1960s.[27] In the 1970s, both organizations were involved in the most influential labor conflicts, and those struggles were initiated by the resisting workers, who were educated by the worker priests.[28] JOC adapted the "see, judge, act" method in order to serve the suffering workers in the battlefield of life, and individual Christian workers were trained to carry out the mission of an apostle: seeing the hurt, identifying the cause of the pain, and working to make a change.[29]

In 1961, the United Methodist Church in the United States sent Pastor George Ogle, an expert in the urban industrial mission, as a missionary to South Korea, and the industrial mission began in the Korean Methodist Church.[30] In the mid-1970s, Reverend Cho Wha Soon, a worker priest from UIM, was closely involved with one of the most prominent labor conflicts.[31] UIM asked Reverend Cho to serve women workers in the city of Incheon.[32] She did not know the details of the ministry, but she accepted the request when she heard that there was no one else to do this ministry.[33] She told herself, "I should do things others dislike. This is the minimum duty of the Christian faith."[34] She was committed to staying with the sick, the poor, the weak, and the marginalized, and she wanted to imitate the life of Jesus in her pastoral life, always standing on the side of the poor.[35]

UIM offered its personnel one month of basic training before sending them as laborers to the factory.[36] Men served in this context for 1 year and women for 6 months.[37] Pastor Ogle explained to Reverend Cho that the program was not aimed at the evangelization of laborers; rather, it was a training wherein she could experience labor.[38] Pastor Ogle encouraged her to have a humble attitude so as to learn from the laborers.[39] Frequent insult and humiliation characterized the rookie laborer at the factory.[40] She felt ignored and abandoned at work, and her hard labor caused her physical pain, but the experience of labor helped her to understand laborers better than ever before.[41] At first, Reverend Cho worked as a laborer at the factory, and later she became a factory pastor to the young female textile laborers.[42] She would eventually insist that she was not a pastor for laborers; she was a laborer herself.[43] Experiencing the industrial working life enabled UIM pastors to redefine religion, salvation, spirituality, and especially Christology in light of those experiences.[44]

At the textile company, Reverend Cho led small groups of workers in worship, recreation, and conversation.[45] Together, they faced up to their poor working conditions and their useless union, which was run by a small number of men, even though most workers were women.[46] They planned to elect a female union leader, and Reverend Cho intentionally positioned herself in a facilitator role rather than jockeying for position and power:

> In the process (of women workers' participating actively in the labor union) I just motivated them to think for themselves about their own problems and encouraged them in their activities and I did not tell them to do it in this way or in that way. I let them find their way. I did not know any specifics on how to do it. I thought it's more important for women workers to recognize and to solve their problem by themselves. I thought that it's a genuine rebirth and transformation of a person when one can think, stand, say, decide and take the responsibility for oneself, not to follow instructions and to be tamed.[47]

The first-ever female president of a union was subsequently elected in 1972.[48] However, the female union leaders were threatened, and some of them were dismissed.[49] Reverend Cho was eventually arrested, charged with illegal affiliation with the labor movement, and imprisoned.[50] Some female union leaders were arrested on charges of inciting a riot as well.[51] Reverend Cho was put in solitary confinement, and she would eventually describe her cell as a toilet due to its filth and smell.[52] She was given unhygienic bedding and suffered from poor nutrition and lack of water, but other prisoners, including political prisoners, helped her to survive.[53] She was released after three months thanks to the efforts of church organizations who petitioned the government on her behalf.[54]

Regardless of these threats, female workers continued in their struggles. The two most notable examples of female workers' resistance were the "naked protest" and the "feces incident." When female workers went on a strike demanding the release of their arrested colleagues in July 1976, they did so half naked as the police approached.[55] They hoped to prevent the police from approaching them, but the police arrested them with mockery and violence nonetheless.[56] On February 21, 1978, male workers threw feces and urine at women workers in order to disrupt the election of new floor delegates.[57] While the male workers intended to humiliate the female workers in public, they could not break the resisting spirit of the female workers. [58] The young women were no longer powerless, and they began standing up to solve their own problems.

SEXUAL VIOLENCE AGAINST WOMEN SINCE THE 1970S

In 1973, feminist activists launched a rally in protest of Japanese sex tourism, generally known as *kisaeng* tourism at Seoul's Kimpo airport, which is the point of entry for Japanese male tourists. [59] Lee Oojung (1923–2002) was one of the leading figures in this movement. She was a professor, theologian, and activist. She played a leadership role in a variety of Christian ecumenical organizations. [60] She taught at a university before stepping down due to a campus dispute and pressure from the military dictatorship, which was outraged by her global influence regarding human rights and democracy. [61] After that, she continued her courageous engagement in spite of the frequent internment, interrogation, and consistent surveillance. [62]

Shortly after Lee Oojung became the president of Korean Church Women United (KCWU), a petition came to KCWU in response to two tragic incidents: the first was regarding a prostitute who, unable to overcome the perverted abuse of a Japanese tourist, committed suicide and left behind her 11-year-old son. The second had to do with another woman who was found dead after spending the night with a tourist. [63] KCWU replied to this irruption of the powerless into their faith-based community. Back in Japan, feminist campaigners responded by organizing the Women's Group Opposing Kisaeng Tourism in Tokyo, and they staged a protest against Japanese male tourists going on *kisaeng* tour at Tokyo's Haneda airport on Christmas Day in 1973. [64]

In the history of Korea, *kisaeng* marked the border between entertainment and prostitution but eventually turned into prostitution, particularly since the colonizing Japan transplanted its licensed prostitution system to the colonized Korea, which Japan colonized from 1910 to 1945. [65] By the late 1960s, not only the *kisaeng* system but also Japanese colonialism had disappeared on the Korean soil, but the commercially organized sex tourism of Japanese men to South Korea was shamefully named *kisaeng* tourism. [66] At that time, the government condoned the sex industry in order to earn foreign currency for its national economic development. [67] The government failed to protect the human rights of its female citizens, including young girls, and it did not apply its prostitution prevention law to those prostitutes whose customers were foreign tourists in specific hotels and American servicemen in the camp towns called *kijich'on*. [68]

Durebang (My Sister's Place) was founded in 1986 by the Presbyterian Women's Association in order to support the women in the camp towns. [69] It aims for "a place where women could come and be listened to, a safe place where they could pour their hearts out."[70] Faye Moon, the American wife of the minjung theologian and human rights advocate Reverend Moon Dong Hwan, started this ministry.[71] In the 1970s, she worked as a social worker at the drug and alcohol rehabilitation center of the US Army base in Tongdu-chun.[72] There she met with poor women who were mostly "prostitutes, or former prostitutes and a few were married to American soldiers."[73] In her eyes, they were the most excluded group in society, and "no one—not the U.S. military, not the Korean government, and not even Korean activists— had ever listened" to them.[74] She served the soldiers suffering from addictions, but her heart was set on working with those women.[75]

Faye Moon applied for a missionary project in order to raise support for these women, and her proposal was accepted by the US Presbyterian Church.[76] In South Korea, she affiliated with the Presbyterian Church of Korea (PROK), and the Presbyterian Women's Association supervised her project.[77] She began this project with a Korean partner, Ms. Yu Bok-nim.[78] Bonnie Bruner, a Catholic Maryknoll lay missioner from the United States, later joined the project.[79] In the neocolonial relationship between the United States and South Korea, marked by the presence of the American military bases in South Korea after the Korean War (1945–1950), support for the marginalized has been provided by both members of the colonizing and the colonized nation.[80]

They offered the women around the bases "counseling, English classes, and preparation for life in the U.S."[81] In the beginning, only married women visited the center, and the staff ventured into the bars, the clinic, and the clubs to meet more women.[82] They even visited another village, where most of the unmarried women and soldiers from the poorest backgrounds were stationed.[83] They eventually moved their center to this village.[84] Faye Moon said she went to the villages to help others but that she was the one who actually was blessed.[85] She testified that in villages of poverty and despair she saw Jesus "disguised as a woman, a former prostitute, the mother of a small baby boy."[86] She also mentioned that Christ's love was being manifest in "this poor village woman, a woman with little education, but infinite compassion, a woman who showed love and caring to others in a multitude of ways."[87] Bonnie Bruner echoed Faye Moon in suggesting that she learned about God's love through the women in the villages:

> There are many things I'm learning in this village. I witness these women sharing and comforting each other every day. No matter how busy they are, if someone runs into trouble or has a mishap, they share each other's sadness and support one another. Although they are poor, they readily loan money to each other, watch over each other's children and even help teach the children, becoming like extra parents for them. Does this village not come closer to exhibiting Christian values than other places?[88]

In April 1988, the year of the Summer Olympic Games in Seoul, an international conference addressing the issue of "women and tourism" was held by KCWU on Cheju Island.[89] Kisaeng tourism was understood as a form of "neo-*jungshindae*" by Korean feminist scholars, referencing the issue of *jungshindae* during the colonial period.[90] During World War II, young women among occupied and colonized populations were drafted by Japanese forces as sex slaves for the military.[91] In colonized Korea, these women were called *jungshindae* because Korean women were recruited as *Kunro-jungshindae* and told they would work in arms factories or hospitals. There were also women who were sent to work as factory workers, domestic workers, and nurses.[92] In postwar Japan, they were called *juguianfu*, comfort women for the Japanese military.[93] Thus, the terms *jungshindae* and *juguianfu* referred to them as "military sex slaves" and "comfort women." Most of these women were drafted by force or fraud between the ages of 14 and 18.[94] Of these girls, 80 percent came from Korea, 10 percent were from Japan, and others were trafficked in from China, the Netherlands, Indonesia, Burma (Myanmar), Russia, Eurasia, and the Philippines.[95] The Japanese military leaders wanted "a system of sexual release for their soldiers," and they placed the women in the military in order to control their soldiers.[96] They also needed to offer their soldiers some comfort and recreation when they refused to give them their promised vacations.[97]

This academic discussion initiated the jungshindae research unit within KCWU in July 1988, and that unit led to the foundation of the Korean Council for the Women Drafted for Military Sexual Slavery by Japan in November of 1990.[98] On August 14, 1990, Kim Hak-soon, a 67-year-old Korean woman, bore the first public testimony on Japanese wartime atrocities and testified as a comfort-woman-survivor at the office of KCWU.[99] Public apologies from former Japanese government officials and schoolteachers followed from those who were directly and indirectly related to the recruitment of *jungshindae/junguianfu*.[100]

After they were liberated from the Japanese empire in 1945, many suffered physical and mental illnesses.[101] Some could not return home because of their ill health and poor economic conditions.[102] Others committed suicide, and those who did return home typically remained poverty stricken, unmarried, or barren.[103] Whether they returned home or not, some of them became prostitutes in order to survive without any other alternatives.[104] Survivors remained silent due to the fear of shame, humiliation, and social isolation.[105] That trend continued until they began receiving support and encouragement from the feminist movement.[106]

In the beginning, these survivors were merely seen as helpless, miserable victims of sexual violence, but they broke their silence in the wake of the ideological shifts of the 1990s.[107] In the wake of those shifts, one "no longer sees victims of sexual violence as a cause of shame but instead considers the perpetrators as responsible for women's suffering."[108] Only then did these survivors start exercising their agency in the forms of public testimonies, protests, and legal battles. The subject formation of the comfort women as victim-activists has been constructed through intersubjective processes with other subjects.[109] The victim-survivors wanted to be recognized as victims in multiple systems of oppression (i.e., sexism, colonialism, militarism, and racism), but they also wanted to be known as "resilient and hardworking women, who also know how to enjoy life."[110] When the South Korean victim-survivors encountered the victims of civilian massacre and sexual violence carried out by South Korean soldiers during the Vietnam War, they realized that their own nation-state was the victim and victimizer alike.[111] The victim-survivors wanted to support those victims, and they have gradually transformed themselves into human rights activists through interaction with others.[112] In response to the victim-activists' call for support, the Korean Council for the Women Drafted for Military Sexual Slavery by Japan launched the Nabi Fund to support other women suffering from sexual violence in conflicts.[113]

WOMEN MIGRANTS SINCE THE 1990S

In Seoul, on a winter day in 1995, 13 Nepalese industrial trainees tied themselves up with chains and protested outside the Myeongdong Cathedral.[114] They chanted, "We are not slaves."[115] KCWU participated in this protest, and this incident led Korean participants from KCWU to be concerned with issues of migrant workers.[116] KCWU established the Counseling Center for Foreign Women in 1996.[117]

Women Church was founded in 1989 as an alternative church aimed at reforming the broader church's sexism.[118] Chung Sook Ja, the senior pastor of Women Church is Korean-Japanese and settled in South Korea through a marriage to a Korean husband.[119] In 1995, Reverend Chung attended the Asia International Symposium, Ecumenical Association of Third World Theologians, which was held in Indonesia and faced heavy criticism by an Indonesian economist regarding the economic exploitation of Indonesian workers by Korean companies operating on its soil.[120] When Reverend Chung came back home, she visited the Masuk furniture industrial complex, where many migrant laborers were working.[121] The reality she encountered there was much worse than she expected: migrant workers were not protected by the law, and they were fired when injured rather than sent to a doctor.[122] Women workers were exposed to sexual violence in the workplace.[123] She also became interested in the issue of female migrants.[124] In 1997, Women Church opened the Women's Center for Migrant Workers in order to offer space and programs such as night school, a nursery, Korean-language education, and computer education to female migrant workers from Namyangju, a town north-east of Seoul.[125] Reverend Chung has devoted herself to migrant women workers' movements in light of her experiences of discrimination as a Korean-Japanese in Japan and a foreign student in South Korea.[126] In 2005, the Migrant Women Church was established.[127]

Since the late 1990s, foreign women have come to the camp town as victims of human trafficking through fraudulent employment, and Durebang began to support their human rights.[128] KCWU, Durebang, and Seumteo investigated the actual conditions of foreign women working in the entertainment industry in 1999, 2001, and 2002, and they found that 89 percent of the camp town's prostitutes were foreign women.[129] They noted exploitation and abuse of foreign women in the entertainment industry.[130]

KCWU organized a symposium to commemorate the first anniversary of the foundation of the Counseling Center for Foreign Women, and Reverend Han Kuk-Yeom, who has been involved with the movements for the oppressed women and the minjung, was invited to make a presentation.[131] When she was working on her presentation, she learned of these female migrant workers facing human rights issues.[132] She asked herself, "Who is the one that is the most oppressed in this land?" Her answer was "the migrant workers."[133] Thus, she opened the Seoul Migrant Worker's Center in September 1996.[134] In 2000, the House of Women Migrant Workers, affiliated with Seoul Migrant Worker's Center, was opened as the first shelter for female migrants, and Reverend Han began to meet female marriage migrants there.[135] Their situation was quite dire, and she started to concentrate on the issues affecting them.[136] At the end of 2001, she changed the name of the shelter from the House of Women Migrant Workers to the Women Migrants Human Rights Center of Korea (wmigrant hereafter).[137]

In 2004, international marriages accounted for over 10 percent of marriages in South Korea.[138] Among the number (348,688) of the international marriages between 1990 and 2008, there were 243,937 foreign wives and 104,751 foreign husbands.[139] The foreign brides mainly come from China, Vietnam and the Philippines, Japan, Cambodia, Thailand, Mongolia, and Uzbekistan.[140] While some couples enjoy a happy marriage, other couples perpetuate oppressive elements in their international marriages. The Supreme Court in South Korea noted as the chief causes of high divorce rates in international marriages, in which a bridegroom pays all the expenses and brings a bride from a less developed country, the cultural differences and the lack of communication due to language barriers.[141] Foreign brides have suffered from classism, racism, sexism, poverty, assimilation, patriarchy, and domestic violence, as well as physical, verbal, and emotional abuses.[142]

Wmigrant has concentrated its efforts to support the human rights of female marriage migrants such as campaigns to improve legal protection, the monitoring of government multicultural policies, the operations of the hotline and the domestic violence shelter, campaigns against sexism and racism, and the transnational solidarity movements working with migration-related international organizations.[143] In the center, female marriage migrants have been empowered through a variety of competency programs.[144] Some of them became migrant activists and they started to organize self-help groups and take an active role in politics.[145] A memorial service for two murdered Chinese-Korean female marriage migrants was held in front of the Daehan-mun gate of the Deoksugung Palace in Seoul on July 18, 2012, and more than 70 groups united to organize the event.[146] Unfortunately, the murder of female marriage migrants has not yet ended.[147] Another memorial service was held on December 30, 2014, for seven female migrants including female marriage migrants who were killed.[148] The service was entitled "We Did Not Come to Be Killed," and it was organized by female marriage migrant leaders.[149]

In Cologne, Germany, Agisra (Arbeitsgemeinschaft gegen International Sexuelle und Rassistische Ausbeutung, Organization against International Sexual and Racial Exploitation) is a counseling center for female migrants and refugees that advocates for their human rights.[150] It was founded in 1975 by Jae-Soon Joo-Schauen, who first migrated to Germany from South Korea to work as a nurse and then entered the university to study education.[151] Agisra stands as a good example of the possibilities of grassroots leadership: migrant women establish and run the organization for other migrant women, and they campaign against discrimination based on their own experience.[152] As with the example of Agisra, wmigrant also aims at supporting female marriage migrants as they walk out from the margins.[153] Wmigrant's slogan is "From the margin to the subject."[154] In this process, female marriage migrants are transformed from victims of human trafficking and domestic violence to subjects of their own lives.[155]

CONCLUSION

Christian women who put faith in action have been in solidarity with marginalized women in South Korea since the 1960s. However, it is not my intention to claim that women's movements have been exclusively supported by Christian female activists in South Korea. I do not have sufficient statistical data to defend this claim, and it does not seem that they have played the most influential roles in those movements. Rather, my research shows that Christian female activists have opened the way for other activists to join the movements.

The oppressed groaned and cried out, and Christians heard it. Sometimes, the oppressed have irrupted into the space of Christianity through their agonies. The spiritual realm seems to remain a space where the voices of the oppressed can be heard. Thankfully, there are still people of faith willing to listen to the cries of suffering, to be concerned about them, and to walk into their lives through concrete action. People of faith in action have taken risks and made themselves vulnerable, interfering in other people's business. People of faith in action have moved out of their comfort zones and have given up their privileges in order to enter into the lives of the oppressed.

As people of faith in action have communicated with the oppressed, they have understood the issues of the oppressed: this is the knowledge acquired through the various experiences. When people of faith in action have supported the oppressed based on practical knowledge, they have been themselves enlightened or evangelized. At the same time, the oppressed have been transformed from being powerless into subjects who are gaining their own agency not only through outside support but also through inside empowerment by overcoming adversity. People of faith in action and the oppressed have built an equal relationship not as donor and recipient, but as co-agents through their interaction with each other.

When people of faith in action have listened attentively to the groans of the oppressed, especially the doubly oppressed and marginalized, the faces of the oppressed have been changed over time. The solidarity of people of faith in action is not limited to a certain group at a certain time. People of faith in action are trying to keep themselves informed about the oppressed in a constantly changing environment. A deeper understanding leads to new understanding. It is an ongoing struggle against one evil following on the heels of another. The seemingly unending task of solidarity has been taken on by people of faith in action from one generation to another.

Since the 1960s, the worker priest tradition in the Western church has been adapted by Asian churches in the struggles of women workers. It is often imagined that the liberation movement of Christian faith is the exclusive property of the Third World, but the struggle for liberation in the Western church predated the rise of liberation theology in Latin America. Revisiting this liberation tradition in the Western church lets us anticipate how the Western churches might move forward in the liberation struggle in their continuously changing context. This example of the faithful interaction between Western and the Third World churches also lets us dream of their further relationships of solidarity, mutual learning, and decolonization, countering the distorted relationships of conflict, hegemonic theology, and cultural imperialism.

Since the 1970s, the enthusiastic support from feminist activists as descendants of the former colonizers has led to an acceleration of decolonization, working together with the former colonized in a postcolonial era. The challenge is not only the Japanese colonialism in the past but also the US neocolonialism of the present. The struggle against neocolonialism has been fueled by the conscientious members of the (neo)colonizing nation, together with the members of the (neo)colonized nation, since the 1980s. At the same time, the formerly colonized or neocolonized should consider themselves with critical and postcolonial eyes and investigate whether they occupy the double positions of the formerly colonized or neocolonized in relationships with other developed countries, and whether they might be part of cultural, political, and economic imperialism in relationships with other developing countries in a new world order.

Liberation theologians struggled with the definition of action for the poor: charity and aid are reconsidered to avoid regarding the poor as objects of pity, and solidarity is adapted instead.[156] The term "empowerment" is also used in feminist liberation theology.[157] Minjung theologians have regarded the oppressed people as the subjects of history, and from this point of view, they have started to understand the history in new ways. Hence, the term subjectivity has become an important theme for their theologizing. Since the 1960s, Christian female activists have strived to stand in solidarity with, to empower, and to make the oppressed stand as subjects. It is, of course, a small number of women (people) who put faith in action and who develop theological reflection on these grounds, but God-praxis is still being carried out through their commitments.

NOTES

1. Gustavo Gutiérrez, "The Irruption of the Poor in Latin America and the Christian Communities of the Common People," in *The Challenge of Basic Christian Communities: Papers from the International Ecumenical Congress of Theology, February 20–March 2, 1980, Sao Paulo, Brazil,* eds. Sergio Torres and John Eagleson (Maryknoll, NY: Orbis Books, 1981), 107f.; Gustavo Gutiérrez, "Option for the Poor," in *Systematic Theology: Perspectives from Liberation Theology,* eds. Jon Sobrino and Ignacio Ellacuría (Maryknoll, NY: Orbis Books, 1996), 22f.

2. Gutiérrez, "Option for the Poor," 22f.

3. Raymond Fung, "Compassion for the Sinned Against," *Theology Today* 37, no. 2 (July 1980): 84.

4. Gutiérrez, "The Irruption of the Poor," 111f.; Gutiérrez, "Option for the Poor," 23f.

5. Suh Nam-Dong, "Towards a Theology of Han," in *Minjung Theology: People as the Subjects of History,* ed. Commission on Theological Concerns of the Christian Conference of Asia (Singapore: CTC-CCA, 1981), 65.

6. Chung Hyun Kyung, "'Han-Pu-Ri': Doing Theology from Korean Women's Perspective," *The Ecumenical Review* 40, no. 1 (1988): 31.

7. Gutiérrez, "Option for the Poor," 22.

8. Chung, "Han-Pu-Ri," 31, 35f.

9. Chung Hyun Kyung, *Struggle to Be the Sun Again: Introducing Asian Women's Theology* (Maryknoll, NY: Orbis Books, 1990), 100f.

10. Chung, *Struggle to Be,* 100f.

11. George E. Ogle, *South Korea: Dissent within the Economic Miracle* (London: Zed Books, 1990), 80.

12. Ogle, 80.

13. Ogle, 80.

14. Ogle, 82f.

15. Ogle, 83.

16. Ogle, 83.
17. Ogle, 83.
18. Ogle, 82.
19. Ogle, 83.
20. Ogle, 87.
21. Gerd-Rainer Horn, *The Spirit of Vatican II: Western European Progressive Catholicism in the Long Sixties* (Oxford: Oxford University Press, 2015), 65.
22. Horn, 61–110.
23. Horn, 68.
24. Horn, 72f.
25. Horn, 78.
26. Ogle, *South Korea*, 88.
27. Ogle, 87.
28. Ogle, 89.
29. Ogle, 88.
30. Cho Wha Soon, *The Joy of Living with Humility* (Seoul: Dosol, 2005), 129.
31. Ogle, *South Korea*, 86f.
32. Cho, *Joy of Living*, 128.
33. Cho, 128.
34. Cho, 128f.
35. Cho, 36f.
36. Cho, 131.
37. Cho, 131.
38. Cho, 132.
39. Cho, 132.
40. Cho, 131–37.
41. Cho, 131–37.
42. Ogle, *South Korea*, 86.
43. Cho, *Joy of Living*, 115.
44. Ogle, *South Korea*, 87.
45. Ogle, 84.
46. Ogle, 84f.
47. Cho, *Joy of Living*, 142.
48. Ogle, *South Korea*, 85.
49. Ogle, 85.
50. Ogle, 85.
51. Ogle, 85f.
52. Cho, *Joy of Living*, 158.
53. Cho, 159–61.
54. Cho, 163.
55. Ogle, *South Korea*, 86.
56. Ogle, 85f.
57. Ogle, 86.
58. Chung, *Struggle to Be*, 28.
59. Caroline Norma, *The Japanese Comfort Women and Sexual Slavery during the China and Pacific Wars* (London: Bloomsbury, 2017), 33.
60. Jim Stentzel, ed. *More than Witnesses: How a Small Group of Missionaries Aided Korea's Democratic Revolution* (Seoul: Korea Democracy Federation, 2006), 52.
61. Lee Munsuk, *A Critical Biography of Yi Ujŏng: I Chose Only One Thing* (Seoul: Samin, 2012), 111f.
62. Stentzel, *More than Witnesses*, 52, 282.
63. Lee, *Biography of Yi Ujŏng*, 145f.
64. Norma, *Comfort Women and Sexual Slavery*, 33.
65. Chunghee Sarah Soh, "Military Prostitution and Women's Sexual Labour in Japan and Korea," in *Gender and Labour in Korea and Japan: Sexing Classes*, eds. Ruth Barraclough and Elyssa Faison (London: Routledge, 2012), 46.

66. Soh, "Women's Sexual Labour," 45.

67. Soh, 45; Seung-Kyung Kim with Kyounghee Kim, *The Korean Women's Movement and the State: Bargaining for Change* (Oxon, UK: Routledge, 2014), 43.

68. Soh, "Women's Sexual Labour," 45.

69. Han Kuk-yeom, *We Are All Strangers: 15 Years of Women Migrants' Human Rights Movement in Korea* (Paju, South Korea: Hanul, 2017), 46f.; Elisabeth Schober, "'The Colonized Bodies of Our Women . . .': Imaginative and Material Terrains of US Military Entertainment on the Fringes of South Korea," in *Gender and Conflict: Embodiments, Discourses, and Symbolic Practices*, eds. George Frerks, Annelou Ypeij, and Reinhilde Sotiria König (Farnham, UK: Ashgate, 2014), 137.

70. Youngme Moon, *To Korea with Love* (Singapore: Stallion Press, 2014), 246.

71. Moon, vii.

72. Moon, 165.

73. Moon, 238.

74. Kim, *Korean Women's Movement*, 42f.

75. Moon, *Korea with Love*, 238.

76. Moon, 242f.

77. Moon, 242f.

78. Moon, 245f.

79. Moon, 260f.

80. Rosemary Radford Ruether, *Christianity and Social Systems: Historical Constructions and Ethical Challenges* (Lanham, MD: Rowman & Littlefield Publishers 2009), 138.

81. Moon, *Korea with Love*, 277.

82. Moon, 250–53.

83. Moon, 251.

84. Moon, 254.

85. Moon, 262.

86. Moon, 266.

87. Moon, 262, 266.

88. Moon, 261.

89. Norma, *Comfort Women and Sexual Slavery*, 33.

90. Norma, 34.

91. Martin A. Klein, *Historical Dictionary of Slavery and Abolition*, 2nd ed. (London: Rowman & Littlefield Publishers, 2014), 120.

92. Alice Yun Chai, "Korean Feminist and Human Rights Politics: The Chongshindae/Jugunianfu (Comfort Women) Movement," in *Korean American Women: From Tradition to Modern Feminism*, eds. Young I. Song and Ailee Moon (Westport, CT: Praeger Publishers, 1998), 238.

93. Chai, 238.

94. Klein, *Dictionary of Slavery and Abolition*, 120.

95. Klein, 120.

96. Chung Hyun Kyung, "Your Comfort vs. My Death," in *Women Resisting Violence: Spirituality for Life*, eds. Mary John Mananzan, Mercy Amba Oduyoye, Elsa Tamez, J. Shannon Clarkson, Mary C. Grey, and Letty M. Russell (Eugene, OR: Wipf and Stock, 2004), 133f.

97. Chung, "Your Comfort vs. My Death," 133.

98. Norma, *Comfort Women and Sexual Slavery*, 34.

99. Chai, "Chongshindae/Jugunianfu Movement," 246.

100. Chai, 246.

101. Chai, 240.

102. Chai, 240.

103. Chai, 240f.

104. Chai, 240.

105. Chai, 243.

106. Chai, 243.

107. Maki Kimura, *Unfolding the "Comfort Women" Debates: Modernity, Violence, Women's Voices* (New York: Palgrave Macmillan, 2016), 205.

108. Kimura, 205.

109. Kimura, 210.

110. Kimura, 213.

111. Kimura, 213f.

112. Kimura, 213f.

113. Kimura, 213.

114. Han, *We Are All Strangers*, 44.

115. Han, 44.

116. Han, 44.

117. Han, 44.

118. Kwok Pui-lan, *Introducing Asian Feminist Theology* (Sheffield, UK: Sheffield Academic, 2000), 111f.; Han, 47.

119. Han, 47.

120. Chung Sook Ja, "The Pastor Is Not a Position but a Role: An Interview with Chung Sook Ja, Head of Namyangju Women's Center for Migrant Workers," interview by Lee Garam, *The Women's NEWS*, March 19, 2014, http://www.womennews.co.kr/news/view.asp?num=68096.

121. Chung, Interview.

122. Chung, Interview.

123. Chung, Interview.

124. Chung, Interview.

125. Chung, Interview; Chung Sook Ja, "We Are the Daughters of God," in *Dissident Daughters: Feminist Liturgies in Global Context*, ed. Teresa Berger (Louisville, KY: Westminster John Knox Press, 2001), 88.

126. Han, *We Are All Strangers*, 47.

127. Chung, Interview.

128. Han, *We Are All Strangers*, 46f.

129. Seumteo is an organization that was divided from Durebang because "the new center was not focused on religion and, instead, brought more of a feminist and nationalist focus to its work against prostitution"; Han, 46f.; Kim, *Korean Women's Movement*, 43.

130. Han, *We Are All Strangers*, 46f.

131. Han, 13.

132. Han, 13f.

133. Han, 14.

134. Han, 14.

135. Han, 14.

136. Han, 14.

137. Han, 15.

138. Ministry of Gender Equality and Family (MOGEF), *Research on Measures to Improve Matchmaking Service for International Marriage* (Seoul: MOGEF, 2010), 1, 4.

139. Seol Dong-Hoon et al., *A Study of the Medium- to Long-Term Prospects and Measures of the Multicultural Family in Korea: On the Focus of the Population Projection of the Multicultural Family in Korea, and the Analysis of Its Socio-Economic Impacts on Korean Society* (Seoul: Ministry for Health, Welfare and Family Affairs, 2009), 8.

140. Seol et al., 11.

141. Han, *We Are All Strangers*, 77.

142. Han, 47–106, 133, 257.

143. Han, 113–226.

144. Han, 233.

145. Han, 242f.

146. Han, 175f. Daehanmun is a favored place for the public protests in the quest for democracy.

147. Han, 177.

148. Han, 177.

149. Han, 177, 230.

150. Agisra, "Flyer," accessed February 4, 2019, https://agisra.org/index.php?de_home.

151. Han, *We Are All Strangers*, 245.
152. Han, 245.
153. Han, 245.
154. Han, 236.
155. Han, 234.
156. Chris Howson, "Liberation Theology," in *The Sage Encyclopedia of Action Research*, eds. David Coghlan and Mary Brydon-Miller (London: Sage, 2014), 2:507–510.
157. Carter Heyward, "Empowerment," in *An A-Z of Feminist Theology*, eds. Lisa Isherwood and Dorothea McEwan (London: Bloomsbury Publishing, 2016), 52–53.

BIBLIOGRAPHY

Agisra. "Flyer." Accessed February 4, 2019. https://agisra.org/index.php?de_home.
Chai, Alice Yun. "Korean Feminist and Human Rights Politics: The Chongshindae/Jugunianfu (Comfort Women) Movement." In *Korean American Women: From Tradition to Modern Feminism*, edited by Young I. Song and Ailee Moon, 237–54. Westport, CT: Praeger Publishers, 1998.
Cho, Wha Soon. *The Joy of Living with Humility*. Seoul: Dosol, 2005.
Chung, Hyun Kyung. "'Han-Pu-Ri': Doing Theology from Korean Women's Perspective." *The Ecumenical Review* 40, no. 1 (1988): 27–36.
———. *Struggle to Be the Sun Again: Introducing Asian Women's Theology*. Maryknoll, NY: Orbis Books, 1990.
———. "Your Comfort vs. My Death." In *Women Resisting Violence: Spirituality for Life*, edited by Mary John Mananzan, Mercy Amba Oduyoye, Elsa Tamez, J. Shannon Clarkson, Mary C. Grey, and Letty M. Russell, 129–40. Eugene, OR: Wipf and Stock, 2004.
Chung, Sook Ja. "The Pastor Is Not a Position but a Role: An Interview with Chung Sook Ja, Head of Namyangju Women's Center for Migrant Workers." Interview by Lee Garam, *The Women's NEWS*, March 19, 2014. http://www.womennews.co.kr/news/view.asp?num=68096.
———. "We Are the Daughters of God." In *Dissident Daughters: Feminist Liturgies in Global Context*, edited by Teresa Berger, 87–104. Louisville, KY: Westminster John Knox Press, 2001.
Fung, Raymond. "Compassion for the Sinned Against." *Theology Today* 37, no. 2 (July 1980): 162–69.
Gutiérrez, Gustavo. "The Irruption of the Poor in Latin America and the Christian Communities of the Common People." In *The Challenge of Basic Christian Communities: Papers from the International Ecumenical Congress of Theology, February 20–March 2, 1980, Sao Paulo, Brazil*, edited by Sergio Torres and John Eagleson, 107–23. Maryknoll, NY: Orbis Books, 1981.
———. "Option for the Poor." In *Systematic Theology: Perspectives from Liberation Theology*, edited by Jon Sobrino and Ignacio Ellacuría, 22–37. Maryknoll, NY: Orbis Books, 1996.
Han, Kuk-yeom. *We Are All Strangers: 15 Years of Women Migrants' Human Rights Movement in Korea*. Paju, South Korea: Hanul, 2017.
Heyward, Carter. "Empowerment." In *An A-Z of Feminist Theology*. edited by Lisa Isherwood and Dorothea McEwan, 52–53. London: Bloomsbury Publishing, 2016.
Horn, Gerd-Rainer. *The Spirit of Vatican II: Western European Progressive Catholicism in the Long Sixties*. Oxford: Oxford University Press, 2015.
Howson, Chris. "Liberation Theology." In *The Sage Encyclopedia of Action Research*, edited by David Coghlan and Mary Brydon-Miller, 2:507–10. London: Sage, 2014.
Kim, Seung-Kyung, with Kyounghee Kim. *The Korean Women's Movement and the State: Bargaining for Change*. Oxon, UK: Routledge, 2014.
Kimura, Maki. *Unfolding the "Comfort Women" Debates: Modernity, Violence, Women's Voices*. London: Palgrave Macmillan, 2016.
Klein, Martin A. *Historical Dictionary of Slavery and Abolition*. 2nd ed. London: Rowman & Littlefield Publishers, 2014.

Kwok, Pui-lan. *Introducing Asian Feminist Theology*. Sheffield, UK: Sheffield Academic Press, 2000.

Lee, Munsuk. *A Critical Biography of Yi Ujŏng: I Chose Only One Thing*. Seoul: Samin, 2012.

Ministry of Gender Equality and Family (MOGEF). *Research on Measures to Improve Matchmaking Service for International Marriage*. Seoul: MOGEF, 2010.

Moon, Youngme. *To Korea with Love*. Singapore: Stallion Press, 2014.

Norma, Caroline. *The Japanese Comfort Women and Sexual Slavery during the China and Pacific Wars*. London: Bloomsbury, 2017.

Ogle, George E. *South Korea: Dissent within the Economic Miracle*. London: Zed Books, 1990.

Ruether, Rosemary Radford. *Christianity and Social Systems: Historical Constructions and Ethical Challenges*. Lanham, MD: Rowman & Littlefield Publishers, 2009.

Schober, Elisabeth. "'The Colonized Bodies of Our Women . . .': Imaginative and Material Terrains of US Military Entertainment on the Fringes of South Korea." In *Gender and Conflict: Embodiments, Discourses, and Symbolic Practices*, edited by George Frerks, Annelou Ypeij, and Reinhilde Sotiria König, 133–50. Farnham, UK: Ashgate, 2014.

Seol, Dong-Hoon, Moon-Hee Suh, Sam-Sic Lee, and Myoung-Ah Kim. *A Study of the Medium- to Long-Term Prospects and Measures of Multicultural Family in Korea: On the Focus of the Population Projection of Multicultural Family in Korea, and the Analysis of Its Socio-economic Impacts on Korean Society*. Seoul: Ministry for Health, Welfare and Family Affairs, 2009.

Soh, Chunghee Sarah. "Military Prostitution and Women's Sexual Labour in Japan and Korea." In *Gender and Labour in Korea and Japan: Sexing Class*, edited by Ruth Barraclough and Elyssa Faison, 44–59. London: Routledge, 2009.

Stentzel, Jim, ed. *More than Witnesses: How a Small Group of Missionaries Aided Korea's Democratic Revolution*. Seoul: Korea Democracy Federation, 2006.

Suh, Nam-Dong. "Towards a Theology of Han." In *Minjung Theology: People as the Subjects of History*, edited by Commission on Theological Concerns of the Christian Conference of Asia. Singapore: CTC-CCA, 1981.

Part II

On the Move between Identities, Cultures, and Religions

Chapter Six

Holocaust Theology, the Interfaith Ecumenical Deal, and the Unintended Consequences of Jewish-Christian Pilgrimage

Notes from a Jewish Theology of Liberation

Marc H. Ellis

After the 1967 Israeli-Arab war, the Holocaust and Israel became the center of Jewish life in America, Israel, and other parts of the Jewish world. In general, Jewish Holocaust theology, which emerged in the late 1960s and lasted through the 1980s, is a liturgical rendering of the destruction of European Jewry that displaced Judaism as the Jewish community's primary form of religious expression. In Christianity, at least in the United States and Europe, a variation of Holocaust theology emerged in the 1970s, displacing negative stereotypes of Jews and featuring Jewish empowerment in Israel as a primary vehicle for Christianity's repentance. Additionally, Christian Holocaust theology became an essential vehicle for the renewal of Christianity's credibility in the post-Holocaust world. By embracing Holocaust theology, Christians accepted the Jewish liturgy of destruction, for the most part uncritically; it soon became essential to Christian theology and ultimately became the foundation of Jewish-Christian dialogue. A new Jewish-Christian pilgrimage began to Holocaust memorials and museums in America and Europe (including the United States Holocaust Memorial Museum in Washington, DC), to concentration camps in Germany and Poland (including the Auschwitz death camp), and to the state of Israel itself.[1]

Though Jewish and Christian Holocaust theologies, with their profound political implications of support for the state of Israel, privileged Jewish suffering and empowerment in Israel as the essence of these pilgrimages, over the years an unintended consequence occurred. As Israel's settlement of Palestinian land and repression of Palestinians took on a permanent quality, these pilgrimages raised questions about the centrality of the Holocaust and Israel to Jews and Christians. The pilgrimage sites themselves became contested, and what emerged among Jews and Christians of conscience, beginning in the late 1980s and beyond, is a critique of the Holocaust and Israel as they function to hold back a Jewish-Christian solidarity for Palestinian freedom. Having surveyed this landscape of the memory of the Holocaust and Israel's oppression of Palestinians, recently highlighted by the celebration of the movement of the American embassy to Jerusalem, the passing of Israel's Nation-State Law, and Israel's firing upon the Great March of Return in Gaza, all in 2018, the prophetic movement within Jewish life has returned in a dramatic and unexpected way. As well, more Christians, often enshrined in religious denominational structures, have adopted various aspects of the boycott, divestment, and sanctions (BDS) movement. The BDS movement in relation to Israel bears some resemblance to the insurgent South African BDS movement that helped bring down the apartheid regime years ago.[2]

THE HOLOCAUST AND PILGRIMAGE:
A DIVIDED AND TROUBLED LEGACY

When Elie Wiesel, the most famous Holocaust survivor, died in 2016, he left a divided and troubled legacy. As a Holocaust survivor, Wiesel testified to the horrors of the Nazi death camps. As a survivor who kept the memory of the Holocaust alive, though, he was mostly silent about what Israel had done and is doing to the Palestinian people. Christians, especially in the West, also share that divided and troubled legacy. Having been purveyors of anti-Semitism in the past, they are recent converts to solidarity with Jews and are often silent in the face of Israel's onslaught against Palestinians. In fact, Elie Wiesel was a primary architect of what I have called the "interfaith ecumenical deal," a deal Christians accepted almost wholesale as their ticket back to credibility after the Holocaust. Wiesel and his Christian admirers together helped portray Jews as innocent in their suffering *and* in their empowerment. Palestinians were thus cast in a derogatory light. If Israel was part of Jewish and Christian redemption after the Holocaust, those who opposed Israel, for whatever reason, could only be seen as anti-Semites and terrorists. In Jewish and Christian Holocaust theologies, Palestinians are portrayed as the real and symbolic embodiment of post-Holocaust evil.[3]

Wiesel's legacy, indeed the legacy of Holocaust theologians in general, lives on in Israel's continual violence against Palestinians and in Holocaust memorials around the world. Institutions such as the United States Holocaust

Memorial Museum, located in Washington, DC, and the Auschwitz-Birke-nau Memorial and Museum, located in the Auschwitz death camp in Oswie-cim, Poland, dot the American and European landscapes. These sites attract millions of visitors yearly. Ostensibly a teaching tool for the lessons of the Holocaust, the very fact that these sites commemorate the horrors of mass death of Europe's Jews also imbues those visiting with a deep sense of reckoning, eliciting a confessional and mourning spirituality.

Yet to define Holocaust memorial museums as tourist sites imparting lessons for the future is to miss their deeper dimension as sites of pilgrimage. Considering Holocaust memorials as sites of pilgrimage may, at first glance, seem counter-intuitive. Yet if we define pilgrimage as commonly understood in a summation of current scholarship, a second look becomes more evoca-tive. Pilgrimage is a journey of moral or spiritual significance to a location important to a person's beliefs and faith. The connection may be visual or verbal; sites of pilgrimage are found in spaces where miracles were per-formed or witnessed, where a deity is said to live or be housed, or on sites believed to have special spiritual powers. These pilgrimage sites are often commemorated with shrines or temples that devotees are encouraged to visit for their own spiritual benefit. Those who take such journeys are called pilgrims.

Pilgrimage in relation to Holocaust sites is fulfilled only by upending elements of what this definition of pilgrimage proposes. In Holocaust theolo-gy there is no God that can be called on—Where was God in the Holo-caust?—and Judaism and Christianity already have their historic, sacred places. If there are any spiritual powers in Holocaust memorials, they are negative. Instead of life or the renewal of life being the goal of the pilgrim, at Holocaust memorials, death is omnipresent. The questions mass death raises are rarely answered by appeals to religious tradition. Instead, the Holocaust interrogates Judaism and Christianity. If there is an omnipotent and just God, how could six million Jews have been slaughtered without God interfering to stop the killing? And, indeed, since the Holocaust was perpetrated in a thoroughly evangelized and Christian Europe, how did a believing Christian Europe send millions of Jews to their deaths? This interrogation, then, again counter-intuitively, is the essential foundation of the pilgrimage that millions of Jews and Christians make each year to Holocaust memorials.[4]

On the Jewish side, Holocaust theology posits Jewish innocence in the suffering of the Holocaust *and* innocence in Jewish empowerment after the Holocaust in Israel. The logic of Holocaust theology goes something like this: Jews without power in Europe were murdered by the millions without being protected in the nations where Jews lived; after the Holocaust, Jews thus need to be empowered, if only to protect themselves. Israel is said to be that empowerment—a state Jews can call their own, one that protects Jews and provides the context for a renewed life for Jews after the decimation of the Holocaust.

On the Christian side, there is a corresponding logic. In many direct and indirect ways, the long-standing anti-Semitism of Christian theology and culture led to the Holocaust. After the Holocaust, Christians must understand the need for a confession of Christianity's anti-Semitism and a full theological and material repentance toward Jews; this confession admits the guilt of anti-Semitism that enabled the Holocaust and demands a wholesale riddance of the Christian tradition's theological and ritual anti-Semitic elements. If repentance is to be real, it must help enable Jews to survive and thrive after the Holocaust. The state of Israel is Christianity's material expression of repentance for anti-Semitism and the Holocaust.

Nevertheless, Christianity has a more checkered history of discrimination and violence than its embrace of anti-Semitism. The history of Christianity is so riddled with violence and atrocity so that Christians' confessions cannot end with the Holocaust. Observed historically, anti-Semitism, stretching back to the founding of Christianity, is only the beginning of Christianity's need for confession. Christian liberation theologies around the world burst on the scene as Christianity's confession to Jews hit its high mark. These theologies are often carried by the victims of Christianity, who had themselves been conquered by the imperialism and colonialism dominant European Christianity was only too willing to accompany and enable. In the end, anti-Semitism, intimate to Christianity, traveled outward toward others Christianity labeled as heathens and pagans.[5]

THE BIRTH OF JEWISH AND CHRISTIAN HOLOCAUST THEOLOGY

Jewish Holocaust theology began in the 1950s and 1960s with the publications of Elie Wiesel's autobiographical *Night* and Richard Rubenstein's *After Auschwitz*. Soon after, Emil Fackenheim and Irving Greenberg joined the group, with Fackenheim's *God's Presence in History* and Greenberg's seminal essay, "Cloud of Smoke, Pillar of Fire: Judaism, Christianity and Modernity after the Holocaust." These Holocaust theologians helped chart a path for the future of Jewish life after the Holocaust. Though with diverse approaches, all four affirmed the centrality of the Holocaust and Israel in Jewish life, posing the commitment to both as sacred obligations.[6]

Though Jewish Holocaust theology began in the 1950s and 1960s, it became popularly known and adhered to after the 1967 Arab-Israeli war. The anxiety about Israel in the days before the war and its lightning, six-day victory in the war crystallized the importance of Holocaust theology to Jews around the world. It was in the aftermath of Israel's victory that Fackenheim posited the 614th Commandment, an addition to the traditional 613 commandments in Jewish life: "Thou shalt not hand Hitler posthumous victories." Fackenheim's explanation followed: "We are, first, commanded to survive as Jews, lest the Jewish people perish. We are commanded, secondly, to remember in our very guts and bones the martyrs of the Holocaust, lest their memory perish. We are forbidden, thirdly, to deny or despair of God, however much we may have to contend with him or with belief in him, lest Judaism perish." Continuing, "We are forbidden, finally, to despair of the world as the place which is to become the kingdom of God, lest we help make it a meaningless place in which God is dead or irrelevant and everything is permitted." For Fackenheim, to abandon any of these "imperatives, in response to Hitler's victory at Auschwitz, would be to hand him yet other, posthumous victories."[7]

Fackenheim believed that in Israel's 1967 victory the 614th Commandment was promulgated—and obeyed—by the Jewish people, when Israeli soldiers fought bravely and Jews around the world rallied to Israel's defense. Since after the Holocaust, the question of God was unsettled for Jews, Fackenheim asserts that Jews responded to the commanding voice of Auschwitz rather than the commanding voice of Sinai. Wiesel, Rubenstein, and Greenberg took similar positions. After the Holocaust, with the covenant broken, or at least uncertain, Jews around the world had to take responsibility for their own empowerment. In Holocaust theology, commitment to remembrance of the Holocaust and empowerment in Israel became the primary focus of Jews, almost as a sort of sacred obligation. Though almost anything in Jewish history and Judaism itself can be discussed, argued about, or even dismissed, including God, this excluded critical understandings of the state of Israel. Greenberg speaks to this issue directly when he writes that to consciously or unconsciously forget the lessons of the Holocaust, thereby undermining Israel's empowerment, is the excommunicable sin of what he names the Third Era of Jewish history.[8]

Holocaust theology is quite deep on the question of God. In a bold theological assertion, Rubenstein dismissed God as either all powerful, due to God's refusal to come to the aid of Jews in Auschwitz, or lacking the power to stop Auschwitz. Whether it was God's refusal to aid Jews or God's lack of power, God had not lived up to the obligations of God's covenantal partnership with the people Israel. In defiance or need, Rubenstein believed Jews were therefore on their own. Greenberg, in a variation on Rubenstein, proposed a relationship with God that continued but was no longer whole. Instead of seeing the covenant with God as irretrievably broken, Greenberg posits "moment faiths—times when God is present to us and times when we feel God's absence." For Greenberg, after the Holocaust, then, the "easy dichotomy" of theist and atheist moves to the past. Rather, the predominance of presence or absence of God in one's life determines whether or not we are religious or secular. In general, when reading Holocaust theology, one senses that the discussion of Israel's God of History is present only insofar as we affirm that God's presence is past. God remains only as the God That Was.[9]

Christian anti-Semitism is taken to task in Holocaust theology. Though the Nazis are rarely seen as a Christian phenomenon per se, the Holocaust is impossible without the anti-Semitism of Christian history. The death camps were not Christian, but they were impossible without Christianity. As Holocaust theology seeks Jewish affirmation and empowerment after the Holocaust, a positive sensibility for a devastated and beleaguered people, it also calls Christian history to account. In the same vein, Holocaust theologians challenge contemporary Christianity. The past is one thing, the present another. Holocaust theologians believe that the only way for Christianity to exist with credibility in the present is to join in a new solidarity with Jewish history and Jews today. First and foremost, this has to do with Christian support for Israel. To mobilize that support and keep it steady, a revolution in Christian life and theology must occur. Included here is the Christian affirmation of the continuing validity of the Jewish covenant and the Pauline view, at least as it is interpreted today in some Christian circles, of Christians being grafted on to the first and primary covenant of God with the people Israel. This means the end of Christian supersessionism and the Christian demand for the conversion of Jews to belief in Jesus as the Christ. The idea that Jews were the crucifiers of Jesus has to be consigned to the dustbin of a misguided history.

There is much more to say about the first phase of Holocaust theology, roughly spanning from 1966–1974, since this was the time that the Holocaust and Israel became central to Jewish life. In the wake of the 1967 war, Holocaust theology resonated so deeply in Christian life that a parallel theology was beginning to be thought through in the Christian community in America and Europe. By the 1980s, Paul Van Buren, an Episcopal priest, began publishing what would become a three-volume work, *A Theology of the Jewish-Christian Reality*. There were other Christian theologians on this path as well. Stephen Haynes, in his book, *Jews and the Christian Imagination: Reluctant Witnesses*, explores the phenomenon of Christian Holocaust theology, which he believes to be an instance of the witness-people myth's potency in contemporary theological reflection. In designating the concerns and tendencies of this theological movement, Haynes refers to Christian thinkers he regards as Holocaust theologians. Along with Van Buren, Haynes includes John Pawlikowski, Franklin Littell, Alice L. and A. Roy Eckardt, Gregory Baum, Monika Hellwig, Robert Everett, and James Moore. Haynes understands that he is inferring the presence of an intellectual movement from the work of a few authors. He does so because he finds continuities in their writings. Though their visions for the future of Christian theology occasionally diverge, Haynes finds that these theologians agree that the essential failure of historic Christianity is located in its conception and mistreatment of Judaism and Jews. The course correction is obvious for these Christian Holocaust theologians: accept the primacy of the Jewish covenant and embrace the state of Israel.[10]

Thus Jewish and Christian Holocaust theology, in sync and responding to one another, positioned Jews in the privileged position, with Christians regaining their credibility in light of commitment to Jews, Jewish history, the Jewish God of Israel. With an essential solidarity with Jews as the Christian way forward, support for the state of Israel is the place where Christianity stands or falls. The threat of a second Holocaust, which would eliminate Judaism and a credible Christianity altogether, lurks among the shadows of Jewish and Christian Holocaust theologians. That threat emanates from those who seek the destruction of Israel.

THE BIRTH OF JEWISH AND PALESTINIAN LIBERATION THEOLOGY

The convergence of Jewish and Christian Holocaust theology moved far beyond those interested in theology and beyond Jews and Christians interested in religion itself. From the outset, Jewish and Christian Holocaust theology, with its important questions about God and the relationship between Jews and Christians, had political horizons. Jews and Christians involved in the Jewish-Christian dialogue bonded in their political support for Israel and against any entity, country, or movement that was critical of Israeli policies toward Palestinians. Among others, the United Nations was targeted as an anti-Israel entity, but movements for social change—Christian liberation theology emanating from Latin America, for example—were also targeted. In general, Palestinians and their supporters were seen as anti-Semites. "Anti-Semitism" became the watchword for the unwashed, the uncivilized, and the terrorists to be opposed by Jews and Christians.

The catchall phrase for the movement against Israel was the "new anti-Semitism." The naming of the new anti-Semitism in the 1970s took the Jewish-Christian dialogue to a new level. No longer were Jews in the interfaith dialogue primarily concerned with personal, professional, and religious discrimination against Jews; rather, they concerned themselves with the social and political movements that supported the Palestinian struggle for an end to Israel's occupation of East Jerusalem, the West Bank, and Gaza, and the birth of a Palestinian state alongside Israel. Just the mention of Palestinians and their grievances raised hackles in the interfaith ecumenical dialogue. This reached a breaking point with the onset of the first Palestinian Uprising in December 1987, when Palestinians struggling for their rights, the end of Israeli occupation, and a state of their own, were met by the Israeli military with brute force. Interestingly, the Palestinian Uprising arrived at the height of the power of Jewish Holocaust theology and when Christian Holocaust theology was gaining momentum. Looking back, it was at this moment that Jewish and Christian Holocaust theology began their decline. Soon the interfaith ecumenical dialogue built around Jewish and Christian reverence for the Holocaust and uncritical support for the state of Israel began its decline as well.[11]

Before the decline, Jewish and Christian devotion to remembering the Holocaust and supporting Israel as a vehicle for Jewish empowerment and Christian repentance solidified. Plans for the United States Holocaust Memorial Museum began to take shape under President Carter and were chartered by a unanimous act of the US Congress in 1980. A little more than a decade later, the Soviet Union collapsed, freeing Poland and the museum at Auschwitz to open its gates wide and reorient its focus from nationalities imprisoned and murdered under Nazi fascism to concentrate more on the mass murder of Jews there, with numbers placed at a million dead or more. In 1993, the Holocaust Museum in Washington, DC, opened. Millions of Jews and Christians, along with others, made their way to both sites.

But is mass death devotional? This strange inversion has importance for the future of religious life. Auschwitz was both a culmination of an entire history of the Jewish-Christian journey and the possibility of a new beginning. For Jews, obviously, a new beginning was essential. How else could Jews survive without some kind of empowerment? Reliance on God entered a no-go area. Holocaust theology was clear on this. Yet Holocaust theology also insisted that Jews could not rely on humanity for protection either. Where was humanity as Jews were murdered at Auschwitz? The destination of overt anti-Semitism was obvious in the mass death of European Jewry. Beneath and around the overt sensibility lay a profound ambivalence about Jews, which is carried around the world in Christian and Islamic scriptures and culture. This ambivalence entered modern culture and politics, too. Was it by chance that the European Enlightenment carried many of the views of Jews that Christianity and Islam held?

The ending for Jews in the Holocaust was an ending for Christianity as well. The death camps horrified many Christians. If Christianity was not the sole cause of the Nazi hatred of Jews, Christianity certainly enabled it. When it came to Jews, there was not much distinction between the great reformer of Catholicism Martin Luther and the Nazi dictator Adolf Hitler. Reading Luther's long diatribe, *The Jews and Their Lies*, is instructive. One doubts there has ever been a more concentrated, vindictive anti-Semitic argument than the one found in Luther's writings. By comparison, Hitler was inarticulate. What Hitler had, Luther lacked—state power in modern form and thus the means to build and carry out mass industrialized murder of the Jewish population of Europe.[12]

Greenberg posed the challenge of the end of this long history of Jewish-Christian history when he prophetically wrote, in 1974, that after the Holocaust, "no statement, theological or otherwise, should be made that would not be credible in the presence of the burning children."[13] This challenge is difficult, if not impossible to meet head-on. For example, if you want to speak about God, do so, but only if it makes sense to a burning child. Can one then speak about God at all? What statement about God could possibly make sense to a burning child? Greenberg is obviously referencing the burning Jewish children of the Holocaust. Yet, in his later seminal essay, Greenberg specifically opens his horizons to other burning children. In fact, Greenberg cautions against celebrating Passover or Easter after the Holocaust as if the Holocaust had not occurred. The "moment faiths" Greenberg suggests are possible after the Holocaust are characterized by moments of uplift where visions of redemption occur, moments when burning children call redemption to account. Who, then, can honestly celebrate Passover's liberation or Easter's salvation when children of any background, geographical location, culture, or religion are burning?[14]

The Palestinian Uprising of late 1987 into the early 1990s posed such questions to Holocaust theology of the Jewish and Christian variety. Theologically, it was posed directly in two books, my *Toward a Jewish Theology of Liberation* and Naim Ateeks's, *Justice and Only Justice: A Palestinian Theology of Liberation*. Both books were in formation during the pre-Uprising years of the mid-1980s. Both books anticipated and achieved their significance within the Palestinian Uprising. *Toward a Jewish Theology of Liberation* was initially published in 1987, with a second edition in 1989. Ateek's Palestinian theology of liberation was published in 1989. From the point of publication, both authors took to the road, often appearing together to discuss the possibility of a joint future for Jews and Palestinians in Israel-Palestine and a new vision of a joint future for Jews and Christians. Soon we were joined by the well-known feminist and chronicler of the history of Christian anti-Semitism, Rosemary Radford Ruether. She, along with Herman Ruether, published *The Wrath of Jonah: The Crisis of Religious Nationalism in the Israeli-Palestinian Conflict* in 1989. Ateek (a Palestinian Anglican priest who had been made a refugee during the formation of Israel), Ruether (a Roman Catholic feminist), and I (a Jewish American dissident) worked together to challenge the innocence and redemptive aspects of Israel and the interfaith ecumenical dialogue, which censored criticism of what Israel had done and was doing to Palestinians.[15]

PILGRIMAGE TO ISRAEL — AND PALESTINE

With the birth of Jewish and Christian Holocaust theologies, the Holocaust and Israel took on expanded meanings, from historical events ripe for exploration and critical analysis, to events that hinted at, if not assumed, a sacred status. Thinking critically about the Holocaust, especially the way the Holocaust functions to enable power and injustice in the present (in the origins of Israel and its ongoing status vis-à-vis the Palestinian people), became a violation of a sacred taboo. It became blasphemous. For Jews, breaking with Holocaust theology was categorized as Jewish self-hate. For Christians, breaking with Christian Holocaust theology was seen as a return to anti-Semitism. Critical thinkers on both the Jewish and Christian side were thus defined by the mainstream Jewish and Christian progressive establishments, as in a historical continuum of past sins, newly resurrected. Palestinians played their part in this Jewish-Christian sacred drama as well, rendered as terrorists undermining civilization on the political and cultural side and, as the devil incarnate, negative to be sure, though on the Christian evangelical side, somewhat positive in helping to bring on Armageddon and the return of Jesus Christ.[16]

During the first Palestinian Uprising, with the assistance of Jewish and Palestinian theologies of liberation, a counter-pilgrimage narrative began to emerge. Jews and Christians became more aware of the underbelly of the Holocaust/Israel axis. Jews suffered tremendously in the Holocaust; the systematic slaughter of six million Jews remains almost incomprehensible. Yet during this time the focus shifted from the historical dimensions of the mass slaughter of Europe's Jews to how the memory of the Holocaust was being used. In the beginning of Jewish Holocaust theology there were two "never agains." The first, quite rightly, was never again should this happen to the Jewish people. The second, also quite rightly, was that never again should mass death, or anything approximating it, happen to any people. Soon, however, the second admonition was eclipsed by the first, until it dropped from sight. The telling point is that the second still applied to others, for example, the genocide in Rwanda, but rarely, if ever, to Palestinians. Jewish and Christian Holocaust theology covered in silence the state of Israel's birthright and its ongoing expansion. When some Jews and Christians began to speak about Israel's origins in the ethnic cleansing of Palestinians or its ongoing policies regarding Palestinians, the theological and political doors were shut tight. Yet, unexpectedly to Jewish and Christian Holocaust theologians, the draconian measures Israel used to suppress the Palestinian Uprising opened both doors. How the Holocaust functioned and the pretense to Israel's innocence were opened to inspection and critical analysis. In retrospect, the Palestinian Uprising portended the end of Jewish and Christian Holocaust theology.

During the Palestinian Uprising, some Jews and Christians upset with Israel's repression of Palestinians began visiting Israel and Palestine with a new mission of ascertaining what was going on inside the carefully scripted sacred drama presented to them by Jewish and Christian Holocaust theology. Soon travel to Israel was destined less for the sacred sites of Jewish empowerment, which now included Christian holy sites in Jerusalem "safely" under Jewish repression. Rather, tours started to include travel into Palestinian areas under strict Israeli occupation and repression. Through personal encounters with Palestinians under occupation, pilgrims were extracted from a sacred drama of innocence and redemption into a real-life drama of survival under Israeli occupation. During this time, many Jews and Christians encountered the new Israeli historians who were documenting a counter-history that Palestinians knew well: the birth of Israel as fraught with violence and the ethnic cleansing of the Palestinian population. Later, the issue of Israel as an ongoing vestige of Western colonialism came to the fore. The fundamental question had been raised. Had the Holocaust of Jews in Europe given way to Israel's destruction of and continuing occupation of Palestine?[17]

As more and more Jews and Christians visited major areas of Palestinian population, East Jerusalem, the West Bank, and Gaza, in particular, a growing minority of both groups questioned the sacredness, indeed the political injustice, of the Israeli aggression against Palestinians. The issue of what it means to be Jewish within the Israeli oppression could hardly be avoided either. After all, Israel was built for and governed by Jews. The Israeli military was almost exclusively made up of Jews. And the Jewish establishments around the world, beginning with the American Jewish establishment, were die-hard supporters of Israel. They were thus enablers of Israel's political and military policies. The American Jewish establishment was also an enforcer of the interfaith ecumenical deal, which silenced Jewish and Christian dissidents, labeling them as self-haters and anti-Semites.

Over the last decades, a battle has been waged in increasingly angry tones between those who hold fast to Jewish and Christian Holocaust theology, at least the vestiges left of it, and those who seek to transform Holocaust theology and its religious and political power over against Palestinians, first and foremost, and against Jews and Christians who seek another way for Jews and Palestinians to live together in justice and peace. At least in terms of the religious and political narrative of Jewish and Christian Holocaust theology, the dissenters have won. There is little talk in public today about the Holocaust-Israel axis as innocent. Politically, though, dissenters have lost conclusively. As the Holocaust-Israel narrative wanes in its efficacy, Israel's control and power over the Palestinians increases. Concurrent with the narrative's loss, major Arab countries, who were once vocal supporters of Palestinians, have welcomed Israel into their security network. In a strange twist of fate for Palestinians, Israel is now the guarantor of the security of the worst of the Arab regimes, Egypt and Saudi Arabia included.

These days the battle over sacred-political space is fought over the BDS movement and this too, while real, is largely symbolic. The global Left has made Palestine its central issue, which, in terms of size and weight, Palestine cannot carry. Has the global Left made Palestine into their sacred space, meaning that their rhetoric about and travel to Palestine has become an act of pilgrimage in their own right? All of this figures into the ever-evolving religious and political landscape of the (un)Holy Land. This also raises anew the question broached many years ago: Could there be a reconciliation of the suffering of both Jews and Palestinians in Jerusalem if Jerusalem is understood as the broken middle of Israel-Palestine?[18]

The resolution here could be found in small, consequential, steps toward a shared life in Jerusalem, one that features justice and equality as the way forward. In that movement, historical and theological issues would be, for the time being, bracketed. Or perhaps, those issues would assume an evolving configuration as the memory of trauma, displacement, and death remains and recedes, being replaced by new memories of goodness and a shared life, until the assault on Jews or Palestinians becomes an assault on the Other. In this scenario, the broken middle of Jerusalem would no doubt continue as site of pilgrimage, this time to mourn injustice and death while celebrating justice and life everywhere.

NOTES

1. Much of the following discussion of Jewish and Christian Holocaust theologies can be found in my early work, Marc H. Ellis, *Toward a Jewish Theology of Liberation*, 3rd ed. (Waco, TX: Baylor University Press, 2004); Marc H. Ellis, *Beyond Innocence and Redemption: Confronting the Holocaust and Israeli Power: Creating a Moral Future for the Jewish People*, reprint ed. (Wipf and Stock, 2016).

2. For more on the BDS movement see Omar Barghouti, *Boycott, Divestment, Sanctions: The Global Struggle for Palestinian Rights* (Chicago: Haymarket Books, 2011), https://ebook-central.proquest.com/lib/warw/detail.action?docID=665761.

3. A broad analysis of Elie Wiesel can be found in Mark Chmiel, *Elie Wiesel and the Politics of Moral Leadership* (Philadelphia: Temple University Press, 2001). For my recent writing on Wiesel's legacy see Marc H. Ellis, "From Holocaust Theology to a Jewish Theology of Liberation: On the Theo-Politics of Jewish Empowerment," in *T & T Clark Companion to Political Theology* (New York: T & T Clark, 2019): 3–16.

4. For my reflections on my "pilgrimage" to Auschwitz see Marc H. Ellis, *Ending Auschwitz: The Future of Jewish and Christian Life* (Louisville, KY: Westminster John Knox Press, 1994).

5. A fascinating historical take on this process can be found in the work of Latin American Christian Liberation theologian Gustavo Gutiérrez, *Las Casas: In Search of the Poor of Jesus Christ*, trans. Robert R. Barr (Maryknoll, NY: Orbis, 1993).

6. For a discussion of these writings see my third expanded edition of Ellis, *Toward a Jewish Theology of Liberation*.

7. Emil L. Fackenheim, *God's Presence in History: Jewish Affirmations and Philosophical Reflections* (New York: New York University Press, 1970), 84.

8. Irving Greenberg, "On the Third Era of Jewish History: Power and Politics," *Perspectives*, 1987.

9. I explore this theme in relation to the Holocaust and the explosion of the Jewish prophetic in Marc H. Ellis, *Finding Our Voice: Embodying the Prophetic and Other Misadventures* (La Vergne: Wipf and Stock, 2018).

10. Stephen R. Haynes, *Reluctant Witnesses: Jews and the Christian Imagination* (Louisville, KY: Westminster John Knox Press, 1995).

11. The new anti-Semitism remains a feature of those Jews and Christians who label Palestinians as a terrorist threat. For an early example of this see Nathan Perlmutter and Ruth Perlmutter, *The Real Anti-Semitism in America* (New York: Arbor House, 1984).

12. Richard Rubenstein's take on the issue of Luther and anti-Semitism is instructive in relation to Holocaust theology. See Richard L. Rubenstein, *The Cunning of History: The Holocaust and the American Future* (New York: Harper and Row, 1975).

13. Irving Greenberg, "Cloud of Smoke, Pillar of Fire: Judaism, Christianity and Modernity after the Holocaust," in *Auschwitz: Beginning of a New Era?: Reflections on the Holocaust*, ed. Eva Fleischner (New York: Ktav, 1977), 23.

14. I use Greenberg's image of burning children in relation to the Israeli decimation of Gaza in 2014 in Marc H. Ellis, *Burning Children: A Jewish View of the War in Gaza* (Eugene, OR: Wipf and Stock, 2017).

15. Naim Stifan Ateek, *Justice and Only Justice: A Palestinian Theology of Liberation*, 1st ed. (Maryknoll, NY: Orbis Books, 1989); Rosemary Radford Ruether and Herman Ruether, *The Wrath of Jonah* (Minneapolis, MN: Augsburg Fortress, 1989).

16. For an important contribution to the literature critical of Christian Zionism see Robert Ora Smith, *More Desired Than Our Own Salvation: The Roots of Christian Zionism* (Oxford: Oxford University Press, 2013).

17. One of the new Israeli historians is Ilan Pappé. See Ilan Pappé, *The Ethnic Cleansing of Palestine* (Oxford: Oneworld, 2015).

18. For an in-depth review of how BDS has functioned within this reversal see Nathan Thrall, "BDS: How a Controversial Non-Violent Movement Has Transformed the Israeli-Palestinian Debate," *The Guardian*, August 14, 2018, sec. News, https://www.theguardian.com/news/2018/aug/14/bds-boycott-divestment-sanctions-movement-transformed-israeli-palestinian-debate.

BIBLIOGRAPHY

Ateek, Naim Stifan. *Justice and Only Justice: A Palestinian Theology of Liberation*. 1st ed. Maryknoll, NY: Orbis Books, 1989.

Barghouti, Omar. *Boycott, Divestment, Sanctions: The Global Struggle for Palestinian Rights*. Chicago: Haymarket Books, 2011. https://ebookcentral.proquest.com/lib/warw/detail.action?docID=665761.

Chmiel, Mark. *Elie Wiesel and the Politics of Moral Leadership*. Philadelphia: Temple University Press, 2001.

Ellis, Marc H. *Beyond Innocence and Redemption: Confronting the Holocaust and Israeli Power: Creating a Moral Future for the Jewish People*. Reprint ed. Wipf and Stock, 2016.

———. *Burning Children: A Jewish View of the War in Gaza*. Eugene, OR: Wipf and Stock, 2017.

———. *Ending Auschwitz: The Future of Jewish and Christian Life*. Louisville, KY: Westminster John Knox Press, 1994.

———. *Finding Our Voice: Embodying the Prophetic and Other Misadventures*. La Vergne, TN: Wipf and Stock, 2018.

———. "From Holocaust Theology to a Jewish Theology of Liberation: On the Theo-Politics of Jewish Empowerment." In *T & T Clark Companion to Political Theology*. New York: T & T Clark, 2019.

———. *Toward a Jewish Theology of Liberation*. 3rd ed. Waco, TX: Baylor University Press, 2004.

Fackenheim, Emil L. *God's Presence in History: Jewish Affirmations and Philosophical Reflections*. New York: New York University Press, 1970.

Greenberg, Irving. "Cloud of Smoke, Pillar of Fire: Judaism, Christianity and Modernity after the Holocaust." In *Auschwitz: Beginning of a New Era?: Reflections on the Holocaust*, edited by Eva Fleischner. New York: Ktav, 1977.

———. "On the Third Era of Jewish History: Power and Politics." *Perspectives*, 1987.

Gutiérrez, Gustavo. *Las Casas: In Search of the Poor of Jesus Christ*. Translated by Robert R. Barr. Maryknoll, NY: Orbis, 1993.

Haynes, Stephen R. *Reluctant Witnesses: Jews and the Christian Imagination*. Louisville, KY: Westminster John Knox Press, 1995.

Pappé, Ilan. *The Ethnic Cleansing of Palestine*. Oxford: Oneworld, 2015.

Perlmutter, Nathan, and Ruth Perlmutter. *The Real Anti-Semitism in America*. New York: Arbor House, 1984.

Rubenstein, Richard L. *The Cunning of History: The Holocaust and the American Future*. New York: Harper and Row, 1975.

Ruether, Rosemary Radford, and Herman Ruether. *The Wrath of Jonah*. Minneapolis, MN: Augsburg Fortress, 1989.

Smith, Robert Ora. *More Desired Than Our Own Salvation: The Roots of Christian Zionism*. Oxford: Oxford University Press, 2013.

Thrall, Nathan. "BDS: How a Controversial Non-Violent Movement Has Transformed the Israeli-Palestinian Debate." *The Guardian*, August 14, 2018, sec. News. https://www.theguardian.com/news/2018/aug/14/bds-boycott-divestment-sanctions-movement-transformed-israeli-palestinian-debate.

Chapter Seven

La Morenita

The Ambiguous Identity of Our Lady of Guadalupe

Wanda Deifelt

Mary is a patron saint in nearly all Latin American and Caribbean countries.[1] The idea of patron saints harks back to the ancient tradition of tutelary deities, that is, spirits or divine entities that guard or protect a particular place, nation, person, or occupation. The location of Mary's apparitions in Latin America and the Caribbean islands reveals the notion that deities and spirits have certain places of manifestation and areas of dominion in which they perform. Mary's titles are usually connected to the location of her apparition and the circumstances of her presence, thus offering an indication of context and construction of identity. What happens to patron saints when their worshipers migrate? The reality of global migration has widened the scope and presence of Mary throughout the world. In this process, what is emphasized, what is disregarded, and what are the continuities in Marian devotion as Mary journeyed from the Middle East to the Americas?

MARY AND THE FEMININE DIVINE

The figure of Mary, the mother of Jesus, is a multifaceted and malleable persona, as evidenced by the way her apparitions envelop local culture. She is also the embodiment and representation of racial, ethnic, and cultural tensions, as she becomes the site where class, race, ethnicity, and religious identity meet.[2] Mary is certainly an ambiguous figure. Ever since she was named Theotokos (Mother of God) at the council of Ephesus in 431 C.E., her role in the church has been complex. Whereas the clergy preferred to focus on the theological dispute over Mary as Theotokos or Christotokos (birth giver of Christ), the local population was more concerned with the connection between Mary and Artemis (the goddess of fertility).[3] While the clergy focused on her virginity as a support for a growing ascetic movement, the laity celebrated Mary's fertility and maternal role.

By being both virgin and mother, the figure of Mary is capable of bringing together seemingly contradictory expectations. From the outset, the veneration of Mary has been deeply syncretic, allowing for the incorporation of elements of local cultures (such as goddess, fertility, and female wisdom) into the official theological teachings.[4] It is not surprising that many of Mary's shrines and places of pilgrimage are caves and mounds, places traditionally identified with the female divine. Based on anthropological studies, religion scholars have been able to ascertain that the figure of Mary incorporated many aspects of native cultures. Already in the sixteenth century, Bernardino de Sahagún suspected that through the Virgin of Guadalupe the indigenous population had found a disguised manner to worship Tonantzin, a lunar mother goddess.

While the European colonial enterprise was concerned whether bodies had souls (that is, if indigenous and African enslaved peoples were made in the image of God and could be saved),[5] the indigenous (and eventually the African matrix as well) introduced the question whether spirits and other deities could have a material form of bodies. Mary's multiple apparitions in Latin America and the Caribbean seem to corroborate this indigenous outlook. Mary serves as a a close connection between the conditions of the native indigenous population under colonial domination, the celebration of a female deity after the Christian missionaries' attempt to expel indigenous expressions of the feminine divine, and a claim of national (including, perhaps, class and cultural) affirmations of divine revelations among the downtrodden and colonized.

THE VIRGIN OF GUADALUPE

Guadalupe is probably the best-known Latin American representation of Mary. According to legend and tradition, on the morning of December 9, 1531, an indigenous peasant named Juan Diego had a vision at the Hill of Tepeyac (now a suburb of Mexico City). Juan Diego was an Aztec convert to Christianity. The maiden in the vision spoke to him in his native Nahuatl language and identified herself as the Virgin Mary, "mother of the very true deity," and asked that a church be built at that site so that the poor and sick could come there to receive her blessing and intercession.

Juan Diego sought out the bishop of Mexico City, Fray Juan de Zumárraga, and repeatedly presented Mary's wish to the bishop, but was rejected again and again. Eventually, the bishop instructed him to return to

Tepeyac Hill and ask the lady for a miraculous sign to prove her identity. The first sign she gave was the healing of Juan's uncle. The Virgin also told Juan to gather flowers from the top of Tepeyac Hill, which was normally barren at that time of the year. Juan followed her instructions and found roses, not native to Mexico, blooming there. The Virgin arranged the flowers in his cloak (*tilma*), and when Juan Diego opened his cloak before the archbishop on December 12, the flowers fell to the floor, and on the fabric was the image of the Virgin of Guadalupe. [6]

This account is seen as the charter myth of Mexican Catholicism. The canonization of Juan Diego in 2002, by Pope John II, was interpreted by many Mexicans as an acknowledgment of the indigenous element in Mexican Catholicism. The Virgin appeared not to a Spanish conqueror or priest, but to a humble indigenous man. She spoke in Nahuatl, the language of the conquered people. She is dark skinned (known affectionately as La Morenita, the little dark one). She appears standing on a crescent moon, aureoled by the sun, a symbol reminiscent of the woman in the book of Revelation but also known in Aztec representation. The supporting angel's wings recall the Aztec eagle. The location of her apparition, Tepeyac, was home to the cult of Tonantzin, mother of Aztec deities. At the ceremony of Juan Diego's canonization, Pope John Paul II entered the basilica serenaded by a song, composed by a priest, in which Guadalupe was referred to as Tonantzin, La Morenita. [7]

In spite of the fervent devotion toward Mary, there are reservations regarding the historical accuracy of the events surrounding the apparition of the Virgin of Guadalupe to Juan Diego, including those voiced by the former abbot of the Basilica of Guadalupe (eventually leading to his resignation). [8] Contesting the claims of supernatural authorship, an analysis of the painting on the cloth reveals to be "a human product fashioned with materials easily obtained in mid sixteenth-century New Spain."[9] Additionally, the bishop approached by Juan Diego in the account was not consecrated until 1534, and there is no mention of the apparition of the Virgin to Juan Diego in the bishop's own writings. The earliest documented evidence for her apparition dates from 1648, when priest and theologian Miguel Sánchez offered a description and interpretation of the Virgin's apparition in his publication *Imagen de la Virgen María*. [10] An account in Nahuatl was published a year later, in 1649, by Luis Laso de la Vega, the vicar of the chapel of Our Lady of Guadalupe. [11]

MARY'S JOURNEY FROM SPAIN TO MEXICO

The presence of Mary in Latin America and the Caribbean is not accidental. The image of the Virgin Mary was emblazoned on Hernan Cortés's banner in the same way as the Spanish Guadalupe had been during the Reconquest from the twelfth century forward. In New Spain, her image was used to reclaim pagan spaces for Christianity and justify military conquest. Along with crosses, small-scale effigies and engravings of the Virgin Mary were mounted over altars formerly dedicated to pre-Hispanic deities. The triumph of the Christian faith was expressed both physically and symbolically with new shrines typically erected on or near the foundations of pre-Columbian temples. One such shrine at Tepeyac, just north of Tenochtitlan (Mexico City), was dedicated to "Our Lady" from its inception. [12]

When Hernan Cortés arrived in Mexico, in 1519, in search of the wealth he envisioned this new land could provide, he was aware of the hierarchical structure put in place by the Aztec empire. Many of the groups conquered by the Aztecs were dissatisfied, and alliances with those subjugated by the Aztecs allowed the Spanish to conquer the Aztec empire after a two-year struggle. "They were hated and feared by the subordinate groups, many of which felt that the Aztec's obsession with human sacrifice had totally perverted the religion." [13] This is in part what enabled the Spaniards to conquer Mexico. The Nahuatl sector of society was willing to ally with the Spanish because they saw it as a way to escape Aztec oppression.

Historically, however, the conquest of Aztecs is explained through the indecisiveness of the Moctezuma II, the Aztec ruler (recorded in the *Florentine Codex* years after the fact), who interpreted the arrival of the Spaniards as an indication of a cataclysmic disaster and a return of Quetzalcoatl and other deities to earth. [14] This account is largely seen as a historical oversimplification. Camilla Townsend, for instance, disagrees with the explanation that the Aztecs were in awe of the Spaniards and considered them gods because Quetzalcoatl was predicted to return on the day that Cortés arrived on the new continent. She criticizes this trend among historians who imply that the Aztecs were ignorant natives, so in awe of the Spaniards that it rendered them unable to make rational tactical decisions. [15] This explanation is paired with the description of the Spaniards who, with their superior intellect, were easily able to overtake the Aztecs despite overwhelming disparities in the size of their armies. [16]

The assistance of indigenous enemies of the Aztecs, military weaponry at the disposal of the conquistadors, and the devastation of the native population caused by European-brought diseases should also be considered. In addition, the Aztec defeat needs to be understood through a religious lens:

> The Aztecs desperately needed to understand, within the framework of their cosmology, the disaster that had befallen them; the only explanation that made any sense was that their gods had been defeated by a more powerful Christian god. From that point on, the formerly powerful warriors of Central Mexico posed little if any threat to the conquerors. [17]

In this battle of the deities, the Virgin of Guadalupe played a crucial role. However, the lack of any visual similarity between the Romanesque sculpture of a black Madonna in Extremadura, Spain, and the two-dimensional painting of Guadalupe in Mexico has puzzled scholars for centuries. The iconography of the Tepeyac Guadalupe is a hybrid image, drawing from St. John's vision in Revelation as well as the Assumption of Mary and other symbolic expressions of her purity (the doctrine of Immaculate Conception). Jeanette Peterson's theory is that the making of the Mexican Virgin of Guadalupe draws from three overlapping themes: the Mulier Amicta Sole ("woman clothed with sun" from Revelation 12:1), the Assumption of the Virgin (which establishes her purity and freedom from corruption), and the Tota Pulchra (all beautiful), drawing from her virginity and sinlessness (Song of Songs 4:7). Without established doctrinal or biblical guidelines, artists combined, adapted, and enhanced Marian portraits.

> In all three types Mary is shown between heaven and earth, neither wholly earthbound nor remotely transcendental, as a body figure who mediates both spheres. It is a trio of Marian themes, the Mulier Amica Sole, Assumption of the Virgin, and the Tota Pulchra that may have impacted the making of the Mexican Virgin of Guadalupe. [18]

Before being the patron saint of Latin Americans, Mary was the patron saint of the Spaniards. In New Spain, the Virgin Mary was introduced by Spanish masters as their patroness. Religion and secular powers were inseparable to the early colonizers, and Cortés did bring a large amount of pictures and statues of the Virgin, which he presented as representations of divine mission and Spanish rule. Mary was "the embodiment of Spanish sovereignty in a cosmic confrontation of supernatural forces, with the Spaniards intent upon dethroning the old gods and replacing them with Mary in the native temples and sacred places." [19]

About the time of the conquest of Mexico, a reverence for Mary had blossomed in Castile. With numerous apparitions reported in Spain, Mary was no remote figure; she was the object of widespread public devotion. While God and Christ were feared more than loved, Mary was understood to be the beloved intercessor who could soften the harsh judgement of God. Christ's representation as either a child or on the cross (hence, too vulnerable and impotent to intervene on people's behalf), and the understanding of God as a distant, brooding eminence, made Christianity a source of fear and judgment. Mary, on the other hand, was a sympathetic advocate. Her popularity was such that she eclipsed all other saints during this time. Nearly two-thirds of all miracles were attributed to her. [20]

The popularity of Mary in New Spain cannot be attributed solely to Catholic and colonial indoctrination. Paradoxically, the indigenous devotion to

Mary (in her various forms) in the colonial period shared striking resemblance with folk belief in sixteenth-century Spain. This Marian devotion combined elements of popular religiosity that crossed the oceans, making Mary an ambiguous figure, combining seemingly contradictory characteristics: she was simultaneously virgin and mother, beautiful and humble, and a protector of both Spaniards and indigenous people. She became a patron saint on both sides of the Atlantic.

As for the connection between the apparition and the name "Guadalupe," there is no definite answer. Ondina and Justo González present three possible explanations.[21] One theory is that Guadalupe is a Spanish adaptation of the Nahuatl title *coatlaxopeuh* or *coatlalopeuh* ("the one who crushes the serpent") used by the Virgin in her conversation with Juan Diego. The pronunciation *"quatlasupe"* could be associated with "Guadalupe," and the serpent could be a reference to the plumed serpent Quetzalcoatl. Another theory is that the Mexican Guadalupe is named after the shrine of Guadalupe in Extremadura, Spain, from where many Spanish settlers came. Yet a third theory is that for the indigenous population, Mary was the Aztec goddess Tonantzin disguised as the Virgin Mary.

In Mexico, veneration of Mary Immaculate (of which Guadalupe is one representation) was strong in territories assigned to the Franciscans and Augustinians in the sixteenth and seventeenth century.[22] The Franciscans, for instance, showed Mary as a symbol of charity and redemption. However, the devotion to the image of Guadalupe slowly moved away from her representation as the patroness of the conquistadores to the Virgin of the conquered indigenous people.[23]

INDIGENOUS DEITIES AND SPIRITUALITY

If there is a general agreement on the silence of Guadalupe's apparition from 1531 until the next century, when the legend of Juan Diego was formulated and published, by 1555–1556 there is evidence of Guadalupe's growing popularity at the Tepeyac shrine. "A larger chapel was built and the devotion to the Virgin of Guadalupe was reoriented from her Spanish roots to a distinctly novel American off-shoot."[24] The embrace of Guadalupe appears to reconcile the tension between her role as a patron saint of the colonizer and her apparition to the indigenous Juan Diego. While both sides could claim her, Mary's archetypical role of mother offers a solution to this tension. She introduces herself as Virgin Mary, "mother of the very true deity." She is a nurturing and accepting figure, sweet and tender, who can grant the wishes of her devout children on both sides of the Atlantic. But what aspects of Mary's apparition as the Lady of Guadalupe resonate with indigenous deities? Are

Guadalupe's maternal attributes an oversimplification of the multilayered understandings of the indigenous divine?

Tonantzin, revered as "Our Mother" by the Nahuatl-speaking Aztecs, was associated with Guadalupe. In Aztec cosmology, there was one all-encompassing deity who was simultaneously one and many, male and female.[25] People prayed to both "mother" and "father," entities that were seen as complementary but not necessarily opposite. This gender pairing is represented throughout the Aztec pantheon, specifically with the creator divinities and the divinities of death and the underworld.[26] One was not necessarily superior to the other, but they were two sides of the same thing. Some divinities changed gender or were androgynous, which suggests a gender continuum (at least in the realm of the divine). In many cases, gods and goddesses were independent and were not part of a couple.

The mother goddess was the most important female deity in the Aztec religious system. While male gods remained distinct entities, the goddess— however many her manifestations—was always one.[27] On the most basic level she was Tlaltecuhtli, the Earth Lady. Burr C. Brundage describes her as "the palpable rock and soil and slime upon which men moved and into which they were lowered at death."[28] Most often she was called Tonantzin or "Our Holy Mother." Tonantzin was worshipped as the "giver of life and death," and her connection to motherhood and death is emphasized within her many manifestations. Chicomecoatl (goddess of agriculture and nourishment), Xochiquetzal (goddess of fertility and beauty), and Citlalicue (creator goddess who, along with her husband Citlalatonac, created earth and stars, as well as darkness and death) are additional manifestations of the feminine divine. The goddess Tonantzin was not only a mother of deities, but also a mother of the people. She represents their roots and where they came from, the one who was there at their birth and to whom they can turn when they lost their sense of autonomy and identity.[29]

Some of her manifestations are also deities associated with love and female sexual power, such as Xochiquetzal, depicted as a virginal bride and goddess of fertility. Brundage describes her by saying "her connection with delight and sexual passion is always most prominent and her identity as Mother is never lost."[30] There is an additional side to the feminine divine, connected to the Aztec custom of human sacrifice. Godesses such as Coatlicue ("Serpent Skirt," who gave birth to the moon, stars, and Huitzilopochtli, the god of the sun and war, patron of the city of Tenochtlitan), Cihuacoatl ("Snake Woman," who helped Quetzalcoatl create the human race by grinding up bones and mixing them with his blood), and Itzpapalotl ("Obsidian Knife Butterfly," the goddess who ruled over paradise and the place where humans were created) are often described as dreadful and blood-thirsty deities, whose insatiable thirst justifies the need for continual human sacrifice.[31]

In this idea of the feminine divine there are obvious contradictions between innocent sexuality and erotic power, between the goddess as mother and destroyer, and between the goddess as one who gives birth to the people and demands human sacrifice. Yet these paradoxical representations in the Aztec cosmology resonate with the moral expectations regarding Mary. She too is simultaneously virgin and mother, an unattainable reality for all other women. The connection with snakes and sin echoes the Judeo-Christian explanations for the fall of humanity and a suffering world. Marian devotion affirms Mary as the new Eve, that is, the one who redeems the first woman (who allegedly introduced sin into the world). Whereas the Aztec cosmology maintains the tension between opposites and builds on the contradiction of good and bad, Christianity separated them by allocating sinfulness to Eve and redemption to Mary.

MARY AND EVE, GUADALUPE AND MALINCHE

The early church fathers established a parallel between Eve and Mary. Whereas Eve was the second in the order of creation but the first one to sin, Mary is the one who redeems Eve.[32] Blamed for her initiative in engaging the serpent in the Garden of Eden and seducing Adam to eat from the forbidden fruit, Eve has been portrayed as the anti-model for women. Mary, on the other hand, is the ideal embodiment of women's moral code: both virgin and mother. In the words of Irenaeus, "the good news of the truth announced by an angel to Mary, a virgin subject to a husband, undid the evil lie that seduced Eve, a virgin espoused to a husband."[33] Thus, Mary supersedes and redeems the first woman. Whereas Eve was seduced into disobedience by the serpent, Mary was persuaded into obedience by the angel.

According to Gloria Anzaldúa, the same parallel applied to Guadalupe and La Malinche. Guadalupe is seen as the mediator between "the Spanish and the Indian cultures," "the Chicanos and the white world," and "the human and the divine."[34] Guadalupe's role as a positive mediator is contrasted by the role that Malinche (Malinali/Malintzin) played in the Spanish conquest. Malinche served as a translator and bore Cortes's children. Her reputation has changed over the years, but she comes to be portrayed as an evil or scheming temptress in the wake of the Mexican Revolution. La Malinche is Guadalupe's monstrous double. Like Eve, Malinche is intellectually and sexually dominated, held up as the prostitute that Chicanas will become if they fail to abide by the moral norms of virginity or motherhood upheld by Mary and Guadalupe. Castigated for their voices and sexuality, Eve and La Malinche are scapegoats for the divisions created by patriarchal cultures. Anzaldúa interprets Guadalupe as the virgin in the *virgen/puta* split.[35] She can paradoxically embody the options of nun and mother in Chicano culture.

Still today, in Latin America, there are two distinct sets of gender expectations for men and women. While men are indoctrinated to comply with *machismo*, women are expected to comply with *marianismo*.[36] *Machismo* refers to the exacerbated traits of masculinity; that is, that men are supposed to be self-reliant, aggressive, and able to provide for, protect, and defend their family while also sexually prowling outside of their own family. The counterpart of *machismo* is *marianismo*, the cult of the virgin and mother Mary. The values of *marianismo* are passivity, sexual purity, and motherhood. The moral strength of *marianismo* derives from enduring adversities and living a life of sacrifice in the name of motherhood and family.

MARY: SYMBOL OF OPPRESSION OR LIBERATION?

For many, Our Lady of Guadalupe "stands as a symbol of freedom, cultural autonomy and the struggle for human dignity."[37] A close examination of the rise of the cult of the Virgin of Guadalupe suggests many close connections with the condition of the native population under Spanish colonial domination. Indeed, it is a common assumption that the Virgin of Guadalupe came especially for the indigenous people of Mexico in order to validate and liberate them. "The image is an expression of compassion and the relief of Nahuatl suffering."[38] The Virgin's face shows all of indigenous people of Mexico that she is one of them and not one of the conquerors.

She has likewise been seen as a vindication not only of Indians' self-conscious resistance to the transformation of their homeland into "New Spain," but also of the "female self-image" in resistance to patriarchal dominance represented by the Spanish conquistadors and missionaries. Evidently, the identification of the site of the apparition with a native female deity, whom the Spanish Christian missionaries had sought to expel before she returned to their Indian converts in the borrowed guise of the Mother of God, was also at work in the struggle.[39]

Jeanette Rodriguez describes the encounter between Guadalupe and Juan Diego as a "conversation between equals."[40] After Juan Diego fails to convince the bishop, he asks Guadalupe if she would rather choose a different messenger, but she refuses. According to Rodriguez, this affirmation contradicts the internalized feeling of worthlessness resulting from perpetual domination. His own sense of agency is affirmed when Juan Diego is offered the opportunity to choose if he wants to do what the Virgin asks of him. Jeanette Rodriguez interprets the attempt of the bishop's servants to take away Juan Diego's flowers as a symbolic representation of oppression. She writes, "The conquerors and dominant culture have already taken his land, his goods, his city, his form of government, and his reason for being and acting."[41] The symbolism inherent in the story and image of the Virgin of Guadalupe depicts her as a source of hope for the Nahuatl people, thereby reconceptualizing and giving new value to a figure originally introduced by the conquistadors.

As a feminine deity, Guadalupe is depicted as a powerful entity, with connections to the supreme divine that existed in Aztec cosmology. Through Guadalupe, the Nahuatl were able to hold on to their mother goddess (in her multiple iterations) and also absorb attributes of other deities onto her, such as the creator and sun gods. In this sense, Guadalupe provides a powerful model of womanhood. She inspires devotion that eventually extends to an entire nation. However, her power can only be exercised within the confines of Christianity. It is not surprising, then, that she is depicted in humility, as a very humble rather than intimidating virgin. Through her humility, she yields power to Christianity and to what the church represents. The awe-inspiring power of the goddess is domesticated through Guadalupe.

In her image, her eyes are turned down to show that she is not proud. This can also be interpreted as paying attention to the lowly of society. In this case, it allows Juan Diego to address her in familiar terms. Given the environment, where the indigenous people of Mexico have lost their autonomy and sense of worth, her humility is significant because she takes up the role of intercessor. Through her divinity, she is able to restore the lowly to full membership in society and in heaven. The caveat is, of course, that this model of mediation also sanctions the secular channels of colonial rule. A mestiza deity functions as an intermediary, an intercessor on behalf of those who are socially and politically disenfranchised.

There is a clear connection between Guadalupe and the feminine divine. She is the embodiment of Tonantzin-Coatlicue, goddess of the cosmos, sacred guardian of paradise, a deity of fertility and creation. The feminine divine is mother, temptress, virgin, and killer at once. She is good and bad, impersonal and personal, pure and devious. These contradictory qualities are embodied within the Aztec conception of the feminine divine. But this complex nature of the Aztec goddess is simplified in the Guadalupe narrative. She is reduced to being a virgin and a mother, and she becomes the unattainable model for all women, who are supposed to find self-worth through virginity and motherhood. Guadalupe becomes the archetype of *marianismo* in Latin America.

Her domestication is also evident in the encounter with Juan Diego. Guadalupe needs a man to intervene on her behalf to an even more powerful man (the bishop). Power and authority are male prerogatives. Thus, she becomes part of a worldview in which the good of the family and the country is more important than the good of women. While Guadalupe empowers the conquered indigenous people, she also limits the scope of women's action to the private realm of home and family. As a symbol, she carries within herself the paradox of affirmation and negation. She embodies both the power of fertility and reproduction as well as the humility and subservience of women. She is a symbol that simultaneously heralds freedom and signifies submission.

OUR LADY OF GUADALUPE BEYOND MEXICAN BORDERS

As the border between Mexico and the United States was moved and migration from Mexico northwards increased, so did Guadalupe's presence beyond Mexico. Guadalupe represents not only a connection to the Roman Catholic faith but also a cultural and national emblem of Mexican identity. Her presence is ubiquitous: there are images of Guadalupe in the kitchens of Mexican restaurants, suburban living rooms, dashboards of trucks, or wallets in back pockets. But while Our Lady of Guadalupe is heralded as sustenance and spiritual strength for many Mexicans living in the United States, she is also mainstreamed through institutional Roman Catholic practice. An example of the latter is the Shrine of Our Lady of Guadalupe in La Crosse, Wisconsin.[42]

The shrine is not particularly related to Mexican immigrants or even to the apparition of Guadalupe at Tepeyac. The construction of the site was an inspiration of Cardinal Raymond Leo Burke, who wanted to establish a place of pilgrimage in the diocese. The connection to Guadalupe is nominal, since the shrine identifies more with the Marian tradition than the Mexican cultural heritage. In 1999, a request for the construction of the shrine was sent to the Vatican, and the Holy See gave the project its approval. The site "pays homage to the Blessed Virgin Mary, under the title of Our Lady of Guadalupe, Mother of America and Star of the New Evangelization; honors Our Blessed Mother as the Patroness of the Unborn . . ."[43] In the description, Mary's attributes as mother are extended beyond the Mexican people (she is titled Mother of America) and her motherhood encompasses even unborn children. The magazine newsletter of the shrine is named *Tepeyac*, but the focus of the publication is primarily shrine news and has no connection to the Mexican or indigenous experience of that site.[44] Its institutional and ecclesial character is highlighted through its first-class relics for public veneration, adoration chapel, memorial to the unborn, and the possibility of receiving plenary indulgence for visiting the shrine.

As a malleable symbol, Our Lady of Guadalupe can be institutionally appropriated. However, also from this space she continues to serve as refuge and sustenance for groups who have been historically disenfranchised. Her relevance for Hispanic spirituality is undeniable. It is said that La Morenita speaks "to us, for us, and of us."[45] Guadalupe, as a source of pride, strength, resistance, and hope, has moved beyond the confines of Mexican nationality (although it may have started this way) and extended her influence in the Latinx community and beyond. As a form of Chicana feminist resistance—reclaimed by authors and activists such as Gloria Anzaldúa—to a figure that reinforces traditional teachings regarding motherhood and virginity, Our Lady of Guadalupe is a multifaceted figure. She is a source of faith and empowerment as well as compliance. She is a figure that combines multiple identities and ambiguities. She goes beyond the either-or of borders and cultures. Her strength comes from being a malleable symbol, able to accommodate to new times and places. As people migrate, she is capable of migrating along with them. In each new context, she is rediscovered and redefined.

NOTES

1. Our Lady of Luján in Argentina, Copacabana in Bolivia, Aparecida in Brazil, Carmel of the Maipú in Chile, Rosary of Chiquinquirá in Colombia, Charity of El Cobre in Cuba, Altagracia in the Dominican Republic, Presentation of El Quinche in Ecuador, Perpetual Help in Haiti, Guadalupe in Mexico, Miracles of Caacupé in Paraguay, Divine Providence in Puerto Rico, Coromoto in Venezuela, etc.

2. Wanda Deifelt, "Maria: Uma Santa Protestante," *RIBLA* 46 (2003): 119–21.

3. The fact that Mary was declared the Mother of God in Ephesus is relevant, since this city had Artemis (or Diana) as its patron. By giving Mary such high honor, as to be named Theotokos, she was receiving the attributes of Artemis and being elevated into the official teachings of the church. But the figure of Mary also embodies contradictions and reflects ecclesial power struggles. For instance, the fact that she conceived without sexual intercourse led many to associate her with fertility and goddess worship. For more information see Maria Soave Buscemi, "Eles Passarão . . . Eu . . . Passarinha—Ensaio Para Uma Maria-Logia de Resistência," *RIBLA* 46, no. 3 (2003): 101–18.

4. Sabino A. Vengco Jr. addresses the influence of goddess worship in the development of Mariology by stating: "The dogma of Mary as the Mother of God would be the last message from the city of Ephesus to the rest of the world that up to today remains in force. Ephesus therefore became, in this regard, the initial spiritual center of the new cult of Mary the Mother of God, as Ephesus was once the world center of the ancient pagan cult of Artemis, the goddess mother, Magna Mater. As the Christian Church overran paganism everywhere in the Mediterranean world, this could not have happened without something of the pagan culture rubbing on Christianity. That is the question: how much of the cult of female deities of the Mediterranean world became attached to Christianity?" (p. 127). Sabino A. Vengco, "Mary among the Goddesses," *Landas* 19, no. 1 (2005): 119–40.

5. "One way of reconciling those apparently opposed principles was the argument known as the 'civilizing mission,' which suggested that a temporary period of political dependence or tutelage was necessary in order for 'uncivilized' societies to advance to the point where they were capable of sustaining liberal institutions and self-government." See Margaret Kohn and Kavita Reddy, "Colonialism," in *The Stanford Encyclopedia of Philosophy*, ed. Edward N. Zalta (Metaphysics Research Lab, Stanford University, 2017), https://plato.stanford.edu/archives/fall2017/entries/colonialism/.

6. Joseph Kroeger and Patrizia Granziera, *Astec Goddesses and Christian Madonnas: Images of the Divine Feminine in Mexico* (Surrey, UK: Ashgate, 2012), 230.

7. Andrew Beatty, "The Pope in Mexico: Syncretism in Public Ritual," *American Anthropologist* 108, no. 2 (2006): 324–35.

8. In July 1996, the abbot in charge of the Basilica of Our Lady of Guadalupe in Mexico City, the Reverend Guillermo Schulemburg resigned from his position. The resignation followed days of nationwide demonstrations, occasioned by a comment Schulemburg had made in an interview in which he suggested that Juan Diego was "a symbol, not a reality." This statement was enough to send shockwaves throughout Mexico and the Mexican American community in the United States, eventually forcing Schulemburg's resignation. For more details see Roberto Goizueta, "Our Lady of Guadalupe: The Heart of Mexican Identity," in

Religion and the Creation of Race and Ethnicity: An Introduction, ed. Craig R. Prentiss (New York: NYU Press, 2003).

9. Jeanette Favros Peterson, "Creating the Virgin of Guadalupe: The Cloth, the Artist, and Sources in Sixteenth-Century New Spain," *The Americas* 61, no. 4 (April 2005): 573.

10. Marie-Theresa Hernández, *The Virgin of Guadalupe and the Conversos: Uncovering Hidden Influences from Spain to Mexico* (New York: Rutgers University Press, 2014), 119–37.

11. The difference between the two accounts is interpreted as a rise in *criollismo:* "The emphasis on criollismo and the downplaying of the Indian aspect of the story are clear in the differences between the dialogues in the *Imagen* and those in the *Nican mopohua*, which appeared six months later. As they are quoted by Sánchez, the native element is definitely attenuated. In the *Nican mopohua* the Virgin reveals to Juan Diego her wish for a church in tender words: 'I ardently wish and I greatly desire that they build my temple for me here, where I will manifest, make known, and give to people all my love, compassion, aid, and protection, for I am your compassionate mother. . . . There I will listen to their weeping and their sorrows in order to remedy and to heal all their various afflictions, miseries, and torments.' In Sánchez's wording the message is brief and generic. 'I want a house and ermita built for me here, a temple in which to show myself a compassionate mother with you, with yours, with my devotees, with those who seek me in order to remedy their needs.'" Stafford Poole, *Our Lady of Guadalupe: The Origins and Sources of a Mexican National Symbol* (Tuscon: University of Arizona Press, 2017), 114.

12. Peterson, "Creating the Virgin of Guadalupe," 577.

13. Jeanette Rodriguez, *Our Lady of Guadalupe: Faith and Empowerment among Mexican-American Women* (Austin: University of Texas Press, 1994), 2.

14. Justo L. González and Ondina E. González, *Christianity in Latin America: A History* (Cambridge , UK, and New York: Cambridge University Press, 2007), 32.

15. Camilla Townsend, "Burying the White Gods: New Perspectives of the Conquest of Mexico," *American Historical Review* 108, no. 3 (June 2003): 681.

16. Townsend, 673.

17. González and González, *Christianity in Latin America*, 33.

18. Peterson, "Creating the Virgin of Guadalupe," 591.

19. William B. Taylor, "The Virgin of Guadalupe in New Spain: An Inquiry into the Social History of Marian Devotion," *American Ethnologist* 14, no. 1 (1987): 10.

20. Taylor, 11.

21. González and González, *Christianity in Latin America*, 59.

22. González and González, 50–51.

23. See more about the devotion to Mary in Taylor, "The Virgin of Guadalupe in New Spain," 24–25.

24. Peterson, "Creating the Virgin of Guadalupe," 578.

25. Rosemary Ruether, *Goddesses and the Divine Feminine: A Western Religious History*, 1st ed. (Berkeley: University of California Press, 2005), 192.

26. Townsend, "Burying the White Gods," 110.

27. Burr Cartwright Brundage, *The Fifth Sun: Aztec Gods, Aztec World* (Austin: University of Texas Press, 1979), 175.

28. Brundage, 153.

29. Brundage, 154.

30. Brundage, 162.

31. Brundage, 166.

32. Rosemary Radford Ruether, *Sexism and God-Talk: Toward a Feminist Theology* (Boston: Beacon Press, 1983), 167.

33. Irenaeus, "Mary as the New Eve—Irenaeus," Crossroads Initiative, December 9, 2017, https://www.crossroadsinitiative.com/media/articles/mary-as-the-new-eve-st-irenaeus/.

34. Gloria Anzaldúa, *Borderlands/La Frontera: The New Mestiza* (San Francisco: Aunt Lute Books, 1999), 30.

35. Erika Aigner-Varoz, "Metaphors of a Mestiza Consciousness: Anzaldúa's Borderlands/La Frontera," *MELUS* 25, no. 2 (2000): 47–62.

36. Wanda Deifelt, "Beyond Compulsory Motherhood," in *Good Sex: Feminist Perspectives from the World's Religions*, ed. Mary Hunt and Radhika Balakrishnan (New Brunswick, NJ: Rutgers University Press, 2001).

37. Kroeger and Granziera, *Astec Goddesses and Christian Madonnas*, 228.

38. Rodriguez, *Our Lady of Guadalupe*, 44.

39. Professor Jaroslav Pelikan, *Mary through the Centuries: Her Place in the History of Culture* (New Haven, CT: Yale University Press, 1996), 180–81.

40. Rodriguez, *Our Lady of Guadalupe*, 42.

41. Rodriguez, 44.

42. Shrine of Our Lady of Guadalupe, "Pilgrimage," Shrine of Our Lady of Guadalupe, February 13, 2019, https://www.guadalupeshrine.org/visit/pilgrimage. The site advertises: "Whether to venerate a certain saint or ask some spiritual favor; beg for physical cure or perform an act of penance; express thanks or fulfill a promise, the Shrine of Our Lady of Guadalupe welcomes tens of thousands of visitors annually, including individuals, families and organized pilgrimage groups." In addition, visitors to the shrine can also gain plenary indulgence (see Shrine of Our Lady of Guadalupe, "Plenary Indulgence," Shrine of Our Lady of Guadalupe, January 23, 2012, https://www.guadalupeshrine.org/pray/plenary-indulgence). based on the affiliation of the shrine to the Papal Basilica of Saint Mary Major in Rome (Shrine of Our Lady of Guadalupe, "Indulgence Info," accessed January 24, 2019, https://www.guadalupeshrine.org/wp-content/uploads/2015/01/Indulgence-Info-Jan-2015.pdf.).

43. See Shrine of Our Lady of Guadalupe, "Mission Statement," January 17, 2012, https://www.guadalupeshrine.org/about/mission.

44. See Shrine, "Tepeyac Newsletter," March 15, 2019, https://www.guadalupeshrine.org/news/newsletter/tepeyac.

45. Robert Westerfelhaus, "She Speaks to Us, for Us, and of Us: Our Lady of Guadalupe as a Semiotic Site of Struggle and Identity," in *Communicating Ethnic and Cultural Identity*, ed. Mary Fong and Rueyling Chuang (Lanham, MD: Rowman & Littlefield Publishers, 2004), 105–20.

BIBLIOGRAPHY

Aigner-Varoz, Erika. "Metaphors of a Mestiza Consciousness: Anzaldúa's Borderlands/La Frontera." *MELUS* 25, no. 2 (2000): 47–62.

Anzaldúa, Gloria. *Borderlands/La Frontera: The New Mestiza*. San Francisco: Aunt Lute Books, 1999.

Beatty, Andrew. "The Pope in Mexico: Syncretism in Public Ritual." *American Anthropologist* 108, no. 2 (2006): 324–55.

Brundage, Burr Cartwright. *The Fifth Sun: Aztec Gods, Aztec World*. Austin: University of Texas Press, 1979.

Buscemi, Maria Soave. "Eles Passarão . . . Eu . . . Passarinha—Ensaio Para Uma Maria-Logia de Resistência." *RIBLO* 46, no. 3 (2003).

Deifelt, Wanda. "Beyond Compulsory Motherhood." In *Good Sex: Feminist Perspectives from the World's Religions*, edited by Mary Hunt and Radhika Balakrishnan. New Brunswick, NJ: Rutgers University Press, 2001.

———. "Maria: Uma Santa Protestante." *RIBLA* 46 (2003).

Goizueta, Roberto. "Our Lady of Guadalupe: The Heart of Mexican Identity." In *Religion and the Creation of Race and Ethnicity: An Introduction*, edited by Craig R. Prentiss. New York: NYU Press, 2003.

González, Justo L., and Ondina E. González. *Christianity in Latin America: A History*. Cambridge, UK, and New York: Cambridge University Press, 2007.

Hernández, Marie-Theresa. *The Virgin of Guadalupe and the Conversos: Uncovering Hidden Influences from Spain to Mexico*. New York: Rutgers University Press, 2014.

Irenaeus. "Mary as the New Eve—Irenaeus." Crossroads Initiative, December 9, 2017. https://www.crossroadsinitiative.com/media/articles/mary-as-the-new-eve-st-irenaeus/.

Kohn, Margaret, and Kavita Reddy. "Colonialism." In *The Stanford Encyclopedia of Philosophy*, edited by Edward N. Zalta. Metaphysics Research Lab, Stanford University, 2017. https://plato.stanford.edu/archives/fall2017/entries/colonialism/.

Kroeger, Joseph, and Patrizia Granziera. *Astec Goddesses and Christian Madonnas: Images of the Divine Feminine in Mexico*. Surrey, UK: Ashgate, 2012.

Pelikan, Professor Jaroslav. *Mary through the Centuries: Her Place in the History of Culture*. New Haven, CT: Yale University Press, 1996.

Peterson, Jeanette Favros. "Creating the Virgin of Guadalupe: The Cloth, the Artist, and Sources in Sixteenth-Century New Spain." *The Americas* 61, no. 4 (April 2005): 571–610.

Poole, Stafford. *Our Lady of Guadalupe: The Origins and Sources of a Mexican National Symbol*. Tuscon: University of Arizona Press, 2017.

Rodriguez, Jeanette. *Our Lady of Guadalupe: Faith and Empowerment among Mexican-American Women*. Austin: University of Texas Press, 1994.

Ruether, Rosemary. *Goddesses and the Divine Feminine: A Western Religious History*. 1st ed. Berkeley: University of California Press, 2005.

Ruether, Rosemary Radford. *Sexism and God-Talk: Toward a Feminist Theology*. Boston: Beacon Press, 1983.

Shrine of Our Lady of Guadalupe. "Indulgence Info." Shrine of Our Lady of Guadalupe. Accessed January 24, 2019. https://www.guadalupeshrine.org/wp-content/uploads/2015/01/Indulgence-Info-Jan-2015.pdf.

———. "Mission Statement." January 17, 2012. https://www.guadalupeshrine.org/about/mission.

———. "Pilgrimage." February 13, 2019. https://www.guadalupeshrine.org/visit/pilgrimage.

———. "Plenary Indulgence." January 23, 2012. https://www.guadalupeshrine.org/pray/plenary-indulgence.

———. "Tepeyac Newsletter." March 15, 2019. https://www.guadalupeshrine.org/news/newsletter/tepeyac.

Taylor, William B. "The Virgin of Guadalupe in New Spain: An Inquiry into the Social History of Marian Devotion." *American Ethnologist* 14, no. 1 (1987): 9–33.

Townsend, Camilla. "Burying the White Gods: New Perspectives of the Conquest of Mexico." *American Historical Review* 108, no. 3 (June 2003): 659–87.

Vengco, Sabino A. "Mary among the Goddesses." *Landas* 19, no. 1 (2005): 119–40.

Westerfelhaus, Robert. "She Speaks to Us, for Us, and of Us: Our Lady of Guadalupe as a Semiotic Site of Struggle and Identity." In *Communicating Ethnic and Cultural Identity*, edited by Mary Fong and Rueyling Chuang. Lanham, MD: Rowman & Littlefield Publishers, 2004.

Chapter Eight

The Tortilla Wall and Migration Semantics

Eliseo Pérez-Álvarez

PASSPORT AND PASSWORD

Martin Luther stated that the theologian of the cross names things for what they actually are.[1] That is a very relevant reminder for today, as we live under the tyranny of fake news, the cruelty of euphemisms, and the dictatorship of the migration semantics, namely, the constant changing of the meaning of words to the delight of the powers that be. Such constant change of meanings confuses the issue and distracts us from real solutions.

Therefore, in dealing with immigrants who do not own a passport, we need a password to unpack the dehumanizing narratives with which the powerful have veiled this reality. We need to dismantle this narrative from the many layers of lies in which it has been covered and to unveil reality as it has been defined by the "royalty." Such unveiling reveals, for instance, that immigration should be understood, first of all, as the only possible solution available to the 258 million human beings around the planet facing situations of famine and violence. This contradicts rendering migration as "a problem" or "a crisis" by those such as US president Ronald Reagan, who, after the bombing of Granada, simply stated: "It didn't upset my breakfast at all."[2] It comes as no surprise that the Hollywood ex-actor declared the same 1983 the "Year of the Bible," since, due to the resemanticization, Reagan held the Bible in one hand and a rifle in the other . . . in good conscience.[3] As an ex-actor he knew how to play with words without being held accountable to reality, as expressed in the phrase by journalists Amy Goodman and Denis Moynihan, "Arms welcome, arms kill."[4]

Such resemanticization paved the road for ex-reality showman and now president Trump, who has made more than 10,000 misleading statements in 828 days.[5] Needless to say, hundreds of those whoppers refer to immigrants. Post-truth or absolute relativism is pure resemanticization from above.

The first concept that needs to be unveiled is that of immigration. Granted, my own use of the term "immigration," above, is anachronistic—that word was not coined until the Industrial Revolution.[6] However, my use of the term is warranted because even though the concept is new, people have been migrating, immigrating, and transmigrating since time immemorial. Immigration is as old as humanity and even older than that! According to anthropologists, our human ancestors mimicked animals in departing to other lands in search of food and water.[7] From the book of Genesis, we learn that Adam and Eve were asked to leave the Garden (*pardis*, i.e., "walled garden" in Persian) of Eden (Genesis 3:23–24), thus becoming the first immigrants in the history of humanity.

What is at stake is not the concept of immigration but its true meaning. Who holds the power to name reality? Who has the monopoly over the Greek word *sema,* for meaning or semantics? In order to name things as they actually are, as a theologian of the cross should, I propose the following glossary as a password to unlock or unveil the issue of immigration from the many layers of colonialist semantics in which it has been kidnapped. The different categories are nomads, Native Americans, pilgrims, irregulars, immigrants, transmigrants, refugees, exiled, dreamers, and deported, to list a few.

NOMADS: ABRAHAM 1200 B.C.E.

With the exception of Africans, all human beings migrated from the African continent. We really are *homo et mulier Africanis*! Experts estimate that the first human migration took place about 50,000 years ago, as a consequence of hunger due to weather change.[8]

Immigration also played a central role in the text that we Christians hold as sacred. In fact, as Christians our salvation is rooted in the stories and geographies of immigration. Think of Hagar, Sarah, and Abraham, wandering folks, food seekers, dreamers in pursuit of a promised land, who by being willing to become immigrants also became founders of the religions of Islam, Judaism, Rastafarianism, and Christianity. All four religions bear the mark of their immigrant Abraham in the creed: "A wandering Aramean was my ancestor" (Deuteronomy 26:5).

Hagar, the slave migrant thrown to the desert, achieved what nobody did: "I have now seen the One who sees me" (Genesis 16:13). Hagar the invisible was the only one who exchanged looks with YHWH (16:10). This single mother became the mother of countless children of Islam.

Immigration or immigrants also had a central role in the ministry of the prophets of Israel and in the life and proclamation of Jesus. Indeed, immigrants, orphans, and widows were, in Jesus's religion, God's favorites (Deuteronomy 10:18). The Old Testament utopia, or a viable place, is a land where you can stay for good (Deuteronomy 2:15; Isaiah 32:17, 42:6, 49:6, 65:17, 66:22; Ruth 1:8–16), a land where children are not left behind (Isaiah 49:15). The Hebrew scriptures are the origin of utopia. It is ironic to see how that original insight of the Hebrew scriptures is contradicted in modern politics.

The current policy of the state of Israel seems to be one of welcoming immigrants, but with the caveat that almost all of them must be Jews themselves, with the exception of US citizens, who are welcomed as up to 15 percent of the total![9] The manifest destiny semantics used to plunder Palestinian land and reduce its people to nothingness can be seen in the Zionist slogan, "A Landless People for a Peopleless Land,"[10] and in the colonial semantics deployed by Israel's prime minister, Golda Meir, who quipped, "Palestinians? . . . I don't know what it means."[11]

We must return again and again to the nomadic roots of our faith, since we are also "looking forward to the city that has foundations, whose designer and builder is God" (Hebrews 11:10). As religious descendants of Hagar, Sarah, and Abraham, we must never forget that hospitality to the foreigner is an essential part of our faith (Exodus 22:21–24). Hospitality in our congregations must go beyond sharing "wine and cheese" or even just distributing food among those in need. True hospitality is rooted in love of the foreigner. We must love the immigrant as ourselves; in fact, "love for the immigrant" is translated in some English Bibles as "hospitality." Among nomads, hospitality is a matter of life or death; to deny hospitality to the stranger is to deny them the means to survive another day. No wonder that from nomadic times hospitality has been considered a sacrament.

NATIVE AMERICANS, CONFINED, DISPLACED, UPROOTED, RELOCATED

By declaring the territory *terra nullius,* or land of nobody, seventeenth-century Europeans not only grabbed the land of the people who had been living on Turtle Island for ages; they deprived its inhabitants of their humanity as well. Overnight, they became "Indians," "Native Americans," "redskins," and so on. By fencing them into "reservations" (read: concentration camps), Europeans sought to make them invisible. In fact, Europeans monopolized the term "immigrants" and the expression "we are a nation of immigrants" up until February 2018, when the US Citizenship and Immigration Services

(USCIS) deleted it for good.[12] The rest were "illegal aliens," *braceros,* and so forth.

Native Americans were not Indians—they were not from Asian India. Those nations totally reject not only the "doctrine of discovery" but the "scientific" Bering Strait theory, which undermines them and their faithfulness to their own land. To add insult to injury, social institutions such as the church and school came to uproot their children and colonize them into the European image. According to this narrative, Native Americans will never come of age. Take, for example, the name of the Lone Ranger's companion, Tonto, which is the Spanish word for dumb or stupid.

The formula was repeated in the nineteenth century, this time, when 100,000 Mexican people (and 55 percent of Mexican geography) were crossed by the US border. That is, they did not cross the border; the border crossed them! Native Mexicans cannot be illegal in Abya Yala, their native continent. Their lands were expropriated and the exploitation of their labor followed.

As North American citizens, Puerto Ricans were left out of the system at the psychological and cultural levels. Euro–North Americans' psychological wall continually dismissed non-Europeans through the internalization of fear and paranoia.

It is not a coincidence that Arizona, which holds the largest number of Native American nations in the United States, has banned Latino studies. The fact that the largest Native American language in the United States now is Zapoteco, from Oaxaca, Mexico, continues shaking the semantics of the term "immigrant," opening a tear in its veil. The time has come to face it. Hundreds of children from Southern ancient civilizations skip Spanish: they go straight from their native Abya Yala language (such as Aymara, Quechua, Nahuatl, Maya, Guarani, Mapuche, and others) into English.

As long as the empire of the United States refuses to revisit its tailor-made semantics, the Mexican Mouse Speedy González will keep on making fun of the gringo cat Sylvester by converting the border into a revolving door. This animated cartoon character of 1953 was created by Robert McKimson, Fritz Freleng, and Hawley Pratt. It is more relevant than ever with Speedy singing, "¡Ándale! ¡Ándale! ¡Arriba! ¡Arriba! ¡Epa! ¡Epa!" (Hurry up!) while quenching his hunger from a cheese factory guarded by Sylvester right there at the border.[13]

DISCOVERERS, PILGRIMS, PIONEERS, ENTREPRENEURS, SETTLERS, CIVILIZERS, SOJOURNERS, INVESTORS, COLONIZERS, CARPETBAGGERS

Eduardo Galeano describes a history that could have been:

> Christopher Columbus' discovery of America failed because he had neither a
> visa nor a passport. Pedro Álvarez Cabral was not allowed to land in Brazil
> because he could spread smallpox, measles, influenza and other pests un-
> known in the country. Hernán Cortés and Francisco de Pizarro were left with
> the desire to conquer Mexico and Peru because they lacked work permits.
> Pedro de Alvarado bounced in Guatemala and Pedro de Valdivia in Chile
> because neither of them had a certificate of good conduct. The Mayflower
> Pilgrims were returned to the sea, since the coast in Massachusetts did not
> have any open immigration quotas. *La historia que pudo ser.*[14]

In this glossary for understanding immigration from the perspective of the
cross, another concept whose imperial semantics needs to be revealed is the
dual concept of discoverer and civilizer. Europeans did not discover America; they stole it by force and genocide. The true discoverers of this continent
are the people that named it Abya Yala.[15] Not only did the Europeans strip
the original peoples of their lands, but they also judicially, theologically, and
ontologically declared them to be half human and half beast. Nonetheless,
there were a handful of true prophets, such as Antonio de Montesinos and
Bartolomé de las Casas, who called things by their name.

It wasn't until 1537 that the papal bull *Sublimis Deus* by Paul III declared
Native Americans' humanity. With the appropriate interpretive password, it
is not hard to see how the mislabeled discovery was part of the biggest
imperialistic crusade humanity has ever seen. Around the time that Columbus and others were unlawfully crossing the borders of the Americas and
plundering it, Spain had been applying deportation laws in its local territories
against Muslims and Jews. Simultaneously, across the Atlantic, they were
declaring the newfound lands as *terra nullius*—the land of nobody.

Again, the fake semantics are very convenient. From the arrival of the
Europeans and up until 1798 (and sometimes during part of the nineteenth
century), what is now known as the United States of America was known as
Columbia, as the former national anthem "Hail, Columbia" testifies. Notice
how this Latinate deletes Abya Yala and Turtle Island and replaces them
with Columbia, USA, and eventually America. The act of renaming it veils
the violent and criminal past upon which the new country was founded (it
also hides the rightful and legal claims of the original inhabitants who are
still among us today). One hundred years later, in 1892, Francis Bellamy
promoted the fourth centennial of Columbus in a children's magazine with
the Roman salute and the pledge of "under God."

This was not a *terra nullius*, a land of nobody, "discovered and civilized"
by the Europeans. In Nahuatl, one out of 68 Mexican native languages, many
of which had their own respective dialects, this was *Amoxtlapan*, "a land of
books."[16] Despite what many historians or propagandists have tried to make
us believe, the truth is that when Europeans met the great civilizations that
had emerged on these lands, they were not terrified but in awe, speechless,

before the Mesoamerican and Inca civilizations. These were, after all, foundational ancient cultures alongside five more from Nigeria, Mesopotamia, Egypt, China, and India.[17]

By the time the Europeans arrived, Mesoamericans had created the most productive agricultural technique ever known: the *chinampa*. The 750-square-meter floating islet, always humid and rich in humus, produced from 4 to 7 harvests yearly, that is, three thousand kilograms of grain.[18]

The use of the term "Hispanics" to refer to the descendants of those great Mesoamerican civilizations that predated the arrival of the Hispanics, that is, from Hispania, the name for Spain in the Middle Ages, is another example of the veiling of reality through hegemonic semantics. The term goes back to Richard Nixon's thirst for votes; it attempted to homogenize immigrants from 21 countries of origin into a single oppressive name: "Hispanics." This renaming effects a reversal in the judicial nomenclature of immigrant versus native, so that now the native is called illegal and the immigrant native. But the theologian of the cross must call things by their name.

In the same playful but prophetically serious style of Cornel West, who has quipped that Donald Trump "is for real, but not for right," I query Brother West about the semantics of "real." Does he mean that President Donald Trump shares our ontological poverty, or that he is a "real-regal-royalty" king (from the Spanish *realeza,* meaning "royal")? Is he a latecomer to Abya Yala, or a "real-ity" show manager perpetuating these TV programs created in England (i.e., if we grant that category to the 1964 documentary *Seven Up!* which preceded by one year *The American Sportsman*?) Or is he something else?

Northern Europeans who emigrated to Abya Yala quoted the Bible to legitimize their land grabbing: with their imperial semantics, they justified their experience of immigration as their exodus, their war against Canaanites, their redemption of the Prodigal Son, and so on. However, the comedic rendition of those pilgrim narratives by Jon Stewart helps us unveil the underlying truth. He says, in jest: "I celebrated Thanksgiving in an old-fashioned way. I invited everyone in my neighborhood to my house, we had an enormous feast, and then I killed them and took their land."[19] This is a "real-istic" rendition of history.

What happened "for real" in the first "thanksgiving" was that these first European immigrants in North America had become so weak and vulnerable that they would not have survived without some sort of welfare from the local authorities. Ostheologists, who analyze bones, have disclosed information about this period: their sex, race, age, if they were left handed, if they exercised, rode a horse, and so on. Scientists also reported that they ate rodents, leather, and horses. But the myth of discovery and civilization could not be built on such *parrhesia* (speaking truth to power); it had to be veiled with rhetoric to flatter the powerful.

France came out with the tale of its *Mission Civilisatrice* (Civilizing Mission) to bless the plundering of lands. England cooked up the *White Man's Burden* to legitimize the colonization of a legion of countries. Thirteen out of fifteen American colonies broke with England so that they could expand the rigid and frigid geographical borders established by the crown. But in so doing, they did not leave their myths behind; they recontextualized them and turned them into the sacropolitical doctrine of the Manifest Destiny.

The Thirteen Colonies morphed into Columbia, then into the United States of America, and now, from semantic excess, into "America." From that follows the "identity theft" of the rest of the 35 American countries, and the semantic trick to name "real reality." This rebaptizing is covered by layers of stories and narratives, which give it an aura of facticity. Take, for instance, the Plymouth Pilgrims' story; it is a justification of North European immigration at the expense of reducing the other to nothingness. This became explicit when in 1835 Alexis de Tocqueville articulated the concept of American exceptionalism, which has been repeated ad nauseam by all American presidents, including President Barack Obama. What is missing in imperial semantics, and what is veiled in the hostility against new waves of immigrants, is the recollection of the hundreds of acts of interventionism and coup d'état carried out directly or indirectly by the US military and paramilitary forces, which have created the dire conditions that push children and adults to leave their countries. A couple of examples won't hurt. Last century, the United Fruit Company created the "banana republics," which were named by William Sidney Porter in his "The Admiral," a story from his book *Cabbages and Kings* of 1904. Since then, the United States has invaded Honduras seven times to ensure that huge tracts of land, railroads, ports, highways, and streets are clear to put fruits on their tables. Since Guatemala's coup in 1954, this country does not know what social justice is.[20] The same company owned 42 percent of Guatemala's land, and had control of the country's infrastructure. Coincidentally, the UFC had Foster Dulles, that is, Eisenhower's secretary of state, as one of its partners. Guatemalan elites, people's parsimony, Honduran animosity, and US intervention did not allow the destitute president Jacobo Árbenz to continue doing a land reform that would have ended indigenous slavery and eradicated poverty.

The building of a new enemy (i.e., the Mexican immigrant), through Donald Trump's rhetoric, is only the certification that the days of the Pilgrims' narrative are numbered. Currently the United States of America is 63 percent white, 17 percent Latino/a, 12 percent African American, and 12 percent Asian. According to the US Census Bureau of 2012, by 2042, Euro-Americans will be a minority, and by 2060, one out of three people in the United States will be Latino/a.[21] In the meantime, the US penitentiary system profits from undocumented newcomers, including children who, under the current legal system, can be sentenced for life. Things must be called what they are in reality.

ADMINISTRATIVE IRREGULARS, ALIENS, ILLEGALS, *BRACEROS*, ALIENATED, INVADERS, RAPISTS, WETBACKS, UNDOCUMENTED, PAPERLESS, CRIMINALS, INTRUDERS

> This was the guilt of your sister Sodom: she and her daughters had pride, excess of food and prosperous ease, but did not aid the poor and needy. (Ezekiel 16:49)

Colonizing semantics has equated non-European immigrants with criminals. The criminalization of Caribbean and Latin American immigrants has proven to be a juicy multilayered enterprise for gatekeepers. The profitable prison business, the militarization of society, the arms race, the trafficking in drugs and human bodies that included thousands of children, the land grabbing, the blind faith in capitalism, the systemic corruption, the "bank-cracy," and the 1980s new international division of labor are but some of the ramifications of shifting immigration semantics from the category of human rights to that of crime.

First of all, to enter the United States without a visa is not a felony but a civil violation. This does not belong to the legal realm but to the political sphere, which is taken into tow by the market and its thirst for slave labor. "No human being is illegal," declared the International Convention on the Protection of the Rights of All Migrant Workers and Members of Their Families, and it was subscribed to on December 18, 1990, by the United Nations. What is illegal is to request them to show documents, and to put them in prison. In Mexico, the migratory law of February 24, 2011, instead of calling them illegal, names them "administrative irregulars."

Second, how is it that employers of undocumented persons can get away with not being criminalized? Since the 1952 "Texas Proviso" law, it is perfectly legal to exploit the paperless immigrants. In 1986, penalties were added against employers only if they "consciously" hired irregular workers.

Undocumented 12-year-old children can legally break their backs in the agricultural fields. The National Center for Farmworker Health reports agricultural children laboring as early as seven years old, many of them working off the books or under their parents' social security numbers.[22]

Third, the legal system has criminalized solidarity and mercy. US citizens of goodwill are prevented by law from sheltering, transporting, leasing a house, marrying, feeding, and even praying for an immigrant, like a pastor who mentioned that in his sermon and the following day his church council cornered him. Any police officer can act as an immigration agent to check the status of irregular migrants and arrest them.

Last but not least, the semantics that criminalize Latino/a immigrants for some folks means "in gold we trust." The daily cost of each detained is $164 and a large portion of that money goes to private companies, which operate more than half of the detention centers that imprison 34,000 migrants. This is a more than $2 billion yearly profit to the detriment of taxpayer funds.[23] Irregular children can very well become part of the more than 100,000 US imprisoned children.

The neoliberalist digestive systems that eat human beings, with their forked tongues, criminalize hunger immigrants and simultaneously glorify weapons. To buy a weapon is not a problem, yet to buy medicine, there are many hurdles. The Río Grande, according to US semantics (the Río Bravo, in Mexican nomenclature), is now named the Iron River, given the thousands of weapons that travel north to south without any passport. Along the USA-Mexico border alone there are 17,000 armories. The recipients of the weapons are also children already involved in organized crime or in one or another militia.

Undocumented Latino/as have been demonized, but nothing is further from the truth. Workers in irregular situations often are the most solid human beings, who, by sending money to our countries of origin, keep our humanity and economy afloat. Remittances are the first source of revenue for many countries, but they remain silent regarding the injustices inflicted on irregular migrants.

IMMIGRANTS, PEOPLE IN TRANSIT, PEOPLE OF THE WAY, NEIGHBORS

The term "immigrant" emerged alongside the European Industrial Revolution, but US semantics married "immigrants" to "Ellis Island," namely, with European immigration.[24] During the nineteenth and twentieth centuries, Europe exported 55 million people whose main destiny, since 1492, has been the American continent. Hunger played a central role in becoming immigrants. To name one example, between 1870 and 1930, Norway expelled half of its population counting their children.[25]

It must not be forgotten that up until the US Civil War citizenship was exclusively for white folks. Once the massacre was over, African Americans and Chinese were also eligible. However, it was not until 1868, with the Fourteenth Amendment of the Constitution that citizenship was granted on the basis of *jus solis*, or soil right, meaning that one could obtain it by the mere fact of being born on US soil. Nonetheless, semantics hides the racialization of the amendment: nonwhites could not obtain citizenship via *jus sanguinis*, or blood right, as they were simply ineligible. The exception, until Obama's presidency, was Cuba! In 1994–1995, the United States and Cuba signed the "wet foot, dry foot" policy, which allowed Cubans who arrived on US soil to become permanent residents after one year, and eventually citizens. Three days before Obama finished his period as president, he discontinued this agreement.

The amendment also had a class component because poor white European southerners for decades did not qualify either, like the current PIGS: Portugal, Italy, Greece, and Spain.[26] The *Dictionary of Races and Peoples* of 1911, edited by the US Immigration Commission made a catalogue of 45 races, with the Anglo-Saxons at the top and the Italians at the bottom due to their excitable, impulsive, highly imaginative character and scarce adaptability to a highly organized society.[27] Italians were of short stature, heterogeneous, closely related to the Berbers of northern Africa, with some traces of blood from the Hamites. Needless to say, such a taxonomy that excluded other European countries was based on eugenic myths and pseudoscientific facts, or to say the same, on power and control. The acronym PIGS emerged in the 1990s during the European Union integration. It was coined with the agenda of labeling those countries with poor economies.[28] In 1995, those countries were admitted into the borderless Europe. However, in the same year, other European countries such as Romania, Croatia, Bulgaria, and Cyprus, among others, were not accepted in the Schengen Area. Some European countries are more equal than others.

De jure, according to the law, if a child is born on US soil, his or her citizenship is automatically given. De facto, in fact the semantics remain intact, but Trump's politics is making things more difficult. With the sad example of the Dominican Republic that is sending back Haitians who were born after 1929, the EUDO-citizenship statelessness database reports that 18 out of 42 European countries grant nationality based on jus soli. Nonetheless, in practice, fewer countries honor that right. What prevails is the slamming of the door to Jesus himself who comes to them in disguise in the form of immigrant children (Revelation 3:20).

If the word "immigrant" has been monopolized and racialized, the jus solis has been used to inferiorize children and women. Imperial semantics created the term "anchor baby" in the 1980s to name Vietnamese refugees. Later on, the term was applied to stigmatize African American mothers by arguing that they used their children as "objects" of revenue. Ronald Reagan went as far as naming them "welfare queens."

When applied to undocumented mothers, "anchor baby" means that instead of the mother nurturing her baby, the child is the passport to the "horn of abundance." Some Euro-American paranoiacs and other assimilated sisters and brothers see "anchor babies" everywhere. This narrative dismisses children and women by "using" and "instrumentalizing" them as scapegoats.

Tennessee State Representative Curry Todd animalized them: "[Latina pregnant women] multiply like rats."[29] At the end of August 2015, pre-candidate to the presidency and governor of New Jersey, Chris Christie, made a promise to the country: he would go after undocumented people like FedEx tracks packages. David Cameron, England's former prime minister, named immigrants "swarms." England has no constitution, only some documents in lieu of one, and no memory to realize that it holds the record of the most invaded countries in history. Members of Congress cannot seem to endure the fact that the white population of the United States and Europe is not aging; it is already old. Immigrants are the ones revitalizing the country. In the United States, the median age of women is the following: Euro-American, 41, Asian, 35, African American, 32, and Latinas, 25. Perhaps is it not blue blood but, better yet, young blood.

TRANSMIGRANTS

In Spanish, the word "migrant" designates someone who departed within or beyond the country limits, or even further to other countries' borders. However, in our migration glossary we add the category of transmigrant. At this point let us remember that in contradistinction to the "immigrant crisis on the border" semantics, 60 percent of global migrants remain in their country of origin. Furthermore, the crossings into United States were declining during the past decades.

The media sensationalism that comes up with terms like "immigrationalism" or "it's a borderful world" does not correlate to reality. To block immigrants, US semantics keeps legitimating the wall, even though more than 40 percent of 11.5 million undocumented people arrived by plane with different visas and another 10 percent crossed by land with proper documentation and never went back.[30]

Drones will patrol above Mexican soil, sending high-resolution images. MAD, Minuteman American Defense, with at least 1,000 Latino members, will keep alive the semantics of immigrants as criminals. The persecution already takes place everywhere, including in churches. After the Second World War there were seven walls in the planet; today there are 77.[31]

From the Northern semantics the wall means nothing for US immigrants to other countries such as Mexico. A few years ago, US immigrants were requested to show just a driver's license to cross the Mexican border. Currently they need a US passport, but no visa. 25 percent and 15 percent of US immigrants have made their home in Mexico and in the occupied West Bank, respectively.

SEXUAL, IDEOLOGICAL, PROFESSIONAL, WAR, SELF-EXILED, ECONOMIC, CLIMATE, RELIGIOUS, POLITICAL, GOLDEN REFUGEES, TRAFFICKERS, STATELESS

For I was a stranger and you invited me in. (Jesus the Refugee, Matthew 25:45)

In 1951 the United Nations stated that a refugee is a human being who "owing to well-founded fear of persecution for reasons of race, religion, nationality, membership or a particular social group or political opinion, is outside the country of his [sic] nationality and is unable or, owing to such fear, is unwilling to avail himself [sic] of the protection of that country."[32]

This official discourse seems nondiscriminatory; nevertheless, the semantics of the centers of power have used this statement as an ideological mechanism to empty the concept of immigration. Their "think-tanks" keep adding new types of refugees in order to establish who can come in and who must stay out.

According to tendentious ways of classifying refugees, we have the following groups: political refugees (people whose life is in danger), economic refugees (people who were forced to leave searching for a better quality of life), golden refugees (the almighty Southern elites who are looking for a Northern country in which to invest their fortunes), brain-drain refugees (the one million scientists and university professionals living in the United States after being educated in Latin America, 11,000 of them holding Ph.D. degrees from Mexico),[33] religious refugees (people who are escaping religious persecution), and ideological refugees (those who have chosen to mimic the "American way of life").

Regarding your race, class, religion, gender orientation, disabilities, age, or country, the United States might grant you the following visas: the "H-1B" (for people with a high degree of specialization), the "G-4" (for diplomats, though in October 2018 it didn't apply to same-sex couples, the United States' joining the 12 percent of UN members with this heteronormative policy), the "EB-1" (the "genius visa" aimed at fostering business, science, art), the L-1 and EB-5 (which welcome millionaires who create at least ten full-time jobs), the "E" for investors, the "T" for victims of people trafficking, the "J" for exchange programs, the "H" for laborers, the "U" for victims of domestic violence, the "Lottery" for European countries (though Africa has received some lately), the "H2A" for temporary jobs, and "the humanitarian" (a one-year visa featuring the option to apply for asylum).

Now, with the exception of ideological and golden refugees, Puerto Ricans distinguish between persons who had to leave and those who could afford to stay. Aren't those refugee categories artificial? Isn't world immigration a direct result of the economic asymmetry imposed by the almighty banks and corporations? How is it that there is no such thing as hunger refugees, since hunger is the most terrifying weapon of mass destruction? According to Valeria Emmi, hunger is both the defect and effect of forced migration, since 51 countries have reached alarming hunger levels. [34] Current food production is able to feed ten billion people. However, for big business, food is a commodity, not a human right. Each year five million children die due to poor nutrition. 98 percent of hungry people live in "underdeveloped," that is, impoverished, countries. One billion people suffer chronic hunger. [35]

Again, who decides who is a refugee or an immigrant? Who decides who may live and who must be killed? Aylan Kurdi's brother and mother died on a Turkish beach after his father paid $5,000 for them to board a precarious boat. His father could have paid the same amount for the four Kurdis to travel by plane, if only Canada had accepted his application as a refugee!

The theologian of the cross must name things for what they are.

DREAMERS

Henry David Thoreau declared that "it is desirable to cultivate a respect not for the law, so much as for the right." [36] The Development, Relief, and Education for Alien Minors Act is the 2012 political initiative of President Obama to address the 1.8 million people in this category who came to the United States during their childhood. Obama's proselytizing of the Latino vote came right before his re-election. This program works through DACA, that is, Deferred Action for Childhood Arrivals. This measurement issues work permits and defers deportation proceedings against undocumented residents who are no older than thirty and came to the United States when they were younger than sixteen. One of the outcomes was to stop the deportation of 580,000 persons.

The powers that be resemanticized another immigrant category, which revolves around the American Dream. [37] The same dream led the CIA and the US State Department to grab 14,048 children from Cuba in the 1960s to save them from red communism, the so-called "Peter Pan Operation." What is still pending is the eradication of the external debt, aporophobia or hate of the poor, racism, hunger, war, unemployment, and the arms race, which cause children to leave their countries.

The American Dream is feasible only for 5 percent of the US population. Latino/a Dreamers have to face the lie of the "trickle down" heresy, which claims that "the wealthier some people are, the more wealth spreads out to the whole of society." With that, semantics veils the rich, who are given tax deductions. This semantics also justifies that a CEO in this country earns 475 times more than his/her employees. The United States is ninety-third in the world in terms of equality, given the fact that "there's nothing more unequal than the equal treatment of unequals." Two out of three senators and half of the House of Representatives are millionaires, while one out of six people in the United States live in poverty.[38]

"There are no illegal persons," declared the International Convention on Rights Protection of All Immigrant Workers and the Members of Their Families. That was signed on December 18, 1990, in the UN building in New York. International workers have the right to assistance from their consulates, of being in a room separate from prisoners, of not being deported, of not being deprived of their freedom for a long period of time.

The terms "illegality" and "undocumentedness" were fabricated to take advantage of some sisters and brothers. The idea of "alien" was applied to African slaves in the United States and later extended to Mexicans, Chinese, Japanese, and Filipinos.[39] Slaves were alien to themselves; they were the master's private property. That is why suicide, contraceptive remedies, and abortion were prohibited. It was not a moral issue but an economic matter. For instance, in the mid-nineteenth century, after the United States took from Mexico a portion of its territory equivalent to the size of Argentina, abortion was banned in order to repopulate the country. Slaves were considered property, and still more, they were addressed as animals. By denying their humanity, the slave trade was veiled as perfectly legal.[40] Alongside cattle stood chattel, labor workers without the status of humans.

On the other hand, whites employed by other whites had to pay the transatlantic ticket by serving seven years regardless of being able to pay the debt earlier. White workers enrolled into the institution of "indenture," or literally, to stick the *diente* or tooth into their flesh. One out of three died before the contract expired. Indentured whites who survived were given land at the frontier with Native Americans in order to set territorial boundaries. Nonetheless, many freed whites, instead of fighting Native Americans, ended up marrying them. The original inhabitants were granted souls, but souls that would never come of age, since Native Americans remained "in-fants," meaning in Latin voiceless. Their right to speak or to say their word was taken.

For a century and a half, the USA-Mexico border was open since Mexicans were replacing African agricultural labor. What took place was a circular immigration with no access to US citizenship. According to the Pew Hispanic Center, 2005–2010 featured the "punto muerto," or break-even point where 1.4 million Mexicans entered the United States and the same number simultaneously left the country.

For more than 20 years (1942–1964) around five million Mexicans turned the United States into the most profitable agricultural system in the world. But still Mexicans were treated worse than animals; their clothes, bodies, and faces were directly fumigated with DDT and gasoline. Children broke their backs at an early age in the fields.

The label "illegal alien" emerged once the "Bracero Program" (i.e., the ones reduced to their "brazos" or arms) was discontinued on 1964. Needless to say, capitalistic semantics has associated whites with "the minds," and Mexicans with "the arms."[41] Paul's organicistic[42] ecclesiology runs the risk of being interpreted in terms of the doctrine of the great chain of being of white, European, heterosexual, male, well-to-do supremacy: "Just as each of us has one body with many members, and not all members have the same function, so in Christ, we who are many are one body" (Romans 12:4–5). Still more, since Spaniards interpreted labor as being cursed by God (Genesis 3:19), they gladly granted that burden to the Abyalans and uprooted Africans.

With this background, it is expected for immigrant children to be named retainers, criminals, or prisoners of war.

DEPORTED, RETURNED, EXPELLED, REPATRIATED, EXPATRIATED, BANISHED, ROOTLESS

The semantics of the United States as a nation of immigrants has migrated to the United States as a nation of deportees. As a matter of fact, in February 2018 USCIS (US Citizenship and Immigration Services) deleted its old rhetoric: "We are a nation of immigrants."

Due to powerful migrant activism, the US government is considering an immigration reform, which obviously enhances the amnesty element (read: criminal component). In 1986 three million obtained "forgiveness," and from 1994 to 2000 six more amnesties were granted to Nicaraguans, Guatemalans, Salvadorians, and Haitians as "political refugees." The "terms" of the current immigration reform proposal mean a 13-year winding and expensive road to citizenship where one-third of applicants will be deported. Eligible people will get a temporary status for ten years. The militarization of the border will continue. The massive deportation will keep its pace at least until the presidential reelection of November 2020, since Trump has not abandoned his anti-Abyalan immigration crisis rhetoric, which he created during his political presidential campaign. The lucky ones who arrive at the promised land will have to pay the price by accepting their crime and being considered second-class citizens.

Mitt Romney, ex-candidate for the presidency of the United States, was particularly hostile towards Mexicans and Southern immigration in general. He opposed any kind of amnesty and swore to make the lives of undocumented immigrants so miserable that they would deport themselves. According to jus solis semantics, Romney was technically Mexican since his father George was born in Dublán Colony, from the Galeana district in Chihuahua, Mexico. Furthermore, from the jus sanguinis point of view, his grandfather

Miles was an "illegal alien" in Mexico in the 1870s together with his five wives and children.

Needless to say, Romney's semantics privileged the Ku Klux Klan's narrative "keep America American" with a slight swing, "Keep America America," or in the theology of the cross semantics, of calling things what they are, "keep US WASP (white Anglo-Saxon Protestant)." Founded in 1865 as a reaction to the War of Secession, the KKK killed blacks, homosexuals, Jews, and immigrants under the guise of the cross.

Contrary to Romney's xenophobic political campaign, Barack Obama promised to accomplish an immigration reform. Nonetheless, Obama's short memory broke all the records by becoming the "Deporter in Chief," repatriating up to three million people.

Since Mexico is the point of entry of Southern countries to the United States, the Aztec nation is a country of origin, transit, destiny, and return of thousands of immigrants. But it is also a deporting country; it is a nightmare for Central American transmigrants. [43]

How do you otherwise explain the sudden stop of massive infant immigration to the United States, where some 60,000 unaccompanied children arrived in 2014 alone? Mexico not only deported immigrants in transit but also sealed the border with Guatemala. Especially with the signing of the euphemistic North America Free Trade Agreement of 1994, the Aztec country became the US backyard, turning its back on its long tradition of welcoming the immigrant. [44]

Why is it so hard to apply the refugee status to the thousands of children immigrants to the United States from Latin America? Children are running away from gangs such as the infamous Mara Salvatrucha, which originated in the United States and was exported to Central America. Children are escaping *kaos* or disorder, which originated in June 2009 in the Honduras coup d'état, blessed by Hillary Clinton. [45] Aren't the United States and northern Europe experiencing a boomerang effect by supporting anti-democratic Southern regimes, fraudulent elections, impunity, you name it?

SEMANTICS MATTERS

Let your word be "Yes, Yes" or "No, No"; anything more than this comes from the evil one. (Matthew 5:37)

In Jesus Christ there is no longer Jew or Greek. (Galatians 3:28)

The oldest Christian baptismal formula (Galatians 3:26–28) is unequivocal: it is the end of all dividing walls, being geographical, racial, social, religious, and a long et cetera. This sacrament is a permanent reminder that God created the world (Psalm 24) and the feudal lords, rulers, royalty, bankers, corporations, and puppet states went on to create the borders. The resemanticization performed by the regal ended up monopolizing the right to name reality.

To be sure, a central cause of emigration is the plundering of land. That is why Palestinian liberation theology repudiates the "exodus narrative," which legitimizes the invasion of the Israelites into their Canaanite land more than 3,000 years ago and today. It had to be a Native American theologian who urged us to read the Bible from the perspective of the Canaanites,[46] and I would add, from the experience of the Prodigal Son, the Philistines, the pagans, the infidels, the uncircumcised . . . the losers.

When the Israelites expropriated the Palestinian land they did it under a piety disguise like Exodus 22:21, which speaks about "taking care of the stranger" (i.e., the Palestinian, namely, the native inhabitants). Overnight the intruder Israelites became the owners and the Palestinian owners became the intruders. In 1948, after the deportation of 700,000 Palestinians and the devastation of 400 of their towns, took place the birth of the state of Israel with imported Jews from Russia and Ethiopia.[47] Nonetheless, the liberating news of Jesus is that the Exodus imperialistic speech was replaced by Jesus's beatitude: "The powerless will inherit the land" (Matthew 5:5). Jesus's "land reform" was more in tune with Isaiah's (65:25) prophetic thunder against the wolf or empire and the lion or super-powers: "The wolf and the lamb shall feed together, the lion shall eat straw like the ox; but the serpent, its food shall be dust."

It is not an anachronism to consider the Pentateuch, Joshua, Judges 1, 2 Samuel, and 1 and 2 Kings as "Zionists texts," since they continue to be quoted in order to bless the ongoing plundering of Palestinian land by the Zionist Jews. From that follows that the "Ahab and Naboth" (1 Kings 21) story is the crux of the matter not only for liberation theologies but for grasping global migrations.

King Ahab is the modern Zionist state of Israel, which is stealing the land of Naboth, namely the Palestinian people. Elijah is the theologian of the cross whose yes is yes and no is no, whose speech is euphemism free. Furthermore, Elijah is the prophet who takes the side of the abused Arabs. This liberating interpretation of scripture shows us the method of how "the Bible can be reclaimed for Palestinian Christians."[48]

Only in Mexico the 1994 US, Canada, and Mexico "Free Trade Agreement" has expelled 4.8 million peasants from their lands.[49] Millions of landless Abyayalans were forced to emigrate to the US empire. In their new place, instead of Latino/a immigrants being a threat to the United States, isn't the opposite true? In the United States, 50.7 million Latino/as form a country within a country, which, in itself would be the fourteenth-largest world economy with a purchasing power of over $1 trillion.

God's semantics recognizes no geographical walls, and there are no second-class citizens. Instead, there is a sacramental relation with the other, as the refugee on the Greek island of Patmos pointed out: "After this I looked, and there before me was a great multitude that no one could count, from every nation, tribe, people and language, standing before the throne and before the Lamb" (Revelation 7:9). And the most meaningful: Greeks do not have to become Jews (Acts 15). Jewishness is fine; Samaritanism is also acceptable (Luke 10:25–37). Judaism is all right; the Syrophoenician woman's religion is well recognized.

It is our mission as organic[50] theologians of the cross to join congregations and social organizations to undress the fake anti-immigrant narratives;[51] to maximize our usually weekday idle church facilities to provide legal, psychological, linguistic, and labor advice and services; to offer showers, shelter, and meals alongside lifting the pilgrims' self-value; to accompany irregular immigrants to get their I.D. and warn them about the risks of hanging their country of origin flags, placing identity stickers, having broken taillights, listening to loud music while driving, and wearing shiny clothes while walking; to tell them about their right to remain silent, to not open the door, to film raids, or to apply for asylum to avoid deportation; and to remind them to keep one foot on the current evil system (Galations 1:4) and the other on new ground of the "new wine in new wineskins" (Mark 2:22).

As prophets we have to go from the *puerta* to the portal. In 1517, Luther nailed on the *puerta* (door) of Wittenberg Castle Church his 95 revolutionary theses, which "went viral" thanks to the printing press. Almost five centuries after, Bradley Manning, a 22-year-old USA army intelligence analyst, also appealed to knowledge and consciousness. Being stationed in Iraq, he felt the urgency to leak 750,000 files to the WikiLeaks portal in order to raise awareness about the evils of war.

As an antidote to omnipresent fake news and toxic social nets, Daniel Ellsberg, Gary Web, now Chelsea Manning, Julian Assange, Edward Snowden, and Glenn Greenwald are but a few of the champions of parrhesian semantics. This Greek word composed of *pan* and *rhema* has to do with *parrhesiazesthai*, that is, "the activity of saying everything" or *parrhesiastés*, namely, the one who says everything (Acts 28:31). Granted, the circa 6,000 worldwide mass media are owned by six people; however, we are not orphans of theologians of the cross who speak truth to power to keep the free press and free speech afloat regardless of risking their lives.[52]

In order to transform reality, let's begin from the beginning by calling things by their name and act accordingly in togetherness.

NOTES

1. Theodore G. Tappert and Martin Luther, eds., "Heidelberg Disputation # 21," in *The Book of Concord: The Confessions of the Evangelical Lutheran Church* (Philadelphia: Fortress Press, 1992).

2. Ronald Reagan's expression after bombarding the country of Granada, the motherland of Malcolm X's mother. Francis X. Clines, "It Was a Rescue Mission, Reagan Says," *The New York Times*, November 4, 1983.

3. UPI, "Civil Liberties Union Calls Reagan's Year of the Bible 'Illegal,'" *The New York Times*, November 25, 1983.

4. Amy Goodman and Denis Moynihan, "The Migrant Crisis: Arms That Welcome, Arms That Kill," Truthdig: Expert Reporting, Current News, Provocative Columnists, September 10, 2015, https://www.truthdig.com/articles/the-migrant-crisis-arms-that-welcome-arms-that-kill/.

5. Glenn Kessler, Salvador Rizzo, and Meg Kelly, "President Trump Has Made More than 10,000 False or Misleading Claims," *Washington Post*, accessed May 3, 2019, https://www.washingtonpost.com/politics/2019/04/29/president-trump-has-made-more-than-false-or-misleading-claims/.

6. Charles Hirschman and Elizabeth Mogford, "Immigration and the American Industrial Revolution from 1880 to 1920," *Social Science Research* 38, no. 4 (December 1, 2009): 897–920, https://doi.org/10.1016/j.ssresearch.2009.04.001.

7. Marcela Torres Rezende, "A Alimentação Como Objeto Histórico Complexo: Relações Entre Comidas e Sociedades," *Estudios Históricos* 1, no. 33 (2004): 175–79.

8. Spencer Wells, "Out of Africa," *The Hive*, June 12, 2007, https://www.vanityfair.com/news/2007/07/genographic200707.

9. Newsweek Team, "Study: 15% of West Bank Settlers Are American," *Newsweek*, August 28, 2015, https://www.newsweek.com/israel-settlements-us-americawest-bankpalestine-washingtonisraelmiddle-601001.

10. Adam Garfinkle, *Jewcentricity: Why the Jews Are Praised, Blamed, and Used to Explain Just about Everything* (Hoboken, NJ: John Wiley and Sons, 2009), 265

11. Golda Meir, "Interview with Golda Meir," *The Sunday Times*, June 15, 1969.

12. Aviva Chomsky, *Undocumented: How Immigration Became Illegal* (Boston: Beacon Press, 2014).

13. Carolina Moreno, "Is Speedy Gonzales a Mexican Hero or a Stereotype in Cartoon Form?," HuffPost, April 7, 2016, https://www.huffpost.com/entry/is-speedy-gonzales-a-mexican-hero-or-a-stereotype-in-cartoon-form_n_5706a852e4b0537661890eaa.

14. Eduardo Galeano, *The First Americans*, 2012, https://dotsub.com/view/61cfc39f-6ac7-4879-a1e0-1cb1815d92b0.

15. Eliseo Pérez-Álvarez, "La Milpa from Abya Yala: An Epistemological Rupture in the Context of Oikos, i.e., Economy, Ecology and Ecumenism," in *Life-Enhancing Learning Together* (Nam-gu, Daegu, South Korea: Less Press and Life in Beauty Press, 2016).

16. Iranyela Anai Lopez Valdez, Mutacion de un libro de artista hacia un espacio digital, Mexico: Tesis, ICONO, 2015, 35.

17. David Carrasco, *Religions of Mesoamerica: Cosmovision and Ceremonial Centers*, Religious Traditions of the World (Prospect Heights, IL: Waveland Press, n.d.), accessed April 29, 2019.

18. Pérez-Álvarez, "La Milpa from Abya Yala."

19. Jon Stewart, a quoted in Tracy López, "Modern Day Pilgrims," *Latinaish* (blog), November 24, 2010, https://latinaish.com/2010/11/24/modern-day-pilgrims/.

20. Gregorio Selser, *El Guatemalaza: La Primera Guerra Sucia* (Argentina: Editorial Universitaria, 1961).

21. US Census Bureau Public Information, "U.S. Census Bureau Projections Show a Slower Growing, Older, More Diverse Nation a Half Century from Now," accessed April 29, 2019, https://www.census.gov/newsroom/releases/archives/population/cb12-243.html.

22. National Center for Farmworker Health, Inc., "Child Labor in Agriculture" (National Center for Farmworker Health, Inc., 2018), http://www.ncfh.org/uploads/3/8/6/8/38685499/fs-child_labor.pdf.

23. Brianna Lee, "The Expensive Business of Immigration Detention in the U.S.," *International Business Times*, September 11, 2014, sec. World, https://www.ibtimes.com/expensive-business-immigration-detention-us-1685018.

24. Chomsky, *Undocumented*.

25. Jean Luc Piccard, "Refugiados, Europa e Hipocresia," Taringa!, September 23, 2015, http://localhost:3000/+info/refugiados-europa-e-hipocresia_hllvu.

26. Chomsky, *Undocumented*.

27. Elnora C. Folkmar, ed., *Dictionary of Races and Peoples* (Washington, DC: Government Printing Office, 1911).

28. Roberto M. Dainotto, *Europe (In Theory)* (Durham, NC: Duke University Press, 2007), 2.

29. CNN Wire Staff, "Tennessee Lawmaker Calls Some Illegal Immigrants 'Rats,'" CNN, November 12, 2010, http://www.cnn.com/2010/US/11/12/tennessee.lawmaker.remark/index.html.

30. Jon Greenberg, "Ramos: 40% of Undocumented Immigrants Come by Air," @politifact, September 8, 215AD, https://www.politifact.com/punditfact/statements/2015/sep/08/jorge-ramos/ramos-40-undocumented-immigrants-come-air/.

31. Kim Hjelmgaard, "From 7 to 77: There's Been an Explosion in Building Border Walls since World War II," *USA Today*, May 24, 2018, https://www.usatoday.com/story/news/world/2018/05/24/border-walls-berlin-wall-donald-trump-wall/553250002/.

32. United Nations High Commissioner for Refugees, "Convention and Protocol Relating to the Status of Refugees" (United Nations High Commissioner for Refugees, n.d.), https://www.unhcr.org/protection/basic/3b66c2aa10/convention-protocol-relating-status-refugees.html.

33. One third of USA Nobel Prize winners are foreigners.

34. Xiii Rapporto, "Indice globale fame: Emmi (Cesvi), 'esiste un nesso evidente tra migrazioni forzate e fame' | AgenSIR," AgenSIR—Servizio Informazione Religiosa, October 11, 2018, https://agensir.it/quotidiano/2018/10/11/indice-globale-fame-emmi-cesvi-esiste-un-nesso-evidente-tra-migrazioni-forzate-e-fame/.

35. Hilal Elver, "Why Are There Still So Many Hungry People in the World?," *The Guardian*, February 19, 2015, sec. Global development, https://www.theguardian.com/global-development/2015/feb/19/why-hungry-people-food-poverty-hunger-economics-mdgs.

36. Henry David Thoreau, "Resistance to Civil Government," in *The Norton Anthology of Literature*, ed. Nina Baym, 5th ed. (New York: Norton, 1999), 853.

37. Eliseo Pérez-Álvarez, *El Muro de Tortilla: Migración y Mitos* (Mexico City, Mexico: Comunidad Teológica, 2019).

38. Andrew Katz, "Congress Is Now Mostly a Millionaires' Club," *Time*, January 9, 2014, http://time.com/373/congress-is-now-mostly-a-millionaires-club/.

39. David Bacon, *The Right to Stay Home: How US Policy Drives Mexican Migration* (Boston: Beacon Press, 2013); Ched Myers and Matthew Colwell, *Our God Is Undocumented: Biblical Faith and Immigrant Justice* (Maryknoll, NY: Orbis Books, 2012).

40. Edward Long, *The History of Jamaica: Reflections on Its Situation, Settlements, Inhabitants, Climate, Products, Commerce, Laws, and Government in Three Volumes*, 3 vols. (Montreal: McGill-Queen's University Press, 2003).

41. Tracie McMillan, *The American Way of Eating: Undercover at Walmart, Applebee's, Farm Fields and the Dinner Table*, 1st ed. (New York: Scribner, 2012).

42. The organicistic concept of society preaches that there's an analogy between society and a human biological body (i.e., some people are the mind and others the subaltern). Within the Christological realm we have the Apollinarianism heresy, which states that Jesus was psychologically divine and bodily human. In hegemonic semantics this means that the ruling classes are the divines with no need of repentance at all. See Eliseo Pérez-Álvarez, "In Memory of Me: Hispanic/Latino Christology beyond Borders," in *Teología En Conjunto: A Collaborative Hispanic Protestant Theology*, ed. Loida Martell-Otero and José David Rodríguez (Louisville, KY: Westminster John Knox Press, 1997), 37.

43. Hernández Alejandro, *Amarás a Dios sobre todas las cosas* (México, D.F: Planeta Publishing, 2013).

44. José Maria Murià, *De No Ser Por México* (Mexico City, Mexico: Porrúa, 2019). In the late 1930s Mexico sheltered more than 30,000 political refugees from Spain who were running away from their civil war.

45. Roberto Quesada, *Nunca entres por Miami* (CreateSpace Independent Publishing Platform, 2014).

46. Robert Allen Warrior, "A North American Perspective: Canaanites, Cowboys, and Indians," in *Voices from the Margin: Interpreting the Bible in the Third World*, ed. R. S. Sugirtharajah, 25th anniversary ed. (Maryknoll, NY: Orbis Books, 2016), 289.

47. Mitri Raheb, *Faith in the Face of Empire: The Bible through Palestinian Eyes* (Maryknoll, NY: Orbis Books, 2014), 42.

48. Naim Stifan Ateek, *Justice and Only Justice: A Palestinian Theology of Liberation*, 1st ed. (Maryknoll, NY: Orbis Books, 1989), 86–87, 64–65.

49. Ana de Ita, "Detrás de La Cortina de Nopal: TLCAN y Agricultura," Globalización, July 2, 2017, https://www.globalizacion.ca/detras-de-la-cortina-de-nopal-tlcan-y-agricultura/.

50. Here I'm following Gramsci concept of the organic intellectual, as the scholar who remains connected to the subaltern class. Cf. Antonio Gramsci, *Selections from the Prison Notebooks* (London: The Electric Book Company, 1999), 132.

51. Amanda Marcotte, "Why People Believe Donald Trump's Immigration Lies—And Why It's Time to Fight Back with Truth," *Salon*, July 5, 2018, https://www.salon.com/2018/07/05/publics-false-view-of-immigrants-is-shaped-by-trump-propaganda-time-to-fight-back-with-some-truth/.

52. Eliseo Pérez-Álvarez, "From Luther to Manning: Conscience, Parrhesia and the Press," *The Living Lutheran*, October 2017.

BIBLIOGRAPHY

Alejandro, Hernández. *Amarás a Dios sobre todas las cosas*. México, D.F: Planeta Publishing, 2013.

Ateek, Naim Stifan. *Justice and Only Justice: A Palestinian Theology of Liberation*. 1st ed. Maryknoll, NY: Orbis Books, 1989.

Bacon, David. *The Right to Stay Home: How US Policy Drives Mexican Migration*. Boston: Beacon Press, 2013.

Carrasco, David. *Religions of Mesoamerica: Cosmovision and Ceremonial Centers*. Religious Traditions of the World. Prospect Heights, IL: Waveland Press, n.d. Accessed April 29, 2019.

Chomsky, Aviva. *Undocumented: How Immigration Became Illegal*. Boston: Beacon Press, 2014.

Clines, Francis X. "It Was a Rescue Mission, Reagan Says." *The New York Times*, November 4, 1983.

CNN Wire Staff. "Tennessee Lawmaker Calls Some Illegal Immigrants 'Rats.'" CNN, November 12, 2010. http://www.cnn.com/2010/US/11/12/tennessee.lawmaker.remark/index.html.

Dainotto, Roberto M. *Europe (In Theory)*. Durham, NC: Duke University Press, 2007.

Elver, Hilal. "Why Are There Still So Many Hungry People in the World?" *The Guardian*, February 19, 2015, sec. Global development. https://www.theguardian.com/global-development/2015/feb/19/why-hungry-people-food-poverty-hunger-economics-mdgs.

Folkmar, Elnora C, ed. *Dictionary of Races and Peoples*. Washington, DC: Government Printing Office, 1911.

Galeano, Eduardo. *The First Americans*, 2012. https://dotsub.com/view/61cfc39f-6ac7-4879-a1e0-1cb1815d92b0.

Goodman, Amy, and Denis Moynihan. "The Migrant Crisis: Arms That Welcome, Arms That Kill." Truthdig: Expert Reporting, Current News, Provocative Columnists, September 10, 2015. https://www.truthdig.com/articles/the-migrant-crisis-arms-that-welcome-arms-that-kill/.

Gramsci, Antonio. *Selections from the Prison Notebooks*. London: The Electric Book Company, 1999.

Greenberg, Jon. "Ramos: 40% of Undocumented Immigrants Come by Air." @politifact, September 8, 215AD. https://www.politifact.com/punditfact/statements/2015/sep/08/jorge-ramos/ramos-40-undocumented-immigrants-come-air/.

Hirschman, Charles, and Elizabeth Mogford. "Immigration and the American Industrial Revolution from 1880 to 1920." *Social Science Research* 38, no. 4 (December 1, 2009): 897–920. https://doi.org/10.1016/j.ssresearch.2009.04.001.

Hjelmgaard, Kim. "From 7 to 77: There's Been an Explosion in Building Border Walls since World War II." *USA Today*, May 24, 2018. https://www.usatoday.com/story/news/world/2018/05/24/border-walls-berlin-wall-donald-trump-wall/553250002/.

Ita, Ana de. "Detrás de La Cortina de Nopal: TLCAN y Agricultura." Globalización, July 2, 2017. https://www.globalizacion.ca/detras-de-la-cortina-de-nopal-tlcan-y-agricultura/.

Katz, Andrew. "Congress Is Now Mostly a Millionaires' Club." *Time*, January 9, 2014. http://time.com/373/congress-is-now-mostly-a-millionaires-club/.

Kessler, Glenn, Salvador Rizzo, and Meg Kelly. "President Trump Has Made More than 10,000 False or Misleading Claims." *Washington Post*. Accessed May 3, 2019. https://www.washingtonpost.com/politics/2019/04/29/president-trump-has-made-more-than-false-or-misleading-claims/.

Lee, Brianna. "The Expensive Business of Immigration Detention in the U.S." *International Business Times*, September 11, 2014, sec. World. https://www.ibtimes.com/expensive-business-immigration-detention-us-1685018.

Long, Edward. *The History of Jamaica: Reflections on Its Situation, Settlements, Inhabitants, Climate, Products, Commerce, Laws, and Government in Three Volumes*. 3 vols. Montreal: McGill-Queen's University Press, 2003.

López, Tracy. "Modern Day Pilgrims." *Latinaish* (blog), November 24, 2010. https://latinaish.com/2010/11/24/modern-day-pilgrims/.

Marcotte, Amanda. "Why People Believe Donald Trump's Immigration Lies—And Why It's Time to Fight Back with Truth." *Salon*, July 5, 2018. https://www.salon.com/2018/07/05/publics-false-view-of-immigrants-is-shaped-by-trump-propaganda-time-to-fight-back-with-some-truth/.

McMillan, Tracie. *The American Way of Eating: Undercover at Walmart, Applebee's, Farm Fields and the Dinner Table*. 1st ed. New York: Scribner, 2012.

Meir, Golda. "Interview with Golda Meir." *The Sunday Times*, June 15, 1969.

Moreno, Carolina. "Is Speedy Gonzales a Mexican Hero or a Stereotype in Cartoon Form?" HuffPost, April 7, 2016. https://www.huffpost.com/entry/is-speedy-gonzales-a-mexican-hero-or-a-stereotype-in-cartoon-form_n_5706a852e4b0537661890eaa.

Murià, José Maria. *De No Ser Por México*. Mexico City, Mexico: Porrúa, 2019.

Myers, Ched, and Matthew Colwell. *Our God Is Undocumented: Biblical Faith and Immigrant Justice*. Maryknoll, NY: Orbis Books, 2012.

National Center for Farmworker Health, Inc. "Child Labor in Agriculture." National Center for Farmworker Health, Inc., 2018. http://www.ncfh.org/uploads/3/8/6/8/38685499/fs-child_labor.pdf.

Newsweek Team. "Study: 15% of West Bank Settlers Are American." *Newsweek*, August 28, 2015. https://www.newsweek.com/israel-settlements-us-americawest-bankpalestinewashingtonisraelmiddle-601001.

Pérez-Álvarez, Eliseo. *El Muro de Tortilla: Migración y Mitos*. Mexico City, Mexico: Comunidad Teológica, 2019.

———. "From Luther to Manning: Conscience, Parrhesia and the Press." *The Living Lutheran*, October 2017.

———. "In Memory of Me: Hispanic/Latino Christology beyond Borders." In *Teología En Conjunto. A Collaborative Hispanic Protestant Theology*, edited by Loida Martell-Otero and José David Rodríguez. Louisville, KY: Westminster John Knox Press, 1997.

———. "La Milpa from Abya Yala: An Epistemological Rupture in the Context of Oikos, i.e., Economy, Ecology and Ecumenism." In *Life-Enhancing Learning Together*. Nam-gu, Daegu, South Korea: Less Press and Life in Beauty Press, 2016.

Piccard, Jean Luc. "Refugiados, Europa e Hipocresia." Taringa!, September 23, 2015. http://localhost:3000/+info/refugiados-europa-e-hipocresia_hllvu.

Quesada, Roberto. *Nunca entres por Miami*. CreateSpace Independent Publishing Platform, 2014.

Raheb, Mitri. *Faith in the Face of Empire: The Bible through Palestinian Eyes*. Maryknoll, NY: Orbis Books, 2014.

Rapporto, Xiii. "Indice globale fame: Emmi (Cesvi), 'esiste un nesso evidente tra migrazioni forzate e fame' | AgenSIR." *AgenSIR—Servizio Informazione Religiosa*, October 11, 2018. https://agensir.it/quotidiano/2018/10/11/indice-globale-fame-emmi-cesvi-esiste-un-nesso-evidente-tra-migrazioni-forzate-e-fame/.

Rezende, Marcela Torres. "A Alimentação Como Objeto Histórico Complexo: Relações Entre Comidas e Sociedades." *Estudios Históricos* 1, no. 33 (2004): 175–79.

Selser, Gregorio. *El Guatemalaza: La Primera Guerra Sucia*. Argentina: Editorial Universitaria, 1961.

Tappert, Theodore G., and Martin Luther, eds. "Heidelberg Disputation # 21." In *The Book of Concord: The Confessions of the Evangelical Lutheran Church*. Philadelphia: Fortress Press, 1992.

Thoreau, Henry David. "Resistance to Civil Government." In *The Norton Anthology of Literature*, edited by Nina Baym, 5th ed. New York: Norton, 1999.

United Nations High Commissioner for Refugees. "Convention and Protocol Relating to the Status of Refugees." United Nations High Commissioner for Refugees, n.d. https://www.unhcr.org/protection/basic/3b66c2aa10/convention-protocol-relating-status-refugees.html.

UPI. "Civil Liberties Union Calls Reagan's Year of the Bible 'Illegal.'" *The New York Times*, November 25, 1983.

US Census Bureau Public Information. "U.S. Census Bureau Projections Show a Slower Growing, Older, More Diverse Nation a Half Century from Now." Accessed April 29, 2019. https://www.census.gov/newsroom/releases/archives/population/cb12-243.html.

Warrior, Robert Allen. "A North American Perspective: Canaanites, Cowboys, and Indians." In *Voices from the Margin: Interpreting the Bible in the Third World*, edited by R. S. Sugirtharajah, 25th anniversary ed. Maryknoll, NY: Orbis Books, 2016.

Wells, Spencer. "Out of Africa." *The Hive*, June 12, 2007. https://www.vanityfair.com/news/2007/07/genographic200707.

Chapter Nine

Power of the Powerless?

Theological Reflections on Pilgrimage in the Experience of Roman Catholic Latino/a Migrants in the United States

Gemma Tulud Cruz

FAITH ON THE MOVE

In earlier times, particularly in the West, religions had such clear geographical locations that one could categorically say Europe or the United States was Christian. Contemporary migration, however, has muddled this claim. In the case of the United States, the very title of Diana Eck's book *A New Religious America: How a "Christian Country" Has Become the World's Most Religiously Diverse Nation* points to this blurring of religious boundaries based on geography.[1] Most Asian migrants, for example, do not give up the religions of the East and the subcontinent like Hinduism, Buddhism, and Islam just as many Afro-Caribbean and Afro-Brazilian migrants do not give up Santeria and Candomblé, which are hybrids of African religion and European Christianity. Migrants build their own places of worship, celebrate their own festivals, and conduct the religious service in their own language. In some cases they, or their religious authorities, even import a priest, pastor, or religious leader from their country of origin.

William Portier maintains that human life has a religious dimension such that wherever we find human beings, we usually find a god or gods, religious behavior, and religious faith.[2] Muslims and Christians alone account for more than half of the world's population. This continuing role and power of religion in the lives of human beings live on—perhaps even in more constructive and creative forms—in migration and in the lives of migrants. In what follows, I explore the continuing, constructive, and creative role and power of religion in the lives of Catholic Latino/a migrants in the United States (especially those of Mexican descent) as they are reflected in their traditional and reimagined practice of pilgrimage vis-à-vis the conditions and challenges of the migration experience. Using Roman Catholic theological perspectives, I will then endeavor to interrogate the nature of power in their experience of pilgrimage.

THE PROBLEMATIC CONTEXTS OF
LATINO/A MIGRATION TO THE UNITED STATES

Latino/a migration to North America has a long and complex history. Contrary to the popular Frontier Thesis, it began, even if sparsely, in the early 1500s—a century before England's colonial explorations of the region.[3] Much of the migration afterwards is linked to the United States itself. This is particularly true for Mexicans, given that at least a third of Mexico was taken by the United States after the war in 1848.

To be sure, the economic and sociopolitical woes that beset a number of Latin American countries, most of which have connections to US geo-political and macroeconomic interests, heavily account for waves of Latino/a migration to the United States. The US transformation of the Puerto Rican economy from an agrarian-based system to an industrialized one in the period ranging from the late 1940s to the late 1980s led to significant social dislocations that resulted in the mass migration of Puerto Ricans to the US mainland. The Cuban Revolution in 1959 led to the first mass migration of Cubans to the United States, supported and encouraged by the US government since it opposed the Castro regime during the height of the Cold War. The support meant that Cubans were given automatic residency upon arrival in the United States.

In the case of Central America, a combination of direct political and economic interventions by the United States led to large-scale migrations. These interventions, which often had disastrous results that forced large numbers of people to move, include the US military invasion in Nicaragua in 1894, 1896, and 1910; US occupation of the country from 1912 to 1933; US troops' entry into Honduras in 1903, 1907, 1911, 1912, 1919, and 1924, most of which were in response to internal conflict over electoral outcomes; and the US government's influence in the secession of Panama from Colombia so as to be able to build the Panama Canal largely for US companies, such as the United Fruit Company (now Chiquita Banana). Economic interests also lay at the heart of the US intervention in Guatemala in 1954, which resulted in the establishment of a brutal military dictatorship. The United States also supported a similarly brutal regime in El Salvador, and both interventions led to the development of strong guerrilla movements in both countries. The result was civil war and extreme violence, both of which led to massive social dislocation and the beginning of large-scale Guatemalan and Salvadoran migration to the United States.[4]

There are, of course, internal factors as well. In addition to grinding poverty, gang violence figures heavily in contemporary migration to the United States from El Salvador and Honduras. In the case of Mexico, the Mexican Revolution in 1910 and the explosion of drug-related violence, prompted by the government's assault on drug cartels since 2006, led to waves of migration, too. Nevertheless, it cannot be denied that the legacies of the Bracero Program, which ran from the 1940s to the 1960s,[5] the more recent H2A (or agricultural worker) visa, and the North American Free Trade Agreement (NAFTA), which has displaced and disillusioned small Mexican farmers forcing many to cross unauthorized into the United States to find work, account for the (continuing) migration of a significant number of Mexicans to *el norte*.[6]

Whether authorized or unauthorized, many past and present Latino/a migrants face various challenges and risks, including death, during border crossing, especially for those who cross via the southern border. In 1994, Operation Gatekeeper militarized the westernmost section of the southern border with ten-foot-high steel walls, long sections of secondary and tertiary fences, heat sensors, electronic vision detection devices, Black Hawk helicopters patrolling, and thousands of additional Border Patrol agents.[7] It shifted the crossing points eastward to mountainous and remote desert terrain, exposing migrants to extremes of heat and cold leading to a significant rise in deaths. A similar "prevention through deterrence strategy" was implemented in 1993 by doubling the number of Border Patrol agents stationed along the southwest border, again to push migrants away from major urban areas and out into the desert where they could be more easily apprehended. This led to a dramatic rise in desert deaths, especially in southern Arizona, where migrants have to walk as much as fifty miles in temperatures that can reach 120 degrees in summertime.[8] Mexican authorities estimate there were 5,607 deaths between 1994 and 2008, while the Border Patrol has reported 4,111 deaths in border areas since 1998, not counting those reported first to local authorities.[9]

What is worse, the death-dealing conditions do not end after migrants have crossed the border—Latino/as have become the face of unauthorized (a.k.a. illegal) immigration. The year 1954's "Operation Wetback" was a national effort to crack down on illegal immigration. Those who looked to be of Latin American descent were routinely rounded up and sent to Mexico. Indeed, racism and discrimination have plagued Latino/a communities in various spheres of social life (e.g., in schools such as San Diego's Santana

High School where groups of white students would wear T-shirts reading "White Power" or "Youth Klan Core.")[10] As one migrant notes:

> I have stowed away in baggage compartments of buses and almost suffocated in a boxcar; I almost froze to death in the mountains and baked to death in the deserts; I have gone without food and water for days, and nearly died on various occasions. As difficult as these are, these are not the hardest parts of being a migrant. The worst is when people treat you like you are a dog, like you are the lowest form of life on earth.[11]

Indeed, Latino/a migrants have faced unjust and exclusionary policies and practices.[12] The worst perhaps is when such experiences of discrimination occur, of all places, in churches. Take the case of the following Mexican immigrants who had to ask the bishop for their own church because they were rejected by the members of the local Roman Catholic Church:

> It was really hard work and long days, still we were happy to have our Sundays free. Yet, even then we could not feel at home in the Catholic Church since we were denied pews at Our Lady of Perpetual Help (pseudonym). The Italians would tell us, "all seats are taken." No matter how early we arrived the pews were always reserved for Italians. That is why we asked the Bishop for our own church.[13]

To be sure, religion plays a central, public, and often constructive role in the lives of Latino/as. It can serve as a means of coping and resistance against the problematic conditions of migration in the United States, and it is to that role of religion in the lives of Latino/as, particularly among Latino/a Catholics, that this essay now turns.[14]

PILGRIMAGE AND THE MIGRATION EXPERIENCE AMONG ROMAN CATHOLIC LATINO/AS IN THE UNITED STATES

"Pilgrim," the root word of "pilgrimage," comes from the Latin word *peregrinus*, which means "wanderer" or "stranger." Ian Bradley offers various definitions of pilgrimage: (1) a departure from daily life on a journey in search of spiritual well-being; (2) an individual summons to know God more fully; (3) a spiritual journey to which the pilgrim joyfully responds "yes" to God's invitation; (4) a provisional, transitory state, often taken as a metaphor for the journey of life; and (5) a reminder that all things in this world are temporary and that everything is in motion.[15] A simpler, more traditional definition would be that it is a journey to some sacred place or shrine undertaken as an act of devotion. This essay subscribes to Richard Scriven's broader conceptualization of pilgrimage based on what he posits as the common features of existing definitions of the term. For Scriven, it is both appropriate and useful to consider pilgrimage as the combination of four interrelated characteristics: movement, place, belief, and transformation.[16] In this section I attend to the literal and figurative, or the more traditional and more modern, expressions of pilgrimage as reflected in the experience of Catholic Latino/a migrants in the United States (particularly those of Mexican descent) in connection with the problematic contexts of their migration experience.

THE MIGRATION EXPERIENCE AS PILGRIMAGE

As a form of meaningful movement, the very act and experience of migration on the part of migrants in search of a better life could be considered a pilgrimage. For many migrants, crossing the border means leaving behind much of what gives meaning, value, and cohesion to their lives. Indeed, even when they do not suffer or die in their perilous physical journeys, they undergo some form of death culturally, psychologically, socially, and emotionally. They suffer an agonizing movement from belonging to nonbelonging, from relational connectedness to family separation, from being to nonbeing, from life to the threat of death, literally and figuratively, which they endure and survive with the help of their religious faith.

What is striking is that migrants still decide to take the journey despite the possible difficulties and dangers that await them. In the words of Julio, "We are aware of the dangers, but our need is greater. There's always the risk of dying in the desert but the desire to survive and keep going is even more important. It's a gamble."[17] To be sure, the journey that migrants undertake is more than a trip. It is not a vacation nor a sojourn. As a people who brave unforgiving deserts and merciless seas and then struggle against death-dealing conditions in destination countries in their unwavering search for "greener pastures" or their own "promised land," migrants experience mobility as a spiritual journey, as a pilgrimage.

First and foremost, the world, for most Latino/a migrants, is a religious universe; God's grace permeates the earth and meets us constantly in *lo cotidiano* (daily life), be it in their relationships, in the created world, or in the events of their daily lives. This deep religious faith is a wellspring of hope and courage that they draw from well before the journey begins.[18] As a migrant reveals, "When we started the journey the first thing we did was make the sign of the cross."[19] For Latino/a migrants, particularly those moving to the United States from Mexico through the desert, migration is a physical journey through a spiritual landscape marked with deep faith and populated, as often as not, with angels, demons, and a crowd of folk saints, and motivated by a sense of divine purpose.[20] Like the desert fathers and mothers in ancient Christianity, migrants discover that the desert is a place that often strips them of illusions about life, a place for purification that helps them realize central truths about who they are before God.[21] As Cesar reminisces,

> When I was in the desert I thought about Jesus' temptation. It was like God was testing me in some way. . . . For me the temptation was not to trust God, to give up, to admit defeat, to allow myself to die in the desert. But I couldn't do it. . . . I felt God was calling me to fight, to keep going, to suffer for my family. I did not want to let myself be conquered by death least of all.[22]

Christian spiritual commentators speak of a model of Christian life as ascent toward God. In the case of Cesar and the hundreds of undocumented Latino/a migrants who have crossed and continue to cross into the United States through the desert, the quest for well-being and justice ironically entails a further descent into the valley of death where they are forced to surrender everything. They literally put their lives in the hands of God, whom they believe will uphold, guide, and protect them even as evil threatens to crush them.

These difficult, meaningful, and, to a certain extent, transforming journeys that undocumented migrants undertake remind us of the character of Christian life as a journey, as a constant coming and going, as a continuous departure and arrival, and of Christian life as a process. A pilgrimage unites the seeker and the traveler, and, to the extent that these journeys force migrants to struggle to survive and, to a certain extent, find a better life in their destination countries their journeys are a pilgrimage in the wilderness. They are like Israel in the wilderness, embarking on a journey believing that the promised land lay ahead. As Chad Rimmer contends, "In the wilderness, nations are recreated, people are renamed, sacrifices are made, callings are discerned, spiritual acumen is honed, God's grace is revealed, and God's people are renewed."[23] This perspective challenges us to rediscover the God of revelation as a God of the journey, of going out to another place as Abraham, Jesus, Paul, and countless Christian missionaries over the ages did.

THE *POSADA* AND VIA CRUCIS

Away from their home country and in search of company, intimacy, identity, and better living conditions, Catholic Latino/a migrants in the United States find in religion a formidable anchor for their lives. Consequently, religious acts, rituals, symbols, and institutions permeate and inform many aspects of their lives. In fact, in their new home country, religious affiliation, religious assembly, and religious practices constitute some of the most powerful means available to them in living out their identity and searching for communal acceptance and social integration. One of the most vivid expressions of the vital role religion plays in their lives is in the practice of religious rituals in response to the problematic contexts of their migration experience, all of which could be considered pilgrimage.

To be sure, migrants also go on pilgrimage in the more traditional sense of the term. Oftentimes, this involves a visit to a shrine, basilica, or place associated with Jesus, Mary, or a saint to whom the migrant or migrant community has a special devotion. It is not uncommon among Cuban American Catholics, for example, to travel to Miami to visit the Shrine of Our Lady of Charity. Moreover, such pilgrimages are not limited to sacred sites in the United States; migrants sometimes travel all the way back to their country of origin to go on pilgrimage (e.g., to the Basilica of Our Lady of Guadalupe in Mexico City).[24] This is also seen in the devotion of many Mexican Catholics, both in the United States and Mexico, to Saint Toribio Romo, who is considered as the patron saint of undocumented migrants. In fact, hundreds of testimonies are written out and displayed in Santa Ana de Guadalupe's hilltop chapel in Jalisco, Mexico, which Toribio Romo helped design and build. Toribio Romo was not well known outside of the Jalisco highlands. All that has changed since stories of his benevolent ghost began to appear sometime in the 1970s.[25]

Catholic Latino/a migrants also utilize other forms of popular piety, which fit Scriven's broader description of pilgrimage because they involve meaningful journeys. That is, they entail movement from one place to another in a way that is rooted in faith and oriented toward a quest for social justice and transformation. Let us take a look at a couple of these practices.

The first is the Via Crucis or Way of the Cross. In "The Real Way of Praying: The *Via Crucis*, Mexicano Sacred Space, and the Architecture of Domination," Karen Mary Davalos argues that the practice of the Via Crucis by Mexican-Americans in the Pilsen and Little Village neighborhoods in Chicago is a witness to "a theology that is also a politically grounded concept of culture" in the way that it is engaged within a space and architecture of domination experienced by these neighborhoods.[26] Indeed, Via Crucis, as understood and practiced by these neighborhoods, is, in the words of a young Mexican-American, "a re-enactment of a historical event, but it is not a play." Rather, it is a "relieving (of) that moment which is actually happening now."[27] In short, this form of popular piety is also employed as a reflection on and critique of the suffering of these neighborhoods. Consequently, it becomes not simply the Way of the Cross but the *Living* Way of the Cross. My husband and I witnessed a Via Crucis in the Pilsen neighborhood when we were living in Chicago, and I could not help but reflect on the stark contrast when, on our way home riding the train, we were surrounded with more of the spirit of Easter Sunday than Good Friday on the other (affluent) side of the city, as Chicago Cubs fans, complete with all the paraphernalia of a Cubs devotee (no pun intended), boarded the train in animated merriment.

Wayne Ashley describes a similar approach to this Good Friday practice in a primarily Puerto Rican parish in "The Stations of the Cross: Christ, Politics and Processions on New York City's Lower East Side."[28] In what was both a public prayer and critique, participants enact each of the stations in strategically chosen problem areas within the parish: a controversial health clinic, a deteriorating public school, a street corner where drugs are sold, a luxury condominium, and a park associated with danger and vice. By traversing through the neighborhood's volatile areas, participants created two overlapping narratives: one about Christ's suffering, the other about the topography of the East Village and its residents' suffering. What we see here is a cultural practice (outdoor processions are common in Puerto Rico) and traditional text and performance (Stations of the Cross) repositioned and inserted into a new and political discourse such that ongoing social debates and conflicts surrounding housing, welfare, and morality are assimilated into the Christian narrative. Last but not least, there is the Via Crucis del Migrante (Way of the Cross of the Migrant), which human rights and religious activists have organized and staged at the border to denounce the senseless death of so many migrants.[29]

The second form of popular piety employed in a politically creative way by Catholic Latino/a migrants in the United States is the *posada*. *Posada,* which means "inn" or "shelter" in Spanish, is a re-enactment of Mary and Joseph's journey to Bethlehem and their search for an inn or a place to stay. It is a widely celebrated Christmas tradition throughout Latin America, which originated in colonial Mexico. This community tradition takes place on each of the nine nights leading up to Christmas. Today, it continues to be a cherished cultural and religious practice among Mexicans, including those who migrate(d) to the United States. In the United States, however, *posadas* are not confined to Mexican-Americans or migrants of Mexican descent. They are also not limited to literal observances of the ritual, as they carry socio-political and ethical undertones in relation to justice for, as well as solidarity with, people on the move.

One popular, well-known appropriation of this religious practice to dramatize social justice issues associated with immigration policies and practices is the La Posada Sin Fronteras (Posada without Borders). In fact, the idea came from the late Roberto Martinez, who is legendary for his documentation of hundreds of Border Patrol abuses, as a way of communicating the stories of abuses and recontextualizing the bitter drama of immigrant homelessness. Roberto's idea was reimagined by church and immigrant rights activist from Tijuana (Mexico side) and San Diego (US side). This powerful public liturgy has continued each year since an inaugural experiment in 1994. Ched Myers describes and reflects on its character as a "liturgy of resistance" in "Gospel Nativities vs. Anti-Immigrant Nativism":

Groups gather on both sides of the wall, watched carefully by the Border Patrol and, more recently, by anti-immigrant counter-protestors. The US side recites the role of the innkeeper in the litany, the Mexican side that of the Holy Family—and the story comes uncomfortably alive right at the heart of the border war zone. . . . We sing the traditional Posadas litany back and forth across the wall hearing but not seeing one another. To symbolize our solidarity, green ribbons are passed through small holes in the fence. . . . When the liturgy finishes, doves are released and fly off unrestrained by the metal fence, a small sign of hope amidst this free fire zone in the war against the poor, the New Global Economic Order's Berlin Wall.[30]

Myers notes that "at the border fence it becomes a sort of community theatre in real political space that takes on an almost unbearable poignancy, bearing witness to immigrant suffering."[31] The Diocese of San Diego has been doing this for more than twenty years with people from the United States gathering at San Diego's Border Field State Park on one side and people from Mexico gathering at Faro de Playas in Tijuana, leaving only the border wall between them. In 2016, when the migrant crisis in Europe was very much on the minds and hearts of people, the words of San Diego County's Roman Catholic archbishop Robert McElroy shed light on the political character of the observance of this Christmas ritual: "The Gospel tells us that shortly after his birth, Jesus, Mary and Joseph had to flee to Egypt. Thus, they became refugees. . . . [T]hey became illegal emigrants. . . . We are all called to solidarity with those who are undocumented, those who are immigrants, those who are refugees."[32]

A similar reenactment of the *posada* was done in Chicago when about 250 Mexican-American Catholics and people with other religious affiliation used the *posada* to demonstrate the need to change the immigration system. Instead of travelling from house to house, like Mary and Joseph did in their search for an inn, the group traversed the city, stopping at the federal Metropolitan Correction Center, DePaul University, and the Federal Plaza before ending up in St. Peter's Roman Catholic Church. Prayers and dialogues at each stop were tailored to the nature of the public places where they stopped.[33]

LIBERATING RELIGION: THEOLOGICAL PERSPECTIVES ON CATHOLIC LATINO/A MIGRANTS' EXPERIENCE OF PILGRIMAGE

Pilgrimage is a form of popular religion or popular piety in the Roman Catholic tradition.[34] But popular piety has been, at best, ignored and, at worst, dismissed and discouraged (rightfully so in some cases) by social and religious elites due to its associations with the unlettered masses, magic, superstition, and religious ignorance that had somehow not been "Christian-ized."[35] Ernest Henau thinks that this is due to the fact that as a religion that is (1) lived and experienced, (2) not expressed in formulae, and (3) transmitted by means of other forms, popular religiosity leads to insights and intuitions that cannot be adequately contained within the framework of formulated logic. It can, therefore, be easily dismissed as subjective and emotive and therefore downplayed in a mainstream theology concerned with rationality.[36]

The Second Vatican Council, the irruption of the poor in history, and the rise of liberationist theologies helped shift perspectives on popular piety from an elitist to a more pastoral perspective. The document from the plenary assembly in Puebla, Mexico, of the Latin American Catholic Bishops' Conference (CELAM) in 1979 contains some of the most eloquent articulation of this shift in perspectives with regard to popular piety. The Puebla document, for example, contends that popular religion "can give coherence and a sense of direction to life; it is a central factor in creating and maintaining individual and collective identity and could even be an expression of discipleship."[37] It may be regarded, in other words, as a protest against oppression. It could serve as a dissent against the official (read: dominant or institutional) culture and religion and, at the same time, contribute to the symbolic resolution of real-life contradictions.[38] Through it, unsatisfied longings of hope find expression, making it both a means of comfort and a form of protest.

As the poor move across borders, they bring with them their popular religious practices and creatively use those practices as "weapons" to deal with the death-dealing conditions of their migration. This enables the assertion of their identity in their destination country, often through popular religious practices that are being increasingly reimagined, reappropriated, and revalued.[39] Pope Francis himself talks about popular piety in *Evangelii Gaudium* as *locus theologicus*, a source of evangelization and missionary power that one must not underestimate or stifle.[40]

The emphasis and reappropriation of the story of Our Lady of Guadalupe by the Latino/a community in the United States, focusing on the Virgin's "empowerment" of Juan Diego, is an example of this reappropriation and revaluing by engaging the story to serve as a tool for resistance and empowerment. Ana Maria Bidegain points this out in the way the late Virgilio Elizondo and other theologians reframe the story around defense of the rights and dignity of immigrants. Bidegain also notes how the figure of the Virgin of Guadalupe has been strongly bound up with the Latin social movement in the United States since the mobilizations by Cesar Chavez in 1960s in defense of the dignity of immigrant workers.[41]

Indeed, for many Catholic Latino/a theologians in the United States, popular piety denotes "much more than a series of religious practices, symbols, narratives, devotions" but also "a particular worldview, an epistemological framework that infuses and defines every aspect of the community's life" such that it becomes not only a particular way of being "religious" but also a particular way of living life.[42] Popular piety, despite its problematic tendencies, answers this need not only because it serves as support of identity but also because it has liberating potential.[43] As the Puebla document maintains, popular religion can be ambivalent precisely because it is subject to sociohistorical conditions. Moreover, because it is tied up with individual and collective identity, it can also be the cause of the most profound alienation and oppression. It can hold people in the grip of irreversible regression and can have pathological and destructive effects. As such, Christian theology must grapple with it by judging it on its own merits. It must expose and point out the various mechanisms of oppression in church and society that have penetrated it and critically distinguish the various ways of dealing with them so that its liberating potential can be surfaced.[44]

Orlando Espin explicates on this less elitist and more pastoral approach to popular piety in *The Faith of the People: Theological Reflections on Popular Catholicism*. Using primarily the experience of Latino/a Catholics in the United States, Espin contends that popular piety mainly operates on a worldview that the divine, who is encountered in and through the symbols of popular religion, intervenes daily in a world marred by the conflict between good and evil. Espin argues that popular piety could be regarded as an epistemology of suffering[45] insofar as it is the religion of those treated as subaltern by both society and the church. For instance, "Latino popular Catholicism," Espin argues, is "an effort by the subaltern [Latino/as] to explain, justify, and somehow control a social reality that appears too dangerous to confront in terms of and through means other than the mainly symbolic."[46] Mexican-American theologians themselves maintain that the rites and practices that comprise their people's symbolic world not only reinforce their ethnic identity but also function "as a defense and protest against the demands of the dominant culture."[47] This living faith, according to Elizondo, is an expression and/or means of resistance and survival and, for Espin, a source for the development of doctrine.[48]

Like the Israelites' experience in the wilderness, the pilgrim represents a type of mobility long venerated in the Christian tradition.[49] Latino/a migrants' experience somehow continues this tradition since they have a profound experience of God as a pilgrim community. As they, especially the undocumented, move from one reality to another, so does their God, who is not established in a solid temple but shares in their provisional life. God walks alongside them and becomes a pilgrim on the roads of this uneven world, nurturing and blessing them by the power of renewed relationships and community within the household of life.[50] In doing so, these migrants reveal "the underlying reality of the church as a pilgrim people" as they help the people of God view reality and migration itself "not only as a problem but also as grace that . . . transforms the church when its members embrace their poverty as wayfarers in a passing world."[51] They remind all of us of the eschatological destiny of all humanity.

CONCLUSION

The theological reflections on Catholic Latino/a migrants' experience of pilgrimage in this essay point to the reality and importance of power, particularly the power of the powerless. In traditional Christian theology, power often has to do with the majority, with those who wield authority and with those who dictate the course of history. In short, power is usually about domination or those who bring about oppression. Deriving from the Latin word *potere*, which means "to be able," however, power must not be viewed solely as the ability to dominate. It is also present in the ability to resist, and I mean this not in the binary (either/or) way but in an integrated (both/and) manner. Joanne Sharp and coauthors describe this as the domination/resistance couplet. They contend that power operates in "myriad entanglements" and emphasize that "wound up in these entanglements are countless processes of domination and resistance which are always implicated in, and mutually constitutive of one another."[52]

Power, as a dynamic interplay between resistance and domination and as played out in spatial conditions, endlessly circulates. Power, then, is exercised or practiced not only by the powerful through domination, but also by the powerless through resistance. The notion that the poor and oppressed are "without power" is a myth. Christian theology, especially in the past, is guilty of peddling this myth in its presentations of the poor, including migrants, as passive victims, in its focus on their suffering and oppression, and in its portrayal of power as domination. Such attitudes render acts of resistance futile or insignificant.[53] This should be critiqued not only because it is not fully representative of reality, but also because it can be a self-serving agenda of the dominant elite. This kind of rhetoric can be utilized by those who dominate to keep the poor and oppressed in their place.

Furthermore, power, as exercised by Catholic Latino/a migrants in their sociopolitical use of pilgrimage and the *posada* and Via Crucis, is not necessarily the lame, passive, and weak power of defenselessness or powerlessness. It is, rather, an active, liberative, and transformative power. Theology has to take this into account if it is to give justice not just to the full meaning of the term "power" but also to the struggle of the marginal(ized). A meaningful engagement of power, in other words, must recognize power as omnipresent and not simply exercised occasionally by a few, productive and not simply repressive or destructive, private and not just public, consistent with human freedom, and related to justice, love, and ethics.

At the same time, and like popular piety, resistance should be neither trivialized nor romanticized. This means that while we try to critique and destabilize overemphasis on power as domination, or the power that comes from the center, we must not fall into the trap of the other side by resorting to simplistic spatial imagery of the center and margins. It is important, indeed, that we do not resort to a "romance of the margins" or a "romance of the resisters," since this could result in sidestepping, if not escaping from, the responsibilities of power. Power has manifold possibilities. At the same time, it has inescapable responsibilities. Hence, while we talk about power by giving a preferential option for the margins (powerless) and shining a spotlight on their own exercise of power, such an endeavor must not take us away from making the center (powerful) accountable.

Ultimately, the experience of pilgrimage of Catholic Latino/a migrants in the United States teaches us of theology as *via theologica*—theology as always "on the way." Divine wisdom dwells not just in texts or among leaders and institutions; it is found among the people, among the inarticulate, and in their creative struggles to survive and transform relations of domination. Theology, in this way, becomes more than just "faith seeking understanding" but "faith seeking *empowering* understanding."

NOTES

1. Diana L. Eck, *A New Religious America: How a "Christian Country" Has Now Become the World's Most Religiously Diverse Nation* (San Francisco: HarperOne, 2002).

2. William L Portier, ed., *Tradition and Incarnation* (New York: Paulist Press, 1993), 9.

3. John Tutino, *Mexico and the Mexicans in the Making of the United States* (Austin: University of Texas Press, 2012), 1–35.

4. Lisa Garcia Bedolla, "Latino Migration and U.S. Foreign Policy," Text, Center for Latin American Studies (CLAS), July 16, 2014, https://clas.berkeley.edu/research/immigration-latino-migration-and-us-foreign-policy.

5. Justin Akers Chacón and Mike Davis, *No One Is Illegal: Fighting Violence and State Repression on the U.S.-Mexico Border* (Chicago: Haymarket Books, 2006), 139–47 considers the Bracero Program, a guest worker program, as "a twentieth-century caste system."

6. David Bacon, *Illegal People: How Globalization Creates Migration and Criminalizes Immigrants* (Boston: Beacon Press, 2009), 23–26.

7. Akers Chacón and Davis, *No One Is Illegal*, 204.

8. Robin Hoover, "The Story of Humane Borders," in *A Promised Land, a Perilous Journey: Theological Perspectives on Migration*, ed. Daniel G. Groody and Gioacchino Campese, 1st ed. (Notre Dame, IN: University of Notre Dame Press, 2008), 160–61.

9. The number would be even higher if one takes into account the claim of human rights groups that for every dead migrant that has been found at least ten others are missing in the desert. See Spencer S. Hsu, "Border Deaths Are Increasing," September 30, 2009, http://www.washingtonpost.com/wp-dyn/content/article/2009/09/29/AR2009092903212.html.

10. Matthew Colwell, "Defending Human Rights in the Borderlands: Roberto Martinez," in *Our God Is Undocumented: Biblical Faith and Immigrant Justice*, ed. Ched Myers and Matthew Colwell (Maryknoll, NY: Orbis Books, 2012), 181–82.

11. Daniel G. Groody, "Passing Over: Migration as Conversion," *International Review of Mission* 104, no. 1 (April 2015): 49.

12. Matthew Garcia, *From the Jaws of Victory: The Triumph and Tragedy of Cesar Chavez and the Farm Worker Movement*, 1st ed. (Berkeley: University of California Press, 2014).

13. Kathleen Sullivan, "St. Mary's Catholic Church: Celebrating Domestic Religion," in *Religion and the New Immigrants: Continuities and Adaptations in Immigrant Congregations*, ed. Janet Saltman Chafetz and Helen Rose Ebaugh (Walnut Creek, CA: AltaMira Press, 2000), 145.

14. Allan Figuerora Deck SJ, "Latino Migrations and the Transformation of Religion in the United States: Framing the Question," in *Christianities in Migration: The Global Perspective*, ed. Peter C. Phan and Elaine Padilla, 1st ed. (Houndmills, UK, and New York: Palgrave Macmillan, 2015), 268.

15. Ian Bradley, *Pilgrimage: A Spiritual and Cultural Journey*, 1st ed. (Oxford: Lion Books, 2010).

16. Richard Scriven, "Geographies of Pilgrimage: Meaningful Movements and Embodied Mobilities," *Geography Compass* 8, no. 4 (April 2014): 251–52.

17. Daniel G. Groody, *Border of Death, Valley of Life: An Immigrant Journey of Heart and Spirit* (Lanham MD: Rowman & Littlefield Publishers, 2007), 23–24.

18. Jacqueline Maria Hagan, "Faith for the Journey: Religion as a Resource for Migrants," in *A Promised Land, a Perilous Journey: Theological Perspectives on Migration*, ed. Daniel G. Groody and Gioacchino Campese (Notre Dame, IN: University of Notre Dame Press, 2008), 3–19.

19. Daniel G. Groody, "Jesus and the Undocumented Immigrant: A Spiritual Geography of a Crucified People," *Theological Studies* 70, no. 2 (June 2009): 303.

20. Ben Daniel, *Neighbor: Christian Encounters with "Illegal" Immigration* (Louisville, KY: Westminster John Knox Press, 2010), 4.

21. Alex Nava, "God in the Desert: Searching for the Divine in the Midst of Death," in *A Promised Land, a Perilous Journey: Theological Perspectives on Migration*, ed. Daniel G. Groody and Gioacchino Campese (Notre Dame, IN: University of Notre Dame Press, 2008), 65–67.

22. Groody, "Jesus and the Undocumented Immigrant," 305.

23. Chad M. Rimmer, "Prospects for Ecumenism in the 21st Century: Towards an Ecumenical Theology of the Wilderness," *The Ecumenical Review* 60, no. 3 (July 2008): 262.

24. Jeanette Rodriguez, "Devotion to Our Lady of Guadalupe Among Mexican-Americans," in *Many Faces, One Church: Cultural Diversity and the American Catholic Experience*, Peter C. Phan and Diana Hayes, eds. (Lanham, MD: Rowman & Littlefield Publishers, 2004), 83–97. The devotion to Our Lady of Guadalupe has also increasingly become a pan-ethnic phenomenon among Catholic Latino/a migrants. See Ana Maria Bidegain, "Living a Trans-National Spirituality: Latin American Catholic Families in Miami," in *Migration in a Global World*, ed. Solange Lefebvre and Luis Carlos Susin (London: SCM Press, 2008), 103–4.

25. See Daniel, *Neighbor*, 5, for the story on Saint Romo, which many Mexican migrants who cross the desert into the US recount over and over again.

26. Karen Mary Davalos, "The Real Way of Praying: The Via Crucis, Mexicano Sacred Space, and the Architecture of Domination," in *Horizons of the Sacred: Mexican Traditions in U.S. Catholicism*, ed. Timothy Matovina and Gary Riebe-Estrella (Ithaca, NY: Cornell University Press, 2002), 42.

27. "That moment" here refers to suffering. Davalos, 41.

28. This practice, as studied by Ashley in 1989–1990, emerged months after the 1988 anti-gentrification protest in the area. See Wayne Ashley, "The Stations of the Cross: Christ, Politics and Processions on New York City's Lower East Side," in *Gods of the City: Religion and the American Urban Landscape*, ed. Robert A. Orsi (Bloomington: Indiana University Press, 1999), 341–42.

29. Gioacchino Campese cites this ritual and the El Día de los Muertos (All Souls Day) as well as Posada sin Fronteras (Posada without Borders) in Gioacchino Campese, "¿Cuantos Mas?: The Crucified Peoples at the U.S. Mexico Border," in *A Promised Land, a Perilous Journey: Theological Perspectives on Migration*, ed. Daniel G. Groody and Gioacchino Campese (Notre Dame, IN: University of Notre Dame Press, 2008), 272.

30. Chad Myers, "Gospel Nativities vs Anti-Immigrant Nativism," in *Our God Is Undocumented: Biblical Faith and Immigrant Justice*, ed. Ched Myers and Matthew Colwell (Maryknoll, NY: Orbis Books, 2012), 171–73.

31. Myers, 173.

32. Bradley J. Fikes, "'Posada without Borders' Gets More Meaning with Refugee Crisis," *San Diego Union-Tribune*, December 11, 2016, https://www.sandiegouniontribune.com/news/religion/sd-me-posada-border-20161210–story.html.

33. At DePaul University, for example, a young participant spoke about being told to study hard only to find out he cannot attend college because no government financial aid can go to undocumented students. See Michelle Martin, "'Posada' Draws Attention to Immigration Reform," National Catholic Reporter, December 19, 2011, https://www.ncronline.org/news/posada-draws-attention-immigration-reform.

34. Popular piety is the quest for simpler, more direct, and more profitable relationships with the divine. It usually comes in three forms: (1) devotions to Christ, Mary, and the saints, (2) rites related to the liturgical year (e.g., *posada* and Way of the Cross), and (3) institutions and religious objects that are often connected with the first two forms (e.g., rosary, miraculous medal, or the statue of the saint). See Luis Maldonado, "Popular Religion: Its Dimensions, Levels and Types," in *Popular Religion*, ed. Norbert Greinacher and Norbert Mette (London: T & T Clark, 1986), 4.

35. Thomas Tweed, "Identity and Authority at a Cuban Shrine in Miami: Santería, Catholicism, and Struggles for Religious Identity," *Journal of Hispanic/Latino Theology* 4, no. 1 (1995): 27–48.

36. Ernest Henau, "Popular Religiosity and Christian Faith," in *Popular Religion*, ed. Norbert Greinacher and Norbert Mette (London: T & T Clark, 1986), 79.

37. Puebla 450 quoted in Norbert Mette and Norbert Greinacher, "Editorial," in *Popular Religion*, ed. Norbert Greinacher and Norbert Mette (London: T & T Clark, 1986), ix.

38. Cristian Parker writes on how popular religion is the religion of the oppressed and a form of symbolic protest. See Christian Parker, "Popular Religion and Protest against Oppression: The Chilean Example," in *Popular Religion*, ed. Norbert Greinacher and Norbert Mette (London: T & T Clark, 1986), 28–35.

39. Michael Engh SJ, "Companion to Immigrants: Devotion to Our Lady of Guadalupe among Mexicans in the Los Angeles Area, 1900–1940," *Journal of Hispanic/Latino Theology* 5, no. 1 (1997): 37–47.

40. Pope Francis, "Evangelii Gaudium: Apostolic Exhortation on the Proclamation of the Gospel in Today's World," Apostolic Exhortation, November 24, 2013, https://w2.vatican.va/content/francesco/en/apost_exhortations/documents/papa-francesco_esortazione-ap_20131124_evangelii-gaudium.html.

41. Bidegain, "Living a Trans-National Spirituality," 103–4; Groody, *Border of Death, Valley of Life*, 124–29.

42. Roberto Goizueta, "Reflecting on America as a Single Entity: Catholicism and U.S. Latinos," in *Many Faces, One Church: Cultural Diversity and the American Catholic Experience*, Peter C. Phan and Diana Hayes, eds. (Lanham, MD: Sheed and Ward, 2004), 73.

43. Virgilio Elizondo, "Popular Religion as Support of Identity Based on the Mexican-American Experience in the U.S.A.," in *Spirituality of the Third World: A Cry for Life: Papers and Reflections from the Third General Assembly of the Ecumenical Association of Third World*, ed. K. C. Abraham and Bernadette Mbuy-Beya, 1st ed. (Maryknoll, NY: Orbis Books, 1994), 55–63.

44. Puebla 450 as cited in Mette and Greinacher, "Editorial," ix–x.

45. For a more focused treatment of popular religion in relation to suffering see Orlando Espin, "Popular Religion as an Epistemology (of Suffering)," *Journal of Hispanic/Latino Theology* 2, no. 2 (1994): 55–78.

46. Orlando Espin, *The Faith of the People: Theological Reflections on Popular Catholicism* (Maryknoll, NY: Orbis Books, 1997). Espin acknowledges its problematic tendencies by engaging it from a perspective of alienation and hope.

47. Ricardo Ramirez, "Liturgy from the Mexican-American Perspective," *Worship* 51 (July 1977): 296.

48. Virgilio P. Elizondo, "Living Faith: Resistance and Survival," in *Mestizo Worship: A Pastoral Approach to Liturgical Ministry*, ed. Timothy M. Matovina and Virgilio P. Elizondo (Collegeville, MN: Liturgical Press, 1998), 5–21; Orlando Espin, "Mexican Religious Practices, Popular Catholicism and the Development of Doctrine," in *Horizons of the Sacred: Mexican Traditions in U.S. Catholicism* (Ithaca, NY: Cornell University Press, 2002), 139–52.

49. William T. Cavanaugh, *Migrations of the Holy: God, State, and the Political Meaning of the Church* (Eerdmans, 1809), 69–87.

50. Rev. Marga Janete Ströher, "People Are Made to Shine—Not To Suffer," in *The Prophetic Mission of Churches in Response to Forced Displacement of People: A Global Ecumenical Consultation, Addis Ababa, Ethiopia, 6–11 November 1995*, ed. World Council of Churches (Amsterdam: World Council of Churches, 1996), 50.

51. Silvano Tomasi, "The Prophetic Mission of the Churches," in *The Prophetic Mission of Churches in Response to Forced Displacement of People: A Global Ecumenical Consultation, Addis Ababa, Ethiopia, 6–11 November 1995*, ed. World Council of Churches (Amsterdam: World Council of Churches, 1996), 40. For examples on how migrants transform the church see Brett C. Hoover, *The Shared Parish: Latinos, Anglos, and the Future of U.S. Catholicism* (New York: NYU Press, 2014); Gemma Tulud Cruz, "A New Way of Being Christian: The Contribution of Migrants to the Church," in *Contemporary Issues of Migration and Theology*, ed. E. Padilla and P. Phan, 1st ed. (New York: Palgrave Macmillan, 2013), 97–101.

52. Joanne P. Sharp, Paul Routledge, Chris Philo, and Ronan Paddison, "Entanglements of Power: Geographies of Domination/Resistance," in *Entanglements of Power: Geographies of Domination/Resistance*, ed. Joanne P. Sharp, Paul Routledge, Chris Philo, and Ronan Paddison, 1st ed. (London and New York: Routledge, 2000), 1. Walter Wink, *Engaging the Powers: Discernment and Resistance in a World of Domination*, reprint ed. (Minneapolis, MN: Fortress Press, 1992), also discusses how power is not just about domination or oppression but also about how it may be actually engaged and resisted.

53. Kyle A. Pasewark, *A Theology of Power: Being beyond Domination* (Minneapolis, MN: Fortress Press, 1993), 2.

BIBLIOGRAPHY

Akers Chacón, Justin, and Mike Davis. *No One Is Illegal: Fighting Violence and State Repression on the U.S.-Mexico Border*. Chicago: Haymarket Books, 2006.

Ashley, Wayne. "The Stations of the Cross: Christ, Politics and Processions on New York City's Lower East Side." In *Gods of the City: Religion and the American Urban Landscape*, edited by Robert A. Orsi, 341–66. Bloomington: Indiana University Press, 1999.

Bacon, David. *Illegal People: How Globalization Creates Migration and Criminalizes Immigrants*. Boston: Beacon Press, 2009.

Bedolla, Lisa Garcia. "Latino Migration and U.S. Foreign Policy." Text. Center for Latin American Studies (CLAS), July 16, 2014. https://clas.berkeley.edu/research/immigration-latino-migration-and-us-foreign-policy.

Bidegain, Ana Maria. "Living a Trans-National Spirituality: Latin American Catholic Families in Miami." In *Migration in a Global World*, edited by Solange Lefebvre and Luis Carlos Susin, 95–107. London: SCM Press, 2008.

Bradley, Ian. *Pilgrimage: A Spiritual and Cultural Journey*. 1st ed. Oxford: Lion Books, 2010.

Campese, Gioacchino. "¿Cuantos Mas?: The Crucified Peoples at the U.S. Mexico Border." In *A Promised Land, a Perilous Journey: Theological Perspectives on Migration*, edited by Daniel G. Groody and Gioacchino Campese, 271–98. Notre Dame, IN: University of Notre Dame Press, 2008.

Colwell, Matthew. "Defending Human Rights in the Borderlands: Roberto Martinez." In *Our God Is Undocumented: Biblical Faith and Immigrant Justice*, edited by Ched Myers and Matthew Colwell, 179–92. Maryknoll, NY: Orbis Books, 2012.

Cruz, Gemma Tulud. "A New Way of Being Christian: The Contribution of Migrants to the Church." In *Contemporary Issues of Migration and Theology*, edited by E. Padilla and P. Phan, 1st ed. New York: Palgrave Macmillan, 2013.

Daniel, Ben. *Neighbor: Christian Encounters with "Illegal" Immigration.* Louisville, KY: Westminster John Knox Press, 2010.

Davalos, Karen Mary. "The Real Way of Praying: The Via Crucis, Mexicano Sacred Space, and the Architecture of Domination." In *Horizons of the Sacred: Mexican Traditions in U.S. Catholicism*, edited by Timothy Matovina and Gary Riebe-Estrella, 41–68. Ithaca, NY: Cornell University Press, 2002.

Deck SJ, Allan Figuerora. "Latino Migrations and the Transformation of Religion in the United States: Framing the Question." In *Christianities in Migration: The Global Perspective*, edited by Peter C. Phan and Elaine Padilla, 1st ed., 263–80. Houndmills, UK, and New York: Palgrave Macmillan, 2015.

Eck, Diana L. *A New Religious America: How a "Christian Country" Has Now Become the World's Most Religiously Diverse Nation.* San Francisco: HarperOne, 2002.

Elizondo, Virgilio P. "Living Faith: Resistance and Survival." In *Mestizo Worship: A Pastoral Approach to Liturgical Ministry*, edited by Timothy M. Matovina and Virgilio P. Elizondo, 5–21. Collegeville, MN: Liturgical Press, 1998.

———. "Popular Religion as Support of Identity Based on the Mexican-American Experience in the U.S.A." In *Spirituality of the Third World: A Cry for Life: Papers and Reflections from the Third General Assembly of the Ecumenical Association of Third World*, edited by K. C. Abraham and Bernadette Mbuy-Beya, 1st ed., 55–63. Maryknoll, NY: Orbis Books, 1994.

Engh SJ, Michael. "Companion to Immigrants: Devotion to Our Lady of Guadalupe among Mexicans in the Los Angeles Area, 1900–1940." *Journal of Hispanic/Latino Theology* 5, no. 1 (1997): 37–47.

Espin, Orlando. *The Faith of the People: Theological Reflections on Popular Catholicism.* Maryknoll, NY: Orbis Books, 1997.

———. "Mexican Religious Practices, Popular Catholicism and the Development of Doctrine." In *Horizons of the Sacred: Mexican Traditions in U.S. Catholicism*, 139–52. Ithaca, NY: Cornell University Press, 2002.

———. "Popular Religion as an Epistemology (of Suffering)." *Journal of Hispanic/Latino Theology* 2, no. 2 (1994): 55–78.

Fikes, Bradley J. "'Posada without Borders' Gets More Meaning with Refugee Crisis." *San Diego Union-Tribune*, December 11, 2016. https://www.sandiegouniontribune.com/news/religion/sd-me-posada-border-20161210–story.html.

Garcia, Matthew. *From the Jaws of Victory: The Triumph and Tragedy of Cesar Chavez and the Farm Worker Movement*, 1st ed. Berkeley: University of California Press, 2014.

Goizueta, Roberto. "Reflecting on America as a Single Entity: Catholicism and U.S. Latinos." In *Many Faces, One Church: Cultural Diversity and the American Catholic Experience*, edited by Peter C. Phan and Diana Hayes, 69–82. Lanham, MD: Sheed and Ward, 2004.

Groody, Daniel G. *Border of Death, Valley of Life: An Immigrant Journey of Heart and Spirit.* Lanham MD: Rowman & Littlefield Publishers, 2007.

———. "Jesus and the Undocumented Immigrant: A Spiritual Geography of a Crucified People." *Theological Studies* 70, no. 2 (June 2009): 298–316.

———. "Passing Over: Migration as Conversion." *International Review of Mission* 104, no. 1 (April 2015): 46–60.

Hagan, Jacqueline Maria. "Faith for the Journey: Religion as a Resource for Migrants." In *A Promised Land, a Perilous Journey: Theological Perspectives on Migration*, edited by Daniel G. Groody and Gioacchino Campese, 3–19. Notre Dame, IN: University of Notre Dame Press, 2008.

Henau, Ernest. "Popular Religiosity and Christian Faith." In *Popular Religion*, edited by Norbert Greinacher and Norbert Mette, 71–81. London: T & T Clark, 1986.

Hoover, Brett C. *The Shared Parish: Latinos, Anglos, and the Future of U.S. Catholicism.* New York: NYU Press, 2014.

Hoover, Robin. "The Story of Humane Borders." In *A Promised Land, a Perilous Journey: Theological Perspectives on Migration*, edited by Daniel G. Groody and Gioacchino Campese, 1st ed., 160–73. Notre Dame, IN: University of Notre Dame Press, 2008.

Hsu, Spencer S. "Border Deaths Are Increasing," September 30, 2009. http://www.washingtonpost.com/wp-dyn/content/article/2009/09/29/AR2009092903212.html.

Maldonado, Luis. "Popular Religion: Its Dimensions, Levels and Types." In *Popular Religion*, edited by Norbert Greinacher and Norbert Mette, 3–11. London: T & T Clark, 1986.

Martin, Michelle. "'Posada' Draws Attention to Immigration Reform." National Catholic Reporter, December 19, 2011. https://www.ncronline.org/news/posada-draws-attention-immigration-reform.

Mette, Norbert, and Norbert Greinacher. "Editorial." In *Popular Religion*, edited by Norbert Greinacher and Norbert Mette, ix–xi. London: T & T Clark, 1986.

Migrations of the Holy: God, State, and the Political Meaning of the Church by William T. Cavanaugh. Eerdmans, 1809.

Myers, Chad. "Gospel Nativities vs Anti-Immigrant Nativism." In *Our God Is Undocumented: Biblical Faith and Immigrant Justice*, edited by Ched Myers and Matthew Colwell, 159–78. Maryknoll, NY: Orbis Books, 2012.

Nava, Alex. "God in the Desert: Searching for the Divine in the Midst of Death." In *A Promised Land, a Perilous Journey: Theological Perspectives on Migration*, edited by Daniel G. Groody and Gioacchino Campese, 62–75. Notre Dame, IN: University of Notre Dame Press, 2008.

Sharp, Joanne P., Paul Routledge, Chris Philo, and Ronan Paddison. "Entanglements of Power: Geographies of Domination/Resistance." In *Entanglements of Power: Geographies of Domination/Resistance*, edited by Joanne P. Sharp, Paul Routledge, Chris Philo, and Ronan Paddison, 1st ed., 1–41. London and New York: Routledge, 2000.

Parker, Christian. "Popular Religion and Protest against Oppression: The Chilean Example." In *Popular Religion*, edited by Norbert Greinacher and Norbert Mette, 28–35. London: T & T Clark, 1986.

Pasewark, Kyle A. *A Theology of Power: Being beyond Domination*. Minneapolis, MN: Fortress Press, 1993.

Phan, Peter C., Diana Hayes, and Jeanette Rodriguez, eds. "Devotion to Our Lady of Guadalupe among Mexican-Americans." In *Many Faces, One Church: Cultural Diversity and the American Catholic Experience*, 83–97. Lanham, MD: Rowman & Littlefield Publishers, 2004.

Pope Francis. Apostolic Exhortation. "Evangelii Gaudium: Apostolic Exhortation on the Proclamation of the Gospel in Today's World." Apostolic Exhortation, November 24, 2013. https://w2.vatican.va/content/francesco/en/apost_exhortations/documents/papa-francesco_esortazione-ap_20131124_evangelii-gaudium.html.

Portier, William L, ed. *Tradition and Incarnation*. New York: Paulist Press, 1993.

Ramirez, Ricardo. "Liturgy from the Mexican-American Perspective." *Worship* 51 (July 1977): 293–98.

Rimmer, Chad M. "Prospects for Ecumenism in the 21st Century: Towards an Ecumenical Theology of the Wilderness." *The Ecumenical Review* 60, no. 3 (July 2008): 259–70.

Scriven, Richard. "Geographies of Pilgrimage: Meaningful Movements and Embodied Mobilities." *Geography Compass* 8, no. 4 (April 2014): 249–61.

Ströher, Rev. Marga Janete. "People Are Made to Shine—Not to Suffer." In *The Prophetic Mission of Churches in Response to Forced Displacement of People: A Global Ecumenical Consultation, Addis Ababa, Ethiopia, 6–11 November 1995*, edited by World Council of Churches, 44–52. Amsterdam: World Council of Churches, 1996.

Sullivan, Kathleen. "St. Mary's Catholic Church: Celebrating Domestic Religion." In *Religion and the New Immigrants: Continuities and Adaptations in Immigrant Congregations*, edited by Janet Saltman Chafetz and Helen Rose Ebaugh, 125–40. Walnut Creek, CA: AltaMira Press, 2000.

Tomasi, Silvano. "The Prophetic Mission of the Churches." In *The Prophetic Mission of Churches in Response to Forced Displacement of People: A Global Ecumenical Consultation, Addis Ababa, Ethiopia, 6–11 November 1995*, edited by World Council of Churches, 36–43. Amsterdam: World Council of Churches, 1996.

Tutino, John. *Mexico and the Mexicans in the Making of the United States*. Austin: University of Texas Press, 2012.

Tweed, Thomas. "Identity and Authority at a Cuban Shrine in Miami: Santería, Catholicism, and Struggles for Religious Identity." *Journal of Hispanic/Latino Theology* 4, no. 1 (1995): 27–48.

Wink, Walter. *Engaging the Powers: Discernment and Resistance in a World of Domination.* Reprint edition. Minneapolis, MN: Fortress Press, 1992.

Chapter Ten

Toward a Theology of Migration

Luis N. Rivera-Pagán

What does it mean to be a migrant, to have crossed borders? Derek Walcott answers, "I have Dutch, nigger, and English in me, and either I'm nobody, or I'm a nation."[1] Gloria Anzaldúa writes, "To survive the Borderlands you must live sin fronteras. Be a crossroads."[2]

A HOMELESS MIGRANT ARAMEAN

The Bible's first confession of faith begins with a story of pilgrimage and migration: "A wandering Aramean was my ancestor; he went down into Egypt and lived there as an alien" (Deuteronomy 26:5). We might ask, did that "wandering Aramean" and his children have the proper documents to reside in Egypt? Were they maybe "illegal aliens"? Did he and his children have the proper Egyptian social security credentials? Did they speak the Egyptian language properly?

We know at least that he and his children were strangers in the midst of a powerful empire, and that as such they were both exploited and feared. This is the fate of many immigrants. In their reduced circumstances they are usually compelled to perform the least prestigious and most strenuous kinds of menial work. Yet at the same time they awaken the schizophrenic paranoia typical of empires, powerful and yet fearful of the stranger, of the "other," especially if that stranger resides within its frontiers and becomes populous. More than half a century ago, Franz Fanon brilliantly described the peculiar gaze of so many white French people at the growing presence of black Africans and Caribbeans in their national midst.[3] Scorn and fear are entwined in that stare.

The biblical creedal story continues: "When the Egyptians treated us harshly and afflicted us, by imposing hard labor on us, we cried to the . . . God of our ancestors; the Lord heard our voice and saw our affliction . . . and our oppression" (Deuteronomy 26:6). So important was this story of migration, slavery, and liberation for the biblical people of Israel that it became the core of an annual liturgy of remembrance and gratitude. The already quoted statement of faith was to be solemnly recited every year in the thanksgiving liturgy of the harvest festival. It reenacted the wounded memory of the afflictions and humiliations suffered by an immigrant people, strangers in the midst of an empire. This was the recollection of their hard and arduous labor, of the contempt and disdain that are so frequently the fate of the stranger and the foreigner who possess a different skin pigmentation, language, religion, or culture. But it was also the memory of the events of liberation when God heard the dolorous cries of the suffering immigrants. And the remembrance of another kind of migration—one in search of a land where they might live in freedom, peace, and righteousness, a land they might call theirs.

We might ask: Who today might be the wandering Arameans and what strong but fearful empire might Egypt represent these days?

DILEMMAS AND CHALLENGES OF MIGRATION

The United States has expereinced a significant increase in its Latino/Hispanic population. In 1975, little more than 11 million Hispanics made up just over 5 percent of the US inhabitants. Today they number nearly 58 million, around 16 percent of the nation, making Hispanics the largest minority group. Recent projections estimate that by 2050 the Latino/Hispanic share of the US population might be between 26 and 32 percent. This demographic growth has led to a complex political and social debate for it highlights sensitive and crucial issues, like national identity and compliance with the law. It also threatens to unleash a new phase in the sad and long history of American racism and xenophobia,[4] one that, following the Sri Lankan novelist Ambalavaner Sivanandan, might be termed "xeno-racism."[5]

Two concerns have become important topics of public discourse:

1. What to do regarding the growth of unauthorized migration? About a quarter of the Hispanic/Latino adults are unauthorized immigrants. For a society that prides itself on its law and order tradition, this represents a serious breach of its juridical structure.
2. What does this dramatic increase in the Latino/Hispanic population convey for the cultural and linguistic traditions of the United States, its mores and styles of collective self-identification?

Unfortunately, the conversation about these difficult issues takes place in an environment clouded by the gradual development of xenophobic attitudes. There are signs of an increasing hostility to what the Mexican American writer Richard Rodríguez has termed "the browning of America."[6] One can clearly recognize this mind-set in the frequent use of the derogatory term "illegal alien," as if the illegality would define the entire being of the migrant rather than a specific delinquency. We all know the dire and sinister connotations that "alien" has in popular American culture, thanks in part to the sequence of four *Alien* films with Sigourney Weaver fighting back atrocious creatures.[7]

Let me briefly mention some key elements of this emerging xenophobia:

1. The spread of fear regarding the so-called broken borders, the possible proliferation of Third World epidemic diseases, and the alleged increase of criminal activities by undocumented immigrants.[8] A shadowy sinister specter is created in the minds of the public: the image of the intruder and threatening "other." These days that fateful specter is promoted by the president of the United States himself.[9]
2. The xenophobic stance intensifies the post-9/11 attitudes of fear and phobia regarding the strangers, those people who are here but who do not seem to belong here. Surveillance of immigration is now located under the Department of Homeland Security. This administrative merger links two basically unrelated problems: threat of terrorist activities and unauthorized migration.
3. Though US racism and xenophobia have had traditionally different targets—people with African ancestry first (be they slaves or free citizens), marked by their dark skin pigmentation, and foreign-born immigrants second, distinguished by their particular language, religiosity, and collective memory—in the case of Latin American immigrants both nefarious prejudices converge and coalesce (as was also the case with the nineteenth-century Chinese indentured servants, which led to the infamous 1882 Chinese Exclusion Act).[10]
4. There has been a significant increase of aggressive anti-immigrant groups. According to a report by the Southern Poverty Law Center, "'nativist extremist groups'—organizations that go beyond mere advocacy of restrictive immigration policy to actually confront or harass suspected immigrants—jumped from 173 groups in 2008 to 309 in 2009. Virtually all of these vigilante groups have appeared since the spring of 2005."[11]
5. Proposals coming from the White House, Congress, states, and counties have tended to be excessively punitive. Some examples are

a. A projected excluding wall along the Mexican border (compare it to Ephesians 2:14, "Christ . . . has broken down the dividing wall").

b. The criminalization as felony not only of illegal immigration but also of any action by legal residents that might provide assistance to undocumented immigrants.[12]

c. Draconian legislation prescribing mandatory detention and deportation of noncitizens, even for alleged minor violations of law. Arizona's notorious and contentious Senate Bill 1070 is a prime example of this infamous trend. It has been followed by Alabama's even harsher anti-immigrant legislation (House Bill 56), soon to be copied by other states.

d. Proposed legislation to curtail access to public services (health, education, police protection, legal services, drivers' licenses) by undocumented migrants.

e. Some prominent right-wing politicians, including the actual president, have suggested the possibility of revising the first section of the Fourteenth Amendment of the US constitution.[13] Their purpose, apparently, is to deprive the children of immigrants of their constitutional right to citizenship. A campaign against the so-called anchor babies has been part and parcel of the most strident xenophobic campaign in years.

f. A significant intensification of raids, detentions, and deportations. This is transforming several migrant communities into a clandestine underclass of fear and dissimulation. Some legal scholars have even suggested that the United States is becoming a "deportation nation."[14] It brings to mind the infamous Mexican deportation program, authorized in 1929 by President Herbert Hoover. That program led, according to some scholars, to the forceful deportation of approximately one million people of Mexican descent, many of which who were, in fact, American citizens.[15]

g. Congress has been unable to approve the Development, Relief and Education for Alien Minors Act (DREAM Act), that would provide conditional permanent residency to certain deportable foreign-born students who graduate from US high schools, are of good moral character, were brought to the United States illegally as minors, and have been in the country continuously for at least five years prior to the bill's enactment, if they complete two years in the military or at an academic institution of higher learning.

The xenophobia and scapegoating of the "stranger in our midst" have resulted in the chaotic condition that now plagues the immigration system in the United States, judicially, politically, and socially. All recent attempts to enact a comprehensive immigration reform have floundered thanks to the resistance of influential sectors that have been able to propagate fear of the "alien."[16] The increasing support that such phobic anxiety against "outsiders" among substantial sectors of the American public brings to mind Alexis de Tocqueville's astute critical observation: "I know no country in which there is so little true independence of mind and freedom of discussion as in America. . . . In America, the majority raises very formidable barriers to the liberty of opinion."[17]

FROM A CLASH OF CIVILIZATIONS TO A CLASH OF CULTURES

In this social context tending towards xenophobia and racism, the late Professor Samuel P. Huntington wrote some important texts about what he perceived as a Hispanic/Latino threat to the cultural and political integrity of the United States. Huntington was chairman of Harvard's Academy for International and Area Studies and cofounder of the journal *Foreign Policy*. He was also the intellectual father of the theory of the "clash of civilizations," which had disastrous consequences for the foreign policies of George W. Bush presidency.[18]

In 2004, Huntington published an extended article in *Foreign Policy*, titled "The Hispanic Challenge," followed by the lengthy book *Who Are We? The Challenges to America's National Identity*.[19] The former prophet of an unavoidable civilizational abyss and conflict between the "West and the Rest" (specially the Islamic nations) became the apostle of an emerging nefarious cultural conflict inside the United States. Immersed in a dangerous clash of civilizations *ad extra*, this messenger of doom prognosticated that the United States is also entering into a grievous clash of cultures *ad intra*.

American national identity seems a very complex issue for it deals with an extremely intricate and highly diverse history. But Huntington has, surprisingly, a simple answer: the United States is mainly identified by its "Anglo-Protestant culture" and not only by its liberal republican democratic political creed. It has been, according to this historical reconstruction, a nation of settlers rather than immigrants. The first British pioneers transported not only their bodies, but also their fundamental cultural and religious viewpoints, what Huntington designates as "Anglo-Protestant culture." In the formation of this collective identity, Christian devotion—the Congregational pilgrims, the Protestantism of dissent, the Evangelical Awakenings—has been meaningful and crucial. This national identity has also been forged by a long history of wars against a succession of enemies (from Native Americans to Islamic jihadists). There is a certain romantic nostalgia in Huntington's thesis, an emphasis on the foundations of American culture and identity in their continuities rather than its evolutions and transformations.

But the main objective of Huntington is to underline the uncertainties of present trends regarding his nation's collective self-understanding. After the dissolution of the Soviet threat he perceives a significant neglect of American national identity. National identity seems to require the image of a dangerous adversary, what he terms the "perfect enemy." The prevailing trend is supposedly one of a notable loss of US awareness of national identity and loyalty.

Then, supposedly, emerges the sinister challenge of the Latin American migratory invasion. It is not similar to previous migratory waves. Its contiguity, intensity, lack of education, territorial memory, preservation of language, retention of homeland culture, national allegiance and citizenship, its distance to Anglo-Protestant culture, and its alleged absence of a Puritan work ethic make it unique and unprecedented. This immigration constitutes, according to Huntington, "a major potential threat to the cultural and possibly political integrity of the United States."[20] This Harvard professor has discovered and named America's newest "perfect enemy"—the Latin American immigrant!

Huntington's discomfiture regarding the encroachment of Spanish in American public life is intense. He calls attention to the fact that now, in some states, more children are ominously christened José rather than Michael. This increasing public bilingualism threatens to fragment US linguistic integrity. Linguistic bifurcation becomes a veritable menacing Godzilla. He neglects altogether the economic causes for the Latin American migration— its financial and social benefits both for the sending (remittances)[21] and the receiving nations (lower wages for manual jobs).[22] He does not seem to have any concern regarding the process whereby they become new *douloi* and *μέτοικοι*, helots at the margins of society, in a kind of social apartheid, cleaning stores, cooking meals, doing dishes, cutting grass, picking tomatoes and oranges, painting buildings, washing cars, staying out of the way . . .

Obfuscated by Huntington are the consequences of the present trend among metropolitan Third World diasporas of holding dual citizenship. An increasing number of Latin American nations now recognize and promote double citizenship, a process that leads to multiple national and cultural loyalties and to what Huntington classifies, with a disdainful and pejorative tone, "ampersand peoples." Dual citizenship, he rightly recognizes, leads to dual national loyalties and identities. Huntington perceives this trend towards dual citizenship and national fidelity as a violation and disruption of the Oath of Allegiance and the Pledge of Allegiance, essential components of the secular liturgy in the acquisition of US citizenship.[23]

He seems to suggest stricter policies regarding illegal migration, stronger measures to enforce cultural assimilation of legal immigrants, and the rejection of dual citizenship. This perspective is not only utterly archaic; it might also become the theoretical underground for a new wave of xenophobic white nativism.[24] The train has already left that outdated station. What is now required is a wider acceptance and enjoyment of multiple identities and loyalties and, if religious compassion truly matters, a deeper concern regarding the burdens and woes of displaced peoples. The time has come to prevail over the phobia of diversity and to appreciate and enjoy the dignity of difference. For, as Dale Irvin has asserted, "the actual world that we are living in . . . is one of transnational migrations, hyphenated and hybrid identities, cultural conjunctions and disjunctions."[25]

Do Latinos/Hispanics truly represent "a major potential threat to the cultural and possibly political integrity of the United States," as Huntington has argued? Whether what Huntington considers a threat is something to lament, denounce, or celebrate depends on the eyes of the beholder. Maybe, just maybe, it would not be such a bad thing if Latino immigrants prove in fact to be that dramatic and decisive "major potential threat to the cultural and political integrity of the United States."[26]

MIGRATION AND XENOPHOBIA

Migration and xenophobia are serious social quandaries. But they also convey urgent challenges to the ethical sensitivity of religious people and persons of goodwill. The first step we need to take is to perceive this issue from the perspective of immigrants themselves. We must pay cordial (that is, deep from our hearts) attention to their stories of suffering, hope, courage, resistance, ingenuity, and, as so frequently happens in the wildernesses of the American Southwest, death.[27] Many of the unauthorized migrants have become *nobodies*, in the apt title of John Bowe's book, *disposable people*, in Kevin Bales's poignant phrase, or, as Zygmunt Bauman poignantly reminds us, *wasted lives*.[28] They are the empire's new μέτοικοι, *douloi*, modern servants. Their dire existential situation cannot be grasped without taking into consideration the upsurge in global inequalities in these times of unregulated international financial hegemony.

For many human beings the excruciating alternative is between misery in their Third World homeland and marginalization in the rich West/North, both fateful destinies intimately linked together.[29] According to Michael Dillon, "the global capitalism of states and the environmental degradation of many populous regions of the planet have made many millions of people radically endangered strangers in their own homes as well as criminalized or anathemized strangers in the places to which they have been forced to flee."[30]

The situation has been painfully aggravated, with tens of thousands of children and teenagers fleeing poverty and violence from El Salvador, Honduras, Guatemala, or Mexico, daring to survive the gangs of human traffickers, the so-called coyotes, to, at the end of that arduous and dangerous pilgrimage, face detention, contempt, and deportation in the southern frontier of the United States. Their dreadful situation has truly become a humanitarian crisis of epic dimensions.[31]

Will Latinos/Hispanics become the new national scapegoats during these early decades of the twenty-first century? Do they truly represent "a major potential threat to the cultural and political integrity of the United States"? This is a vital dilemma that the United States has up to now been unable to face and solve. We are not called, here and now, to solve it. But allow me, from my perspective as a Hispanic and Latin American Christian theologian, to offer some critical observations that might illuminate our way in this bewildering labyrinth.

XENOPHILIA: TOWARDS A BIBLICAL THEOLOGY OF MIGRATION

We began this essay with the annual creedal and liturgical memory of a time when the people of Israel were aliens in the midst of an empire, a vulnerable community, socially exploited and culturally scorned. It was the worst of times. It also became the best of times: the times of liberation and redemption from servitude. That memory shaped the sensitivity of the Hebrew nation regarding the strangers, the aliens, within Israel. Their vulnerability was not only a reminder of their own past helplessness as immigrants in Egypt but also an ethical challenge to care for the foreigners inside Israel.[32]

Caring for the stranger became a key element of the Torah, the covenant of justice and righteousness between Yahweh and Israel. "When an alien resides with you in your land, you shall not oppress the alien. The alien who resides with you shall be to you as the citizen among you; you shall love the alien as yourself, for you were aliens in the land of Egypt: I am the Lord your God" (Leviticus 19:33f). "You shall not oppress a resident alien; you know the heart of an alien, for you were aliens in the land of Egypt" (Exodus 23:9). "The Lord your God is God of gods . . . who executes justice to the orphan and the widow, and who loves the strangers, providing them food and clothing. You shall also love the stranger, for you were strangers in the land of Egypt" (Deuteronomy 10:17ff). "You shall not withhold the wages of poor and needy laborers, whether other Israelites or aliens who reside in your land in one of your towns. . . . You shall not deprive a resident alien. . . . Remember that you were a slave in Egypt and the Lord redeemed you from there" (Deuteronomy 24:14, 17–18). The twelve curses that, according to Deuteronomy 27, Moses instructs the Israelites to liturgically proclaim at their entrance to the promised land, include the trilogy of orphans, widows, and strangers as privileged recipients of collective solidarity and compassion: "Cursed be anyone who deprives the alien, the orphan, and the widow of justice" (Deuteronomy 27:19).

The prophets constantly chastised the ruling elites of Israel and Judah for their social injustice and their oppression of the vulnerable. Who were those vulnerable persons? The poor, the widows, the orphans, and the foreigners. "The princes of Israel . . . have been bent on shedding blood . . . [and] the alien residing within you suffers extortion; the orphan and the widow are wronged in you" (Ezekiel 22:6f). After condemning with the harshest words possible the apathy and inertia of temple religiosity in Jerusalem, the prophet Jeremiah, in the name of God, commands the alternative: "Thus says the Lord: Act with justice and righteousness. . . . And do no wrong or violence to the alien, the orphan, and the widow" (Jeremiah 22:3). He goes on to reprove the king of Judah with harsh admonishing words: "Thus says the Lord: Act with justice and righteousness and deliver from the hand of the oppressor anyone who has been robbed. And do no wrong or violence to the alien, the orphan, and the widow. . . . If you do not heed these words, I swear by myself, says the Lord, that this house shall become a desolation" (Jeremiah 22:3, 5). The prophet paid a costly price for those daring admonitions.

The divine command to care for the stranger was the matrix of an ethics of hospitality. As evidence of his righteousness, Job affirms that "the stranger has not lodged in the street" for he always "opened the doors of [his] house" to board the foreigner (Job 31:32). It was the violation of the divinely sanctioned code of hospitality that led to the dreadful destruction of Sodom (Genesis 19:1–25).[33] The perennial temptation is xenophobia. The divine command, enshrined in the Torah, is xenophilia—the love for those whom we usually find very difficult to love: the strangers, the aliens, the foreign sojourners.[34]

The command to love the sojourners and resident foreigners in the land of Israel emerges from two sources. One has already been mentioned—the Israelites had been sojourners and resident foreigners in a land not theirs ("for you were strangers in the land of Egypt") and should, therefore, be sensitive to the complex existential stress of communities living in the midst of a nation whose dominant inhabitants speak a different language, venerate dissimilar deities, share distinct traditions, and commemorate different historical founding events. Love and respect towards the stranger and the foreigner are thus, in these biblical texts, construed as an essential dimension of Israel's national identity. It belongs to the essence and nature of the people of God.

A second source for the command of care towards the immigrant foreigner is that it corresponds to God's way of being and acting in history: "The Lord watches over the strangers" (Psalm 146:9ᵃ);[35] "God . . . executes justice for the orphan and the widow and loves the strangers" (Deuteronomy 10:18). God takes sides in history, favoring the most vulnerable: the poor, the widows, the orphans, and the strangers. "I will be swift to bear witness . . . against those who oppress the hired workers in their wages, the widow, and the orphan, against those who thrust aside the alien, and do not fear me, says the Lord of hosts" (Malachi 3:5). Solidarity with the marginalized and excluded corresponds to God's being and acting in history.

How comforting would be to stop right here, with these fine biblical texts of xenophilia, of love for the stranger. But the Bible happens to be a disconcerting book. It contains a disturbing multiplicity of voices, a perplexing polyphony that frequently complicates our theological hermeneutics. Regarding many key ethical dilemmas, we often find in the Bible conflictive and contradictory perspectives. Too frequently we jump from our contemporary labyrinths into a dark and more sinister scriptural maze.

In the Hebrew Bible we also discover statements with a distinct and distasteful flavor of nationalist xenophobia. Leviticus 25 is usually read as the classic text for the liberation of the Israelites, who have fallen into indebted servitude. Indeed, it is, as its famed tenth verse so eloquently manifests: "Proclaim liberty throughout all the land unto all the inhabitants thereof."[36] But it also contains a nefarious distinction: "As for the male and female slaves whom you may have, it is from the nations around you that you may acquire male and female slaves. You may also acquire them from among the aliens residing with you, and from their families . . . and they may be your property. . . . These you may treat as slaves" (Leviticus 25:44–46). And what about the terrifying fate imposed upon the foreign wives (and their children) in the epilogues of Ezra and Nehemiah? They are thrown away, exiled, as sources of impurity and contamination of the faith and culture of the people of God.[37] In the process of reconstructing Jerusalem, "Ezra and Nehemiah demonstrate the growing presence of xenophobia," as the Palestinian theologian Naim Ateek has highlighted. He immediately adds: "Ezra and Nehemiah demonstrate the beginning of the establishment of a religious tradition that leaned toward traditionalism, conservatism, exclusivity, and xenophobia."[38] Let us also not forget the atrocious rules of warfare that prescribe forced servitude or annihilation of the peoples encountered in Israel's route to the "promised land" (Deuteronomy 20:10–17). These all are, in Phyllis Trible's apt expression, "texts of terror."[39]

The problem with some evangelically oriented books (e.g., Matthew Soerens and Jenny Hwang's *Welcoming the Stranger* and M. Daniel Carroll R.'s *Christians at the Border: Immigration, the Church, and the Bible*) is that their hermeneutical strategy evades completely and intentionally those biblical texts that might have xenophobic connotations.[40] Both books, for example, narrate the postexilic project of rebuilding Jerusalem, physically, culturally, and religiously, under Nehemiah, but silence the expulsion of the foreign wives, an important part of that project (Ezra 9–10, Nehemiah 13:23–31).[41] The rejection of foreign wives in Ezra and Nehemiah does not seem too different from modern anti-immigrant xenophobia. Those foreign wives have a different linguistic, cultural, and religious legacy—"half of their children . . . could not speak the language of Judah, but spoke the language of various peoples. And I contended with them and cursed them and beat some of them and pulled out their hair" (Nehemiah 13:24–25).

This conundrum is a constant irritating modus operandi of the Bible. We go to it searching for simple and clear solutions to our ethical enigmas, but it strikes back exacerbating our perplexity. Who said that the Word of God is supposed to make things easier? But have I not forgotten something? If something distinguishes the tradition, it is its Christological emphasis.

What then about Christ and the stranger?

Clues to address Jesus's perspective regarding the socially despised other or stranger can be found in his attitude towards the Samaritans and in his dramatic and surprising eschatological parable on genuine discipleship and fidelity (Matthew 25:31–46). Orthodox Jews despised Samaritans as possible sources of contamination and impurity. Yet Jesus did not have any inhibitions in conversing amiably with a Samaritan woman of doubtful reputation, breaking down the barrier between Judeans and Samaritans (John 4:7–30). Of ten lepers once cleansed by Jesus, only one came to express his gratitude and reverence, and the gospel narrative emphasizes that "he was a Samaritan" (Luke 17:11–19). Finally, in the famous parable illustrating the meaning of the command "love your neighbor as yourself" (Luke 10:29–37), Jesus contrasts the righteousness and solidarity of a Samaritan with the neglect and indifference of a priest and a Levite. The action of a traditionally despised Samaritan is thus exalted as a paradigm of love and solidarity to emulate.

The parable of the judgment of the nations in the Gospel of Matthew (25:31–46) is pure, vintage Jesus. It is a text whose connotations I refuse to reduce to the sort of constraining ecclesiastical confinement we so often see. Jesus disrupts, as he loved to do, the familiar criteria of ethical value and religious worthiness by distinguishing between human actions that sacramentally bespeak divine love for the powerless and vulnerable from those that do not. Who are, according to Jesus, to be divinely blessed and inherit God's kingdom? Those who in their actions care for the hungry, thirsty, naked, sick, and incarcerated—for marginalized and vulnerable human beings. But those who welcome the strangers, who provide them with hospitality, are to inherit the kingdom as well. It also belongs to those who are able to overcome nationalistic exclusions, racism, and xenophobia and are daring enough to welcome and embrace the immigrant, the people in our midst who happen to be different in skin pigmentation, culture, language, and national origins. They belong to the powerless of the powerless, the poorest of the poor, in Franz Fanon's famous terms, "the wretched of the earth," or, in Jesus's poetic language, "the least of these."[42]

Why? Here comes the shocking statement: because they are, in their powerlessness and vulnerability, the sacramental presence of Christ. "For I was hungry and you gave me food, I was thirsty and you gave me something to drink, I was a stranger [*xenos*] and you welcomed me, I was naked and you gave me clothing, I was sick and you took care of me" (Matthew 25:35). The vulnerable human beings turn out to be, in a mysterious way, the sacramental presence of Christ in our midst.[43]

This sacramental presence of Christ becomes, for the first generations of Christian communities, the corner stone of hospitality—*philoxenia*—towards those needy people who do not have a place to rest. This is a virtue insisted upon by the apostle Paul (Romans 12:13).[44] When, in a powerful and imperial nation like the United States of America, its citizens welcome and embrace the immigrant who resides and works with or without some documents required by the powers that be, they are blessed precisely because they are welcoming and embracing Jesus Christ.[45]

The discriminatory distinction between citizens and aliens is broken down. The author of the Epistle to the Ephesians is thus able to proclaim to human communities religiously scorned and socially marginalized: "So then you are no longer strangers and aliens, but you are citizens" (Ephesians 2:19). The author of that missive probably had in mind the peculiar vision of postexilic Israel developed by the prophet Ezekiel. Ezekiel emphasizes two distinctions between the postexilic and the old Israel: the eradication of social injustice and oppression ("And my princes shall no longer oppress my people" [Ezekiel 45:8]) and the elimination of the legal distinctions between citizens and aliens ("You shall allot [the land] as an inheritance for yourselves and for the aliens who reside among you and have begotten children among you. They shall be to you as citizens of Israel; with you they shall be allotted an inheritance among the tribes of Israel. In whatever tribe aliens reside, there you shall assign them their inheritance, says the Lord God" [Ezekiel 47:21–23]). This was not merely theological speculation. Ezekiel himself experienced the tragedy of being an immigrant. He was one of the countless Israelites who suffered forced deportation after the violent invasion of Israel by the Babylonian military forces. Exile and diaspora were the fate of the people of Yahweh and the source of Israel's sacred scriptures.[46]

AN ECUMENICAL, INTERNATIONAL, AND INTERCULTURAL THEOLOGICAL PERSPECTIVE

We need to countervail the xenophobia that contaminates public discourse in the United States and other Western nations with an embracing, exclusion-rejecting perspective of the stranger, the alien, and the "other." I have named this *xenophilia*, a concept that comprises hospitality, love, and care for the stranger.[47] In times of increasing economic and political globalization, when in a megalopolis like New York, Chicago, Dallas, or San Francisco many different cultures, languages, memories, and legacies converge, *xenophilia* should be our duty and vocation. It should be a faith affirmation of our common humanity and of the ethical priority in the eyes of God of those vulnerable beings living in the shadows and margins of our societies.[48]

There is a tendency among many public scholars and leaders to weave a discourse that deals with immigrants mainly or even exclusively as workers, whose labor might or might not contribute to the economic welfare of the American citizens. This kind of public discourse tends to objectify and dehumanize the immigrants. Those immigrants are human beings conceived and designed, according to the Christian tradition, in the image of God. They deserve to be fully recognized as such, both in the letter of the law and in the spirit of social praxis. Whatever the importance of the economic factors for the receiving nation (which usually, as in the case of the United States, happens to be an extremely rich country), from an ethical theological perspective the main concern should be the existential well-being of the most vulnerable and marginalized members of God's humanity, among them those who sojourn far away from their homeland and are constantly scrutinized by the demeaning gaze of many native citizens.

One of the key concerns energizing and spreading the distrust against resident foreigners is fear of their possible consequences on national identity, understood as an already historically fixed essence. We have seen that anxiety in Samuel P. Huntington's assessment of the Latin American immigration as "a major potential threat to the cultural integrity of the United States." It is an apprehension that has spread all over the Western world, disseminating hostile attitudes towards already marginalized and disenfranchised communities of sojourners and strangers. These are perceived as sources of "cultural contamination." What is therein forgotten, though, is, first, that national identities are historical constructs diachronically constituted by exchanges with peoples bearing different cultural heritages and, second, that cultural alterity, the social exchange with the "other," can and should be a source of renewal and enrichment of our own distinct national self-awareness. History has shown the sad consequences of xenophobic ethnocentrism. There have also been intimate links between xenophobia and genocide.[49] As Zygmunt Bauman has so aptly written, "Great crimes often start from great ideas. . . . Among this class of ideas, pride of place belongs to the vision of purity."[50]

The United States tends to play the role of the Lone Ranger. Yet migration and xenophobia are international problems, affecting most of the world community, and they must be understood and faced from a worldwide context.[51] The deportation of Roma people (Gypsies) in France and other European nations is an unfortunate sign of the times. Roma communities are expelled from nations where they are objects of scorn, contempt, and fear, to other nations where they have traditionally been mistreated, disdained, and marginalized. They are perennial national scapegoats, whose unfortunate fate has for too long been silenced.[52] It would also do good to compare the American situation with that prevailing in several European nations, where in the difficult and sometimes tense coexistence of citizens and immigrants and the historically complex conflicts between the Cross and the Crescent resonate. Many of the foreigners happen to be Muslims, venerators of Allah, and are thus subject to insidious kinds of xenophobia and discrimination.[53] Deportation has become a substantial and cruel dimension of public policy in the United States.[54]

Migration is an international problem, a salient dimension of modern globalization.[55] Globalization implies not only the transfer of financial resources, products, and trade, but also the worldwide relocation of peoples, a transnationalization of labor migration, of human beings who take the difficult and frequently painful decision to leave their kin and kith searching for a better future. According to some scholars, we are in the midst of an "age of migration."[56] Borders have become bridges, not only barriers. For, as Edward Said has written in the context of another very complex issue, "in time, who cannot suppose that the borders themselves will mean far less than the human contact taking place between people for whom differences animate more exchange rather than more hostility?"[57]

The intensification of global inequalities has made the issue of labor migration a crucial one.[58] It is a situation that requires rigorous analysis from: (1) a worldwide ecumenical horizon, (2) a deep understanding of the tensions and misunderstandings arising from the proximity of peoples with different traditions and cultural memories, (3) an ethical perspective that privileges the plight and afflictions of the most vulnerable, as "submerged and silenced voices of strangers need to be uncovered,"[59] and (4) for the Christian communities and churches, a solid theological matrix ecumenically conceived and designed.

The churches and Christian communities, therefore, need to address theologically this issue from an international ecumenical and intercultural perspective.[60] The main concern is not and should not be exclusively our national society, but the entire fractured global order, for, as Soerens and Hwang have neatly written, "ultimately, the church must be a place of reconciliation in a broken world."[61] In an age where globalization prevails, there are social issues (migration one of them) whose transnational complexities call for an international ecumenical dialogue and debate. As Susanna Snyder has so aptly written, "A transnational issue requires transnational responses and transnational, global networks such as churches could therefore be key international players."[62] One goal of that worldwide discursive process is the disruption of the increasing tendency of developed and wealthy countries to emphasize the protection of civil rights, understood exclusively as the rights of *citizens*, vis-à-vis the diminishment of the recognition of the human rights of resident noncitizens.[63]

We must also keep in mind another crucial factor: streams of migration are diversifying and strengthening Western and Northern Christianity. According to Brian Stanley, professor of world Christianity at the University of Edinburgh, thanks to massive migrations, "by the year 2012, it is estimated that within the Catholic archdiocese of Los Angeles alone, the Eucharist was being celebrated in forty-two different languages." And he adds,

> The great migrations movements . . . both diversified and even strengthened the Christian presence in northern-hemisphere societies. . . . Migration thus brought to Europe and North America not simple marked interreligious plurality but also greatly enhanced Christian denominational and cultural diversity, with a new infusion of spiritual vitality . . .[64]

Pope Benedict XVI rightly reminded the global community, in his 2009 social encyclical *Caritas in veritate*, of the urgent necessity to develop an international, ecumenical, and theologically humane perspective of migration:

> *[M]igration* . . . is a striking phenomenon because of the sheer numbers of people involved, the social, economic, political, cultural and religious problems it raises. . . . [We] are facing a social phenomenon of epoch-making proportions that requires bold, forward-looking policies of international cooperation. . . . We are all witnesses of the burden of suffering, the dislocation and the aspirations that accompany the flow of migrants. . . . [T]hese laborers cannot be considered as a commodity or a mere workforce. They must not, therefore, be treated like any other factor of production. Every migrant is a human person who, as such, possesses fundamental, inalienable rights that must be respected by everyone and in every circumstance.[65]

NOTES

1. Derek Walcott, "The Schooner 'Flight,'" in *Collected Poems: 1948–1984* (New York: The Noonday Press: Farrar, Straus and Giroux, 1996), 346.
2. Gloria Anzaldúa, *Borderlands/La Frontera: The New Mestiza* (San Francisco: Aunt Lute Books, 1999), 217.

3. Frantz Fanon, *Peau Noir, Masques Blancs* (Paris: Éditions du Seuil, 1952).

4. Charles A. Gallagher and Cameron D. Lippard, eds., *Race and Racism in the United States: An Encyclopedia of the American Mosaic* (Westport, CT: Greenwood Press, 2005); John Higham, *Strangers in the Land: Patterns of American Nativism, 1860–1925* (New Brunswick, NJ: Rutgers University Press, 2011).

5. As quoted in Susanna Snyder, *Asylum-Seeking, Migration and Church* (Burlington, VT: Ashgate, 2012), 93.

6. Richard Rodriguez, *Brown: The Last Discovery of America* (New York: Penguin Books, 2003).

7. Robert W. Heimburger, *God and the Illegal Alien: United States Immigration Law and a Theology of Politics* (Cambridge: Cambridge University Press, 2018), 36. "Today the term 'alien' conjures up extraterrestrial life forms, perhaps threatening or monstrous."

8. David Leonhardt, "Truth, Fiction and, and Lou Dobbs," *The New York Times*, May 30, 2017.

9. See Patrick J. Buchanan's book, with the inflammatory title: Patrick J Buchanan, *State of Emergency: The Third World Invasion and Conquest of America* (New York: St. Martin's Press, 2008).

10. George M. Fredrickson, *Diverse Nations: Explorations in the History of Racial and Ethnic Pluralism* (London: Paradigm Publishers, 2006), http://www.tandfebooks.com/isbn/9781315635125; Stuart Creighton Miller, *The Unwelcome Immigrant: The American Image of the Chinese, 1785–1882* (Berkeley, CA: University of California Press, 1969).

11. Mark Potok, "Rage on the Right," *Intelligence Report*, March 2, 2010, https://www.splcenter.org/fighting-hate/intelligence-report/2010/rage-right.

12. This was one of the most controversial sections of the Border Protection, Anti-Terrorism, and Illegal Immigration Control Act of 2005 (H.R. 4437), a bill approved by the House but not by the Senate. Several religious leaders expressed their objection to it. The Los Angeles Roman Catholic cardinal archbishop Roger Mahoney, in an article published March 22, 2006, in the *New York Times* under the title "Called by God to Help," asserted that "denying aid to a fellow human being violates a law with a higher authority than Congress—the law of God" and warned that the priests of his diocese might disobey the bill in case it would be finally approved.

13. The first sentence of that section reads as follows: "All persons born or naturalized in the United States, and subject to the jurisdiction thereof, are citizens of the United States and of the State wherein they reside." The second sentence of that same first section has also become the center of attention of another key dispute in the United States: whether its tenets of "due process of law" and "equal protection of the laws" preclude any legislative prohibition of gay marriage.

14. Daniel Kanstroom, *Deportation Nation: Outsiders in American History* (Cambridge, MA ; London: Harvard University Press, 2007).

15. Abraham Hoffman, *Unwanted Mexican Americans in the Great Depression: Repatriation Pressures, 1929–1939* (Tucson: University of Arizona Press, 1974); Francisco E. Balderrama and Raymond Rodríguez, *Decade of Betrayal: Mexican Repatriation in the 1930s*, revised ed. (Albuquerque: University of New Mexico Press, 2006).

16. Matthew Soerens and Jenny Hwang provide a succinct and precise summary of several failed attempts to enact a comprehensive immigration legislative and juridical reform. See Matthew Soerens and Jenny Yang, *Welcoming the Stranger: Justice, Compassion and Truth in the Immigration Debate*, revised ed. (Downers Grove, IL: IVP Books, 2018).

17. Alexis de Tocqueville, *Democracy in America* (Oxford: Oxford University Press, 1959), 152.

18. Samuel P. Huntington, "The Clash of Civilizations?," August 31, 2017, https://www.foreignaffairs.com/articles/united-states/1993–06–01/clash-civilizations; Samuel P. Huntington, *The Clash of Civilizations and the Remaking of World Order* (New York: Simon and Schuster, 2011).

19. Samuel P. Huntington, "The Hispanic Challenge," Foriegn Policy, October 28, 2006, https://foreignpolicy.com/2009/10/28/the-hispanic-challenge/; Samuel P. Huntington, *Who Are We?: The Challenges to America's National Identity* (New York: Simon and Schuster, 2005).

20. "The Hispanic Challenge," 33; *Who Are We?* 243.

21. Dilip Ratha, "Dollars without Borders," November 2, 2009, https://www.foreignaffairs.com/articles/2009–10–16/dollars-without-borders. "Remittances are proving to be one of the more resilient pieces of the global economy in the downturn, and will likely play a large role in the economic development and recovery of many poor countries."

22. This is a serious flaw in many ethnocentric critiques of immigration issues according to Francisco Javier Blázquez Ruiz, "Derechos Humanos, Inmigración, Integración," in *Ciudadania, Multiculturalidad e Inmigracion*, ed. José A. Zamora (Editorial Verbo Divino, 2009), 86, 93.

23. Jonathan Sacks, *The Dignity of Difference: How to Avoid the Clash of Civilizations*, 2nd ed. (London: Continuum, 2003).

24. A substantially more nuanced and intellectually complex analysis of the different aspects of immigration in the United States is provided by Alejandro Portes and Rubén G. Rumbaut, *Immigrant America: A Portrait*, 4th ed. (Berkeley and Los Angeles, CA: University of California Press, 2014).

25. Dale Irvin, "The Church, the Urban and the Global: Mission in an Age of Global Cities," *International Bulletin of Missionary Research* 33, no. 4 (October 2009): 181.

26. Yet at least Huntington recognizes the critical urgency of the substantial Latin American immigration for the cultural and political integrity of the United States. Cornel West, in another key text published in 2004, remains cloistered in the traditional white/black American racial dichotomy and is unable to perceive the salience and perils of xenophobia and nativism as a chauvinistic reply to immigration. See Cornel West, *Democracy Matters: Winning the Fight against Imperialism*, reprint ed. (New York: Penguin Books, 2005). Is there any possible conceptual manner of bridging the concerns of the African American ghettos, struggling against color-coded racism, and the growing Latino/Hispanic barrios, facing an insidious cultural disdain? Both communities suffer from a lack of recognition of their genuine human dignity, which should imply more than mere tolerance for their distinctive cultural traits, of socio-economic deprivation and political powerlessness. An always complex and difficult to achieve dialectics between cultural recognition and social-economic redistribution might be the key clue for solving this dilemma. See Nancy Fraser and Axel Honneth, *Redistribution or Recognition?: A Political-Philosophical Exchange*, trans. Joel Golb, James Ingram, and Christiane Wilke (London and New York: Verso, 2003). Ernesto Laclau and Chantal Mouffe emphasize these dialectics in the preface to the new edition of their famed text. See Ernesto Laclau and Chantal Mouffe, *Hegemony and Socialist Strategy: Towards a Radical Democratic Politics*, 2nd ed. (London and New York: Verso, 2014), xviii: "One of the central tenets of *Hegemony and Socialist Strategy* is the need to create a chain of equivalence among the various democratic struggles against subordination . . . to tackle issues of both 'redistribution' and 'recognition.'"

27. Jeremy Harding, "The Deaths Map," *London Review of Books*, October 20, 2011.

28. John Bowe, *Nobodies: Modern American Slave Labor and the Dark Side of the New Global Economy*, 1st ed. (New York: Random House, 2007); Kevin Bales, *Disposable People: New Slavery in the Global Economy* (Berkeley, CA: University of California Press, 2012); Zygmunt Bauman, *Wasted Lives: Modernity and Its Outcasts*, 1st ed. (Cambridge, UK: Polity, 2003).

29. Branko Milanovic, "Global Inequality and the Global Inequality Extraction Ratio: The Story of the Past Two Centuries" (The World Bank, September 1, 2009), http://documents.worldbank.org/curated/en/389721468330911675/Global-inequality-and-the-global-inequality-extraction-ratio-the-story-of-the-past-two-centuries; Peter Stalker, *Workers without Frontiers: The Impact of Globalization on International Migration* (Boulder, CO, and Geneva: Lynne Rienner, 1999).

30. Michael Dillon, "Sovereignty and Governmentality: From the Problematics of the 'New World Order' to the Ethical Problematic of the World Order," *Alternatives: Social Transformations and Humane Governance* 20, no. 3 (Spring 1995): 357.

31. Elizabeth Kennedy, "No Childhood Here: Why Central American Children Are Fleeing Their Homes," American Immigration Council, August 24, 2016, https://www.americanimmigrationcouncil.org/research/no-childhood-here-why-central-american-chil-

dren-are-fleeing-their-homes; Committee on Migration of the United States Conference of Catholic Bishops, "Mission to Central America: The Flight of Unaccompanied Children to the United States," November 2013; "A Guide to Children Arriving at the Border: Laws, Policies and Responses," American Immigration Council, July 12, 2016, http://www.immigrationpolicy.org/research/guide-children-arriving-border-laws-policies-and-responses.

32. José E. Ramírez Kidd, *Alterity and Identity in Israel: The "Ger" in the Old Testament*, reprint ed. (Berlin and New York: De Gruyter, 2012).

33. Sodom's transgression of the hospitality code was part of a culture of corruption and oppression, according to Ezekiel 16:49: "This was the guilt of your sister Sodom: she and her daughters had pride, excess of food, and prosperous ease, but did not aid the poor and needy." The homophobic construal of Sodom's sinfulness, which led to the term "sodomy," is a later (mis)interpretation. See Mark D. D. Jordan, *The Invention of Sodomy in Christian Theology* (Chicago: University of Chicago Press, 1998).

34. José Cervantes Gabarrón, "El Inmigrante en las Tradiciones Bíblicas," in *Ciudadania, Multiculturalidad e Inmigracion* (Editorial Verbo Divino, 2009), 262.

35. This periscope deserves to be quoted in its entirety: "The Lord sets the prisoners free; the Lord opens the eyes of the blind. The Lord lifts up those who are bowed down; the Lord loves the righteous. The Lord watches over the strangers; he upholds the orphan and the widow, but the way of the wicked he brings to ruin" (Psalm 146:8–9).

36. This text is inscribed in Philadelphia's Liberty Bell, a venerated US icon.

37. For a sharp critical analysis of the xenophobic and misogynist theology underlining Ezra and Nehemiah, see Elisabeth Cook Steike, *La mujer como extranjera en Israel: Estudio exegético de Esdras 9–10* (San José, Costa Rica: SEBILA, 2012). Snyder contrasts what she terms "the ecology of fear," exemplified by the banishment of foreign wives (and their children) in Ezra and Nehemiah, with an "ecology of faith," as expressed in the stories of Ruth, a "Moabite woman," and the Syro-Phoenician mother that implores Jesus to heal her daughter. Snyder, *Asylum-Seeking, Migration and Church*, 139–94.

38. Naim Stifan Ateek, *A Palestinian Christian Cry for Reconciliation*, 1st ed. (Maryknoll, NY: Orbis Books, 2008), 132.

39. Phyllis Trible, *Texts of Terror: Literary-Feminist Readings of Biblical Narratives*, 1st ed. (Philadelphia: Fortress Press, 1984).

40. Soerens and Yang, *Welcoming the Stranger*; M. Daniel Carroll R., *Christians at the Border: Immigration, the Church, and the Bible*, 2nd ed. (Grand Rapids, MI: Brazos Press, 2013).

41. Soerens and Yang, *Welcoming the Stranger*, 85; 98; Carroll R., *Christians at the Border*, 83–84.

42. Clark Lyda and Jesse Lyda, *The Least of These*, Documentary, 2009.

43. Regarding Matthew 25:31–46, I am in accord with those scholars, like Gabarrón, "El Inmigrante en las Tradiciones Bíblicas," 273–75. These scholars interpret "the least of these" as referring to the poor, dispossessed, marginalized, and oppressed, and in disagreement with those who limit its denotation to Jesus's disciples, like Carroll R., *Christians at the Border*, 122–23.

44. Peter Phan, "Migration in the Patristic Age," in *A Promised Land, a Perilous Journey: Theological Perspectives on Migration*, ed. Daniel G. Groody and Gioacchino Campese, 1st ed. (Notre Dame, IN: University of Notre Dame Press, 2008), 35–61.

45. There is an instance in which Jesus seems to exclude or marginalize strangers. When a woman, "Gentile, of Syrophoenician origin," implores him to heal her daughter, Jesus declines. But her obstinate, clever, and hopeful response impresses him and leads him to praise her word of faith (Matthew 15:21–28; Mark 7:24–30).

46. Daniel Smith-Christopher, *A Biblical Theology of Exile* (Minneapolis, MN: Augsburg Fortress Publishers, 2002); James M. Scott, ed., *Exile: A Conversation with N. T. Wright* (Downers Grove, IL: IVP Academic, 2017); René Kruger, *La Diáspora: De Una Experiencia Traumática a Paradigma Eclesiológico* (Buenos Aires: Instituto Universitario ISEDET, 2008).

47. Miroslav Volf, *Exclusion and Embrace: A Theological Exploration of Identity, Otherness, and Reconciliation*, 1st ed. (Nashville, TN: Abingdon Press, 1996).

48. William Schweiker, *Theological Ethics and Global Dynamics: In the Time of Many Worlds*, 1st ed. (Malden, MA: Wiley-Blackwell, 2004); Oliver O'Donovan, *The Desire of the Nations: Rediscovering the Roots of Political Theology* (Cambridge , UK, and New York: Cambridge University Press, 1996), 268.

49. Amin Maalouf, *In the Name of Identity* (Cambridge, UK: Polity Press, 1997).

50. Zygmunt Bauman, *Postmodernity and Its Discontents* (Cambridge, UK: Polity Press, 1997), 5.

51. Malise Ruthven, "What Happened to the Arab Spring?," *New York Review of Books*, July 10, 2014, https://www.nybooks.com/articles/2014/07/10/what-happened-arab-spring/: "Of Qatar's population of 2.1 million, 85 percent are listed as 'foreign residents.' Many of these are construction workers from South Asia who work under poor conditions and suffer high casualty rates."

52. European Commission, "Roma in Europe: The Implementation of European Union Instruments and Policies for Roma Inclusion (Progress Report 2008–2010)" (Brussels, April 7, 2010).

53. Giovanni Sartori, *Pluralismo Multiculturalismo E Estranei* (Rizzoli, 2000). Sartori perceives Islamist immigration as irreconcilable with, and thus nefarious for, Western democratic pluralism. His thesis is a sophisticated reconfiguration of the multisecular adversary confrontation between Christian/Western (supposedly open, secular, and liberal) and Islamic/Eastern (allegedly closed, dogmatic, and authoritarian) cultures, a new reenactment of what Edward Said famously named "Orientalism."

54. Bill Ong Hing, *American Presidents, Deportations, and Human Rights Violations: From Carter to Trump* (New York: Cambridge University Press, 2018).

55. A task to which not enough attention has been devoted is the advocacy for the signature and ratification by the wealthy and powerful nations of the 1990 "International Convention on the Protection of the Rights of All Migrant Workers and Members of Their Families," which entered into force on July 1, 2003.

56. Stephen Castles, Hein de Haas, and Mark J. Miller, *The Age of Migration: International Population Movements in the Modern World* (London: The Guilford Press, 2014).

57. Edward W. Said, *The Question of Palestine*, reissue ed. (New York: Vintage, 1992), 176.

58. Some scholars, for example, argue that the North American Free Trade Agreement, which came into force on January 1, 1994, created havoc in several segments of the Mexican economy and deprived of their livelihoods approximately 2.5 million small farmers and other workers dependent on the agricultural sector. The alternative for many of them was the stark choice between the clandestine and dangerous drug trafficking or paying the "coyotes" for the also clandestine and dangerous trek to the North. Ben Ehrenreich, "A Lucrative War," *The New York Review of Books*, October 2010.

59. Snyder, *Asylum-Seeking, Migration and Church*, 31.

60. Raúl Fornet-Betancourt, *Migration and Interculturality: Theological and Philosophical Challenges* (Aachen, Germany: Missionswissenschaftliches Institut Missio, 2004); Jorge E. Castillo Guerra, "A Theology of Migration: Toward an Intercultural Methodology," in *A Promised Land, a Perilous Journey: Theological Perspectives on Migration*, ed. Daniel G. Groody and Gioacchino Campese, 1st ed. (Notre Dame, IN: University of Notre Dame Press, 2008), 243–70.

61. Soerens and Yang, *Welcoming the Stranger*, 174.

62. Snyder, *Asylum-Seeking, Migration and Church*, 205.

63. Fernando Oliván, *El Extranjero y Su Sombra: Crítica Del Nacionalismo Desde El Derecho de Extranjería* (Madrid: San Pablo, 1998).

64. Brian Stanley, *Christianity in the Twentieth Century: A World History* (Princeton, NJ: Princeton University Press, 2019), 340, 356.

65. Benedict XVI, "Caritas in Veritate," n.d., 62.

BIBLIOGRAPHY

"A Guide to Children Arriving at the Border: Laws, Policies and Responses." American Immigration Council, July 12, 2016. http://www.immigrationpolicy.org/research/guide-children-arriving-border-laws-policies-and-responses.

Anzaldúa, Gloria. *Borderlands/La Frontera: The New Mestiza*. San Francisco: Aunt Lute Books, 1999.

Ateek, Naim Stifan. *A Palestinian Christian Cry for Reconciliation*. 1st ed. Maryknoll, NY: Orbis Books, 2008.

Balderrama, Francisco E., and Raymond Rodríguez. *Decade of Betrayal: Mexican Repatriation in the 1930s*. Revised ed. Albuquerque: University of New Mexico Press, 2006.

Bales, Kevin. *Disposable People: New Slavery in the Global Economy*. Berkeley, CA: University of California Press, 2012.

Bauman, Zygmunt. *Postmodernity and Its Discontents*. Cambridge, UK: Polity Press, 1997.

———. *Wasted Lives: Modernity and Its Outcasts*. 1st ed. Cambridge, UK: Polity, 2003.

Benedict XVI. "Caritas in Veritate," n.d.

Bowe, John. *Nobodies: Modern American Slave Labor and the Dark Side of the New Global Economy*. 1st ed. New York: Random House, 2007.

Buchanan, Patrick J. *State of Emergency: The Third World Invasion and Conquest of America*. New York: St. Martin's Press, 2008.

Carroll R., M. Daniel. *Christians at the Border: Immigration, the Church, and the Bible*. 2nd ed. Grand Rapids, MI: Brazos Press, 2013.

Castles, Stephen, Hein de Haas, and Mark J. Miller. *The Age of Migration: International Population Movements in the Modern World*. London: The Guilford Press, 2014.

Committee on Migration of the United States Conference of Catholic Bishops. "Mission to Central America: The Flight of Unaccompanied Children to the United States," November 2013.

Dillon, Michael. "Sovereignty and Governmentality: From the Problematics of the 'New World Order' to the Ethical Problematic of the World Order." *Alternatives: Social Transformations and Humane Governance* 20, no. 3 (Spring 1995).

Ehrenreich, Ben. "A Lucrative War." *The New York Review of Books*, October 2010.

European Commission. "Roma in Europe: The Implementation of European Union Instruments and Policies for Roma Inclusion (Progress Report 2008–2010)." Brussels, April 7, 2010.

Fanon, Frantz. *Peau Noir, Masques Blancs*. Paris: Éditions du Seuil, 1952.

Fornet-Betancourt, Raúl. *Migration and Interculturality: Theological and Philosophical Challenges*. Aachen, Germany: Missionswissenschaftliches Institut Missio, 2004.

Fraser, Nancy, and Axel Honneth. *Redistribution or Recognition?: A Political-Philosophical Exchange*. Translated by Joel Golb, James Ingram, and Christiane Wilke. London and New York: Verso, 2003.

Fredrickson, George M. *Diverse Nations: Explorations in the History of Racial and Ethnic Pluralism*. London: Paradigm Publishers, 2006. http://www.tandfebooks.com/isbn/9781315635125.

Gabarrón, José Cervantes. "El Inmigrante en las Tradiciones Bíblicas." In *Ciudadania, Multi-culturalidad e Inmigracion*. Editorial Verbo Divino, 2009.

Gallagher, Charles A., and Cameron D. Lippard, eds. *Race and Racism in the United States: An Encyclopedia of the American Mosaic*. Westport, CT: Greenwood Press, 2005.

Guerra, Jorge E. Castillo. "A Theology of Migration: Toward an Intercultural Methodology." In *A Promised Land, a Perilous Journey: Theological Perspectives on Migration*, edited by Daniel G. Groody and Gioacchino Campese, 1st ed., 243–70. Notre Dame, IN: University of Notre Dame Press, 2008.

Harding, Jeremy. "The Deaths Map." *London Review of Books*, October 20, 2011.

Heimburger, Robert W. *God and the Illegal Alien: United States Immigration Law and a Theology of Politics*. Cambridge: Cambridge University Press, 2018.

Higham, John. *Strangers in the Land: Patterns of American Nativism, 1860–1925*. New Brunswick, NJ: Rutgers University Press, 2011.

Hing, Bill Ong. *American Presidents, Deportations, and Human Rights Violations: From Carter to Trump*. New York: Cambridge University Press, 2018.

Hoffman, Abraham. *Unwanted Mexican Americans in the Great Depression: Repatriation Pressures, 1929–1939*. Tucson: University of Arizona Press, 1974.

Huntington, Samuel P. "The Clash of Civilizations?," August 31, 2017. https://www.foreignaffairs.com/articles/united-states/1993–06–01/clash-civilizations.

———. *The Clash of Civilizations and the Remaking of World Order*. New York: Simon and Schuster, 2011.

———. "The Hispanic Challenge." Foriegn Policy, October 28, 2006. https://foreignpolicy.com/2009/10/28/the-hispanic-challenge/.

———. *Who Are We?: The Challenges to America's National Identity*. New York: Simon and Schuster, 2005.

Irvin, Dale. "The Church, the Urban and the Global: Mission in an Age of Global Cities." *International Bulletin of Missionary Research* 33, no. 4 (October 2009).

Jordan, Mark D. D. *The Invention of Sodomy in Christian Theology*. Chicago: University of Chicago Press, 1998.

Kanstroom, Daniel. *Deportation Nation: Outsiders in American History*. Cambridge, MA , and London: Harvard University Press, 2007.

Kennedy, Elizabeth. "No Childhood Here: Why Central American Children Are Fleeing Their Homes." American Immigration Council, August 24, 2016. https://www.americanimmigrationcouncil.org/research/no-childhood-here-why-central-american-children-are-fleeing-their-homes.

Kidd, José E. Ramírez. *Alterity and Identity in Israel: The "Ger" in the Old Testament*. Reprint ed. Berlin and New York: De Gruyter, 2012.

Kruger, René. *La Diáspora: De Una Experiencia Traumática a Paradigma Eclesiológico*. Buenos Aires: Instituto Universitario ISEDET, 2008.

Laclau, Ernesto, and Chantal Mouffe. *Hegemony And Socialist Strategy: Towards a Radical Democratic Politics*. 2nd ed. London and New York: Verso, 2014.

Leonhardt, David. "Truth, Fiction and, and Lou Dobbs." *The New York Times*, May 30, 2017.

Lyda, Clark, and Jesse Lyda. *The Least of These*. Documentary, 2009.

Maalouf, Amin. *In the Name of Identity*. Cambridge, UK: Polity Press, 1997.

Milanovic, Branko. "Global Inequality and the Global Inequality Extraction Ratio: The Story of the Past Two Centuries." The World Bank, September 1, 2009. http://documents.worldbank.org/curated/en/389721468330911675/Global-inequality-and-the-global-inequality-extraction-ratio-the-story-of-the-past-two-centuries.

Miller, Stuart Creighton. *The Unwelcome Immigrant: The American Image of the Chinese, 1785–1882*. Berkeley, CA: University of California Press, 1969.

O'Donovan, Oliver. *The Desire of the Nations: Rediscovering the Roots of Political Theology*. Cambridge and New York: Cambridge University Press, 1996.

Oliván, Fernando. *El Extranjero y Su Sombra: Crítica Del Nacionalismo Desde El Derecho de Extranjería*. Madrid: San Pablo, 1998.

Phan, Peter. "Migration in the Patristic Age." In *A Promised Land, a Perilous Journey: Theological Perspectives on Migration*, edited by Daniel G. Groody and Gioacchino Campese, 1st ed., 35–61. Notre Dame, IN: University of Notre Dame Press, 2008.

Portes, Alejandro, and Rubén G. Rumbaut. *Immigrant America: A Portrait*. 4th ed. Berkeley and Los Angeles, CA: University of California Press, 2014.

Potok, Mark. "Rage on the Right." *Intelligence Report*, March 2, 2010. https://www.splcenter.org/fighting-hate/intelligence-report/2010/rage-right.

Ratha, Dilip. "Dollars without Borders," November 2, 2009. https://www.foreignaffairs.com/articles/2009–10–16/dollars-without-borders.

Rodriguez, Richard. *Brown: The Last Discovery of America*. New York: Penguin Books, 2003.

Ruiz, Francisco Javier Blázquez. "Derechos Humanos, Inmigración, Integración." In *Ciudadania, Multiculturalidad e Inmigracion*, edited by José A. Zamora. Editorial Verbo Divino, 2009.

Ruthven, Malise. "What Happened to the Arab Spring?," *New York Review of Books*, July 10, 2014. https://www.nybooks.com/articles/2014/07/10/what-happened-arab-spring/.

Sacks, Jonathan. *The Dignity of Difference: How to Avoid the Clash of Civilizations*. 2nd ed. London: Continuum, 2003.

Said, Edward W. *The Question of Palestine*. Reissued ed. New York: Vintage, 1992.

Sartori, Giovanni. *Pluralismo Multiculturalismo E Estranei*. Rizzoli, 2000.

Schweiker, William. *Theological Ethics and Global Dynamics: In the Time of Many Worlds*. 1st ed. Malden, MA: Wiley-Blackwell, 2004.

Scott, James M., ed. *Exile: A Conversation with N. T. Wright*. Downers Grove, IL: IVP Academic, 2017.

Smith-Christopher, Daniel. *A Biblical Theology of Exile*. Minneapolis, MN: Augsburg Fortress Publishers, 2002.

Snyder, Susanna. *Asylum-Seeking, Migration and Church*. Burlington, VT: Ashgate, 2012.

Soerens, Matthew, and Jenny Yang. *Welcoming the Stranger: Justice, Compassion and Truth in the Immigration Debate*. Revised ed. Downers Grove, IL: IVP Books, 2018.

Stalker, Peter. *Workers without Frontiers: The Impact of Globalization on International Migration*. Boulder, CO , and Geneva: Lynne Rienner, 1999.

Stanley, Brian. *Christianity in the Twentieth Century: A World History*. Princeton, NJ: Princeton University Press, 2019.

Steike, Elisabeth Cook. *La mujer como extranjera en Israel: Estudio exegético de Esdras 9–10*. San José, Costa Rica: SEBILA, 2012.

Tocqueville, Alexis de. *Democracy in America*. Oxford: Oxford University Press, 1959.

Trible, Phyllis. *Texts of Terror: Literary-Feminist Readings of Biblical Narratives*. 1st ed. Philadelphia: Fortress Press, 1984.

Volf, Miroslav. *Exclusion and Embrace: A Theological Exploration of Identity, Otherness, and Reconciliation*. 1st ed. Nashville, TN: Abingdon Press, 1996.

Walcott, Derek. "The Schooner 'Flight.'" In *Collected Poems: 1948–1984*. New York: The Noonday Press and Farrar, Straus and Giroux, 1996.

West, Cornel. *Democracy Matters: Winning the Fight against Imperialism*. Reprint ed. New York: Penguin Books, 2005.

Index

About the Editor and Contributors

Joerg Rieger is Distinguished Professor of Theology, the Cal Turner Chancellor's Chair of Wesleyan Studies, and the Founding Director of the Wendland-Cook Program in Religion and Justice at Vanderbilt University. Author and editor of 23 books, translated into six languages, his most recent books include *Jesus vs. Caesar: For People Tired of Serving the Wrong God* (2018), *No Religion but Social Religion: Liberating Wesleyan Theology* (2018), *Unified We Are a Force: How Faith and Labor Can Overcome America's Inequalities* (with Rosemarie Henkel-Rieger, 2016), and *Faith on the Road: A Short Theology of Travel and Justice* (2015).

* * *

Gemma Tulud Cruz, a native of the Philippines, taught theology for several years in the United States prior to moving to Australian Catholic University in Melbourne, where she now works as Senior Lecturer in Theology. She is author of *Pilgrims in the Wilderness: Toward an Intercultural Theology of Migration* (2010), *Toward a Theology of Migration: Social Justice and Religious Experience* (2014), and a number of peer-reviewed publications on various research interests.

Wanda Deifelt, a native of Brazil, is Professor of Religion at Luther College in Decorah, IA. Her research and publications are on liberation and feminist theologies, ecumenical and interfaith dialogues, and religious pluralism. Her forthcoming book is titled *Embodied Theology*.

Marc H. Ellis has been writing, teaching, and lecturing on Jewish identity, the Holocaust, Israel, Palestine, the prophetic and global issues of justice, peace, and reconciliation for four decades. During this time, he was Professor of Religion, Culture, and Society Studies and Director of the Institute for Justice and Peace at the Maryknoll School of Theology and University Professor of Jewish Studies, Professor of History, and Director of the Center for Jewish Studies at Baylor University. He has written and edited more than twenty-five books, including *Toward a Jewish Theology of Liberation*, now in its third edition, *Unholy Alliance: Religion and Atrocity in Our Time*, *The Future of the Prophetic,* and, most recently, *Finding Our Voice: Embodying the Prophetic and Other Misadventures*. Professor Ellis has lectured around the world and has held visiting positions at Harvard University and the University of London, among others. His work has been translated into ten languages. A Festschrift volume honoring Professor Ellis, *Scholarship in the New Diaspora: The Practices of the Intellectual in Exile*, will appear from Lexington Books/Fortress Academic in 2020.

J. Alice Heo is currently a doctoral student in the Protestant Theological Faculty at the Johannes Gutenberg University Mainz. Her research interests include intercultural theology and hermeneutics, sociology of religion, aesthetics and religion, and migration studies.

M. P. Joseph, professor of ethics at Chang Jung Christian University, Taiwan, is editor of *Theologies and Cultures.* His recent publications include *Theologies of the Non-Person* (2015), and, as editor, *Wrestling with God in Context* (2018).

Deenabandhu Manchala, a theologian from India, has served as program executive at the World Council of Churches in Geneva, Switzerland, coordinating the theological reflection for the Decade to Overcome Violence (2000–2006) and the Just and Inclusive Communities (2007–2014). Currently, he is the area executive for Southern Asia in the Global Ministries of the United Church of Christ and Christian Church (Disciples of Christ) in the United States, and works from Cleveland, Ohio. He holds a doctorate in theology from the South Asia Theological Research Institute, Bangalore, India. He has published many articles in the areas of ecumenism, mission, ecclesiology, justice, peace, and human dignity, and on the issues of the marginalized communities.

Eliseo Pérez-Álvarez is Professor of Systematic Theology at United Theological College of the University of the West Indies in Jamaica. He has been Associate Professor at Seminario Teológico Presbiteriano de México, Seminario Evangélico de Puerto Rico, and Wartburg Theological Seminary. He has done pastoral ministry in Mexico, Puerto Rico, the Virgin Islands, and the United States. He is also the author of a dozen of books. Eliseo received his PhD from the Lutheran School of Theology at Chicago. He studied philosophy and theology in Mexico, the United States, and Denmark.

Luis N. Rivera-Pagán is the Henry Winters Luce Professor of Ecumenics and Mission Emeritus at Princeton Theological Seminary. He is the author of several books, among them *A Violent Evangelism: The Political and Religious Conquest of the Americas* (1992), *Mito exilio y demonios: Literatura y teología en América Latina* (1996), *Ensayos teológicos desde el Caribe* (2013), and *Essays from the Margins* (2014), and the editor of *God, in Your Grace . . . Official Report of the Ninth Assembly of the World Council of Churches* (2007).

George Zachariah serves the Trinity Methodist Theological College, Auckland, Aotearoa/New Zealand as faculty in Theological Studies. He has also served as professor of theology and ethics at the United Theological College, Bangalore, India, and the Gurukul Lutheran Theological College and Research Institute, Chennai, India. He is the author of *Alternatives Unincorporated: Earth Ethics from the Grassroots* (2011) and *Gospel in a Groaning World: Climate Injustice and Public Witness* (2012).